Advance

BUILD A BETTER BUSINESS BOOK

Endorsed by more than 50 successful business authors

"Priceless advice from a business book nerd, destined to save authors time, money and heartache. Anyone who is smart and generous enough to take on writing a business book needs to read Josh's book asap." —**Seth Godin, author of** ***This Is Marketing***

"If you're serious about writing a business book that matters, then look no further. Josh Bernoff's step-by-step approach, backed by years of experience and insider knowledge, will show you how to create a compelling story that connects with readers and drives real change." —**Daniel H. Pink, #1** *New York Times* **best-selling author of** ***When, Drive,*** **and** ***To Sell Is Human***

"Josh gets what countless teachers of this craft seem to forget: Your book should not be fancy packaging for yet another hollow guide, checklist, or personal success story. Your book should share something profound that transforms readers and shapes markets. If that's the business book you aspire to write, start by reading this one." —**Jay Acunzo, author of** ***Break the Wheel: Question Best Practices, Hone Your Intuition, and Do Your Best Work***

"If you're thinking about writing a business book, start here. This book provides the formulas for your success, from concept to writing to launch and all the in-betweens you didn't even know you needed to know." —**Melissa Agnes, author of** ***Crisis Ready: Building an Invincible Brand in an Uncertain World***

"*Build a Better Business Book* is staggeringly useful, and I'm more than a little angry that I had to write six books without it. This is the new, definitive guide to making a business book happen." —**Jay Baer, coauthor of** ***Youtility: Why Smart Marketing Is about Help Not Hype***

"If you care about quality, this indispensable writing guide from respected book coach Josh Bernoff will teach you exactly how to start (and finish!) the business book you've always dreamed of writing. Even after writing nine books myself, I found Josh's advice to be consistently useful and wonderfully non-obvious." —**Rohit Bhargava, three-time *Wall Street Journal* bestselling author and cofounder of Ideapress Publishing**

"Finally, a definitive, complete resource for every author who needs to connect the dots from pitching to writing to publishing to promoting! You don't know what you don't know about developing a book—but Josh does, and now you can too." —**Margot Bloomstein, author of *Trustworthy: How the Smartest Brands Beat Cynicism and Bridge the Trust Gap***

"With this book, Bernoff provides a very actionable plan for aspiring—and published—authors." —**Chris Brogan, author of *Catching Appfire***

"When I write, I feel Josh's presence like Jiminy Cricket on my shoulder, guiding my every word and sentence. Now, he's written the go-to handbook for writing a business book your audience is going to want to read. I will never write another book without this one at my side." —**Todd Caponi, author of *The Transparency Sale* and *The Transparent Sales Leader***

"As the master of writing without bullshit, Josh reveals twenty-four essential areas that demand action when designing a book capable of standing out in a sea of sameness. This is a clear blueprint for aspiring authors who'd prefer to learn the pitfalls before they publish." —**Dave Carroll, author of *United Breaks Guitars: The Power of One Voice in the Age of Social Media***

"Your breakthrough idea deserves a breakthrough bestseller. When you finally decide to write that book, this is the indispensable guide to making it great." —**Dorie Clark, *Wall Street Journal* bestselling author of *The Long Game* and executive education faculty, Duke University Fuqua School of Business**

"Practically anyone can write a business book—and it often feels like practically anyone does. But Josh Bernoff gives you the tools to write a good one ... maybe even a great one." —**Rob Cottingham, cartoonist, Noise to Signal**

"Josh Bernoff has written a remarkable book that explains and demonstrates exactly how to build a better business book. I wish this book had been available before I started writing." —**Don Crawley, author of *The Compassionate Geek***

"Deconstructs the business book into both the profound and the practical in the no-bullshit style that has made Josh Bernoff my go-to for all things writing." —**Liane Davey, bestselling author of *You First* and *The Good Fight***

"Don't even outline your business book without reading this one first. *Build a Better Business Book* is equal parts inspiring and actionable, packed with interesting case studies and tactical advice from a true expert." —**Melanie Deziel, author of *Prove It: Exactly How Modern Marketers Earn Trust***

"Josh Bernoff has written a supremely practical and well-thought-out book for anyone looking to write a business book. From the use of storytelling to working with a coauthor to essential tips in writing, the advice here is invaluable." —**Minter Dial, author of *You Lead: How Being Yourself Makes You a Better Leader***

"Turn your ideas and insights into a must-read business book with Josh Bernoff's start-to-finish guide! Packed with insider tips and practical tactics, this book is a game-changer for both aspiring and seasoned writers." —**Roger Dooley, author of *Friction* and *Brainfluence***

"From the first sentence, I knew I would like this book. Josh knows that how we process information best is via story, and he spins an enticing tale of how you can chronicle your own knowledge and experience to not just teach readers, but captivate them." —**James Fell, author of *On This Day in History Sh!t Went Down***

"Josh served us as an advisor, editor, ghost writer, and therapist. We could not have published without him. *Build a Better Business Book* is the next best thing—it's like having Josh in the room providing crystal clear advice and guidance at every stage of the process." —**Dave Frankland, coauthor of *Marketing to the Entitled Consumer***

"The only thing better than this book is getting an hour of Josh's time to talk about his insights. Don't buy just one copy. Get two so you can share one with a friend." —**Jeff Fromm, five-time author and serial entrepreneur**

"Josh scared the hell out of me by showing me exactly why my previous books didn't really matter—and then put me at ease with a followable guide I can use to write a better business book. This is a book worth reading, re-reading, and using as a GPS for every book I write in the future." —**Phil Gerbyshak, author of *Zero Dollar Consulting***

"Josh Bernoff brings an invaluable mix of clarity, honesty, and actionable insight to the art and science of creating a resonant, relevant business book. In doing so, he has lived up to his own title's lofty ambitions and built the best bible an aspiring business author could ask for." —**Dan Gerstein, founder and CEO of Gotham Ghostwriters**

"With decades of experience as a writer, editor, and strategist, Josh Bernoff has a huge fan club of authors whose ideas he has helped bring to life. Now he gives us the ultimate meta gift: a great book about how to write a great book. Anyone who is thinking about holding their own book in their hands some day should start with Bernoff's insights." —**Diane Hessan, author of *Our Common Ground* and chair of C-Space**

"Authors who succeed must serve their readers well, just as companies must serve their customers. If you want to create a successful book that's useful to your readers, Bernoff's book is a small investment you must make on your way to getting your book published." —**Shep Hyken, *New York Times* bestselling author of *The Amazement Revolution***

"If only this book existed when I was approached to write my own book. It's oozing wisdom right from the table of contents. Josh's 'reader question method' would have saved me months of excruciating rewrites." —**Fotini Iconomopoulos, author of *Say Less, Get More: Unconventional Negotiation Techniques to Get What You Want***

"Josh Bernoff has been my book editor twice, and both times he helped me write a better book. In this new book, he covers everything you need to know to develop, write, publish, and promote your book. I recommend this knowledgeable and clearly written work to any aspiring nonfiction author." —**Shel Israel, author of five business books**

"Most business books are boring. And they're self-serving. The industry needs help! Fortunately for all of us, that helps comes courtesy of Josh Bernoff in *Build a Better Business Book*. I know I won't write my next book without reading this book first!" —**Joseph Jaffe, host of Joseph Jaffe is Not Famous and author of *Built to Suck***

"From this day forward, let's banish boring business books. With this nifty guide, Josh Bernoff raises the bar while showing us what to do. Readers, rejoice." —**Anne Janzer, author of *The Writer's Process* and *Get the Word Out***

"Literally lays the framework out for anyone hoping to show up in a bookstore or at the top of an Amazon bestseller list. I could have used this book when I first started publishing, but now I am going to scream about it from the mountaintops to anybody who will listen. If you're thinking about writing a book, start here!" —**Mitch Joel, founder, ThinkersOne, and author of *Six Pixels of Separation* and *CTRL ALT Delete***

*Advance praise from leading business authors
continues on the last few pages of the book.*

www.amplifypublishinggroup.com

Build a Better Business Book: How to Plan,
Write, and Promote a Book That Matters

Author photo by Ray Bernoff

For more information, please contact:
Amplify Publishing, an imprint of Amplify Publishing Group
620 Herndon Parkway, Suite 320
Herndon, VA 20170
info@amplifypublishing.com

Library of Congress Control Number: 2023934547

CPSIA Code: PRV0423A

ISBN-13: 978-1-64543-255-5

Printed in the United States

Josh Bernoff

BUILD A BETTER BUSINESS BOOK

How to *Plan*, *Write*, and *Promote* a Book That Matters

A COMPREHENSIVE GUIDE FOR AUTHORS

amplify

an imprint of Amplify Publishing Group

CONTENTS

PART I: PREPARE

PART II: RESEARCH AND WRITE

PART III: MANUSCRIPT INTO BOOK

PART IV: SUCCESS

PART I

PREPARE

Chapter 1

Business Books Are Stories

To engage readers, tell a story.

J ay Baer commands attention as he stalks around the stage. He's not a small, quiet guy. He radiates a big, friendly energy; his talks are filled with startling insights and stories that make you smile. He's unforgettable in his exquisitely tailored plaid suit, typically bright purple. And he's so good that he gets around 65 paid speaking gigs a year.

His popular business books fuel that speaking career and send paying clients to the marketing agency he founded, Convince & Convert.

In 2017, Jay was on a roll. His last two books based on counterintuitive marketing ideas were hits. *Youtility: Why Smart Marketing Is about Help Not Hype* (Portfolio, 2013), which explained how brands grow organically by being as useful as possible, was a *New York Times* bestseller. And *Hug Your Haters: How to Embrace Complaints and Keep Your Customers* (Portfolio, 2016) proved that reaching out to your worst, most hostile customers could expand your brand and break down barriers.

It was time for another book to fuel his reputation for great and useful ideas. So Jay decided to deconstruct word of mouth. There were plenty of books on word of mouth, but no one had created a formula for how to build a business that people loved to talk about. Together with coauthor Daniel Lemin, Jay began to investigate examples of companies that had built a "talk trigger" into the way they did business. Think of the warm cookies you get when you check into a DoubleTree hotel, or an oral surgeon who calls patients the week of their appointment to reassure them and answer all their questions, or a theme park that gives out unlimited free soda to every visitor.

These "talkable" people and companies were getting free publicity and driving businesses in ways that traditional marketing couldn't even approach. Jay and Daniel set out to create a clear and compelling set of instructions on how businesses large and small could create talk triggers and become unforgettable (much like Jay's purple plaid suit).

The resulting book was *Talk Triggers: The Complete Guide to Creating Customers with Word of Mouth* (Portfolio, 2018), with a cover featuring a photo of a couple of fuzzy alpacas sharing a secret. Here's how it starts:

Chapter 1: Talk Is Cheap

Do you like chicken? Do you really, really, really like chicken? Do you like chicken as much as Jimmy Buffett likes the beach? If so, The Cheesecake Factory is your perfect restaurant.

Each of the chain's 200 locations offers 85 different chicken dishes. Unsurprisingly, given how many chicken dishes alone it includes, the menu itself runs to 5,940 words long. That is more than 11 percent of the book you are about to read.

You might think that's too long, but for The Cheesecake Factory, it's just right. Why? Because the vastness of the restaurant's menu is so unusual that it compels conversation among its patrons. Menu breadth is its secret customer-acquisition weapon — it hides in plain sight, in the hands of each and every diner.

The menu at The Cheesecake Factory is a talk trigger: a built-in differentiator that creates customer conversations.

Jay and Daniel then tell us what a talk trigger is, how it drives business, how people react to talk triggers, and how you can build one yourself. *Talk Triggers* describes the four criteria for a talk trigger, the five types of talk triggers, and the six steps to create one. It's a complete manual for how to get people talking, and it's both fascinating and useful.

As they describe later in Chapter 1:

> People have the power now in ways that would be unthinkable just a few years ago. That is why the time for talk triggers has never been better — or more necessary. Businesses' ability to unilaterally dictate consumer attitudes and subsequent purchases and loyalties is fraying like the hem of a cheap dress. . . .
>
> One hundred percent of businesses care about word of mouth, but less than 1 percent have a plan for achieving it. That's why we wrote *Talk Triggers*.

The text is dotted with fun examples, like the meeting venue in Antwerp that comes with a free pass to the zoo. You smile, then you think, "We have got to learn to do this." And if your eagerness wanes a bit, there are constant reminders that "same is lame" — that businesses without talk triggers must continually shell out bucks for advertising that generates neither loyalty nor word of mouth. It's a hard pitch to resist.

When the book was done, Jay and Daniel knew that they couldn't just fling it out into the world and hope that Jay's reputation and speeches would spread it. They had to do what they told everyone else to do — make their book talkable. So they sent a bunch of copies to reviewers who had decent-sized followings (including me) in a package that also included a tin of DoubleTree chocolate chip cookies and a cuddly plush alpaca. I wrote about the book on my blog. Four hundred other people posted "shelfies" of them reading the book with their own plush alpacas. For a time in October of 2018, if you were a marketer, you couldn't go anywhere on social media without bumping into a #TalkTriggers shelfie.[1]

Did it work? *Talk Triggers* sold more than 50,000 copies and garnered 168 Amazon reviews, averaging 4.7 stars. In the years that followed, the authors

---

[1] To see more about Jay Baer and Daniel Lemin's successful book promotion, including a collection of *Talk Triggers* shelfies, see my blog post, "Secrets of 3 successful book launches: connecting ideas and people," Josh Bernoff, April 21, 2020. See https://wobs.co/BBBBtriggers.

cleared speaking fees of more than $1 million. And marketers continue to call Jay's firm for help creating their own talk triggers. The book did its job: It spread an idea so broadly that it became part of the marketing lexicon, indelibly connected to the authors.

Stories fuel business books that matter

Talk Triggers isn't successful because Jay Baer and Daniel Lemin are smart.

Oh, they're smart alright. And they're excellent writers. But when it comes to business books, smart and talented by themselves are insufficient.

And while there are a thousand decisions involved in the creation of every successful business book — and I promise, I'll help you with as many of those as I can in the pages that follow — there is one thing that makes all the difference.

Story.

Humans love stories. We want to believe them. We relate to the people in them, imagine ourselves living them, remember them, tell other people about them.

When author Chip Heath conducted an experiment with Stanford University students making presentations, ten minutes after the presentations, only 5% of the audience could remember a statistic, but 63% of the audience remembered the stories.[2]

To be convincing, business books need facts, and data, and reasoning, and advice. But *stories* are what people relate to, remember, and act on. Even though I only shared a few hundred words from Jay and Daniel's book, I know you'll remember the parts that are stories — the story about The Cheesecake Factory's menu, and about the venue that includes a trip to the zoo, and how Jay and Daniel sent me DoubleTree cookies along with their book.

For a business book to matter, it needs to connect with people, motivate them to act, and stimulate them to share the ideas in it. Story is crucial to all of that.

This doesn't mean that you should start your business book with "once upon a time." It's not a fairy tale. But it does mean that when you're planning and

---

2   Cited in *Made to Stick: Why Some Ideas Survive and Others Die* (Random House, 2007) by Chip Heath and Dan Heath, p. 243.

writing your business book, you must consider these five things that relate to stories and narratives.

1. **Who is the audience?** For the readers to relate to the stories in your book, they need to be able to imagine themselves having the experiences you describe and taking the advice you deliver. This demands that you clearly identify your audience. The audience for *Talk Triggers* is marketers. Your audience might be podcasters, or business executives, or new college graduates. But it can't be "everybody," because not everybody will relate to your advice and stories. You are solving a problem; your audience is the group that has that problem and wants to solve it.

2. **What is the idea?** The stories in your book need to have a *point*. That point is your idea — the new way of looking at the world that you've discovered and are sharing. The idea should be new, because why write a book about an idea everyone already knows about? For example, *Talk Triggers* wasn't the first book on word of mouth, but it's arguably the first one that shows systematically how to engineer your business to create it. The idea of a talk trigger is more specific and actionable than vague generalities about word of mouth. Every story in the book is about somebody who created one, how they did it, and how you can do it, too. (For more on how to refine and differentiate your ideas, see Chapter 3.)

3. **Where will the stories come from?** Stories don't just fall from the sky. Authors need to collect them. *Talk Triggers* has 22 case studies; collecting them was crucial to making the book believable and memorable. In your book, the stories may include full case studies, shorter examples of a paragraph or two, and little two-sentence narratives that reinforce a point. But every one of them will be there because you did research to find them: You conducted interviews, researched news articles, or wrote down relevant experiences that you had personally. Unless you are deliberate about collecting stories that reinforce the parts of the idea, the book will be dry and sterile. And books like that don't catch on. (Chapter 9 explains how to find stories and conduct interviews.)

4. **What is the narrative thread of the book?** The best business books don't just contain stories, they *are* stories. The chapters link together to

form a narrative. The narrative in *Talk Triggers* goes like this: Marketers who want ideas to spread need a talk trigger. Otherwise, they're the same as everybody else, and same is lame. Every talk trigger fits four criteria. There are five types of talk triggers. And there are six steps to create one. If you follow this advice, your marketing will succeed, your company will grow, and you will live happily ever after. (To learn more about how to structure your book as a story, see Chapter 6.)

5. **How will you promote your story?** For your book to matter, it needs to reach people. That starts when you seed the world with people who can share your story. That includes both media people who can write about it and regular people who have a lot of friends. That means you need a promotional plan. The core of the *Talk Triggers* promotional plan was getting all those "influencers," like me, to understand the big idea in the book and to talk about it. Your plan won't look just like Jay and Daniel's, but you must have a plan. (For ideas on how to promote your book, see Chapter 21.)

The first chapter must scare the crap out of the reader

The most important part of every story is the beginning, because if the story doesn't suck you in at the start, you'll lose interest.

When it comes to business books, if you don't create urgency in the reader, they will stop reading, and the book will go on the bedside table on the pile that my agent refers to as "guilt mountain." If your book is on guilt mountain (or your ebook is in the digital guilt mountain in the reader's Kindle), it won't be a business book that matters.

The way to start is by scaring the crap out of people. Chapter 1 must be the scare-the-crap-out-of-you chapter.

There are two main ways to scare the crap out of the reader: fear and greed.

Fear looks like this: "Something bad is happening. If you don't act, you could be in big trouble."

Greed looks like this: "You are missing out. If you don't act, you won't take advantage of something great."

You must tap into fear, greed, or both in chapter 1.

In *Talk Triggers*, greed is most prominent. (Jay and Daniel would probably not characterize it as "greed," but marketing is about generating more business, and wanting more is, basically, greed.) The greed in chapter 1 is "If you want your business to get customers talking about it as they do with The Cheesecake Factory, you need a talk trigger."

There's also a little fear. "Same is lame" is fear. Nobody wants to be an ordinary business that competes by being the same as everybody else. If that scares you, you need a talk trigger.

Once you know the fear/greed formula, you'll see it in nearly every business book you read. Here are some excerpts from Chapter 1 of some successful business books:

- **Fear:** "Big data has plenty of evangelists, but I'm not one of them. This book will focus sharply in the other direction, on the damage inflicted by [weapons of math destruction] and the injustice they perpetrate. We will explore harmful examples that affect people at critical life moments: going to college, borrowing money, getting sentenced to prison, or finding and holding a job. All of these life domains are increasingly controlled by secret models wielding arbitrary punishments." *Weapons of Math Destruction: How Big Data Increases Inequality and Threatens Democracy* (Crown, 2016) by Cathy O'Neil, p. 13.

- **Greed:** "I will show that timing is really a science — an emerging body of multifaceted, multidisciplinary research that offers fresh insights into the human condition and useful guidance on working smarter and living better. . . . Think of this book as a new genre altogether — a when-to book." *When: The Scientific Secrets of Perfect Timing* (Riverhead Books, 2018) by Daniel H. Pink, p. 4.

- **Both:** "This book is a guide to the world being created by the new machines, platforms, and crowds. . . . The three rebalancings we describe here will take years, and their end points and exact trajectories are far from clear. But in chaos lies opportunity." *Machine, Platform, Crowd: Harnessing our Digital Future* (W. W. Norton, 2017) by Andrew McAfee and Erik Brynjolfsson, p. 25.

The Gladwell exception

Maybe you're not the kind of person who feels comfortable with fear and greed. Is there any way to create a business book that matters without tapping into fear and greed?

Sure. Take Malcolm Gladwell. Even though he wouldn't describe himself as a business author, businesspeople avidly snap up his books like *The Tipping Point: How Little Things Can Make a Big Difference* and *Outliers: The Story of Success*, scouring them for business insights.

Malcolm Gladwell is an amazingly successful author simply because he is an incredible storyteller. You can't put his books down because they're fascinating. Malcolm Gladwell succeeds, not because of fear or greed, but because he is entertaining.

Couldn't you do that?

No, you couldn't. Because you are not Malcolm Gladwell. (Malcolm, if you're reading this, you're the only person I'm *not* talking to right now. And while you're reading it, go ahead and pick a fight with me, I'm sure the resulting publicity would help attract attention to this book.)

You may imagine that you are as talented as one of the most successful nonfiction authors in the last two decades, but you almost certainly are not.

You could try to write a funny book. It might catch on, and it might spread, and it might get you a few speaking gigs — but if it doesn't tap into fear or greed, in the end, it won't matter. It won't change the way your readers think about the world.

So I'm going to assume that, lacking Malcolm's talent, you'll have to get by the way the other 99.9% of business authors do: by coming up with an awesome new idea and telling stories that people relate to, including tapping into fear and greed. Do that well in your first chapter, and you'll be off to a good start in creating a book that matters.

What you can learn from Dan Bricklin's book experience

Dan Bricklin is one of America's most insightful inventors. In 1978, while in an MBA class at the Harvard Business School, he watched as a professor walked through the tedious process of performing and correcting business calculations. An idea emerged in his mind: Why not create a computerized table that could perform and update calculations automatically?

Dan's conception, created by his programming partner Bob Frankston as software for the Apple II hobbyist computer, was the first electronic spreadsheet: VisiCalc. VisiCalc, more than any other product, turned personal computers from expensive toys into business machines. Microsoft Excel and Google Sheets are direct descendants of Bricklin's groundbreaking idea.

Over the decades, Dan continued to develop successful software products and to observe and comment on developments in the world of computing and technology in blog posts and essays. His blog attracted the attention of editors at the publisher Wiley, and Wiley proposed to publish *Bricklin on Technology*, a book based on Dan's essays and posts, with additional commentary and context. The book was published in 2009. There was no book advance.

Here's how *Bricklin on Technology* begins:

Chapter 1: Introduction: Case Studies and Details

The goal of this book is to help you better understand the juncture between computer technology and people, the process of creating that technology, and the evolution of those innovations. It does this through the use of essays and annotated case studies of people using technologies such as cell phones, blogs, and personal computer productivity tools. . . .

Insight into the forces that govern computer technology, and how that technology affects and is affected by a society made up of people, used to be of concern to just a few insiders. With the new, prominent role that computer technology plays supporting all of society, this insight is now something of interest to a much wider range of people. This book brings a unique perspective to help gain that insight.

When *Bricklin on Technology* came out in 2009, Dan made sure to encourage events where he was speaking to include copies of the book. But there was no concerted publicity campaign. Wiley, the publisher, sent copies to all the usual reviewers but didn't put much emphasis on publicity — not having paid an advance, they had very little skin in the game. In the end, the book sold just a few thousand copies and didn't have a significant impact on Dan's visibility or success as a public speaker.

Was publishing the book worth it?

When I spoke to Dan about working on the book and the launch, he told me it had accomplished some useful goals. He felt that having some of his thoughts in print, as opposed to in online essays and blog posts, made them more permanent — for example, they could be included as references in Wikipedia. And he ended up taking his own advice in the book and developing another software product — an iPhone app for taking notes — that achieved moderate success.

Dan is brilliant and his book is full of fascinating insights. But from where I sit, it could have been a lot more successful. It was a missed opportunity.

Dan doesn't perceive his book as a business book, but his imprint, Wiley, focuses on business books, and books that analyze technology are generally part of the business genre. In this case, *Bricklin on Technology* didn't fit the template of a business book that matters.

The audience was unclear and overly broad — basically, anyone who cares about the impact of technology on society or vice versa. It didn't solve any particular problem for those people.

Ideas were not the problem here. There are plenty of ideas in *Bricklin on Technology*. He analyzes what technology and tools are free and which people will pay for. He examines the dip in CD sales (which would eventually crater) and dismisses the glib explanation that file sharing was responsible. But there is no single driving idea — no "aha" moment. Without a unifying idea, you can't easily tell others what it's about even if you loved the book.

There are certainly a lot of stories here. But the book itself is not a narrative. The essays cluster around some classes of ideas, but they don't naturally lead one into the next.

The promotion was meager, so not enough people learned of the book's existence to give it a chance.

There is certainly no "scare the crap out you" energy in chapter 1, which basically cues you up to receive a bunch of observations and insights but doesn't explain how those will have a significant impact on what you should or should not do next as a businessperson or consumer.

And while you could make the argument that Dan Bricklin is as talented a software developer as Malcolm Gladwell is as a writer, Dan's prose is not at the Gladwell level. There is no shame in this; almost nobody can write that well. So the Gladwell exception doesn't apply.

The problem is not that this is a book of essays or blog posts. Guy Kawasaki's *Reality Check: The Irreverent Guide to Outsmarting, Outmanaging, and Outmarketing Your Competition* (Portfolio, 2008) is in the same format, but it's assembled and organized into a complete manual for getting ahead: "Hardcore information for hardcore people who want to kick ass." Seth Godin's *Small Is the New Big: and 183 Other Riffs, Rants, and Remarkable Business Ideas* (Portfolio, 2006) amounts to a complete essay collection on new ways to think about marketing, as he promises: "I'm certain that you're smart enough to see the stuff you've always wanted to do, buried deep inside one of these riffs. And I'm betting that once inspired, you'll actually make something happen." Both books came out around the same time as *Bricklin on Technology,* and both made a big impact. Guy and Seth made it seem like you were missing out if you didn't take their advice: They scared the crap out of you, at least a little. Dan didn't.

I can't help but wonder what would have happened if Dan had focused his audience, unified his analysis behind an idea, assembled a story around it, and created a little urgency — and then drove that story home with some focused promotion. That would have been more work. But it might have made the difference in this book catching on. We'll never know.[3]

Don't waste your effort

I recently surveyed 242 business authors, of whom about three-fourths had successfully published a book. Among the published authors, 87% agreed that

---

3   Dan is a thoughtful guy regarding media, and upon reading what I wrote, suggested another reason the book didn't catch on: It wasn't the right format for his audience. For various reasons, Dan and Wiley didn't create an ebook version of *Bricklin on Technology.* He wonders if his technical audience was perhaps unwilling to cart around the bulky paper version of the book, which was especially unwieldy for travelers, and might have been more receptive to a version for the then fairly new Kindle ebook format. As a result, if any of his potential readers heard about the book on Twitter or one of the podcasts that interviewed him and wanted to immediately start reading it, they were unable to obtain it in electronic format.

writing a book was a good decision. But as I'll reveal throughout this book, they have many regrets. They found it challenging to organize content and get time to write. They were stymied in their promotional efforts. They were disappointed by their publishers.

Writing a book that matters is hard work, and there are plenty of pitfalls awaiting you. I'll do my best to get you past those pitfalls. But if there's one thing I want you to remember, it's that stories are central. Unless you have a story to tell — and you tell it as a story — people won't easily remember or share your book. And unless you figure out how to scare the crap out of people in chapter 1, they won't read further (unless you're Malcolm Gladwell, of course).

I want you to end up like Jay Baer, with a book that fuels your dreams and puts your ideas into the mainstream conversation of your audience. That's a book that matters. I want to help you avoid ending up like Dan Bricklin, with a book that's a nice statement of your ideas, but that didn't make much of an impact. I want your book journey to be worth it.

The subtitle of this book promises a comprehensive guide for authors. While working on 45 books as author, coauthor, ghostwriter, editor, or writing coach, I've seen a lot go right — and a lot go wrong. I feel compelled to share what I've learned and help other authors. In the remainder of this book, I'll try to give you all the tools you need to create a business book that matters.

I've tried to write the book in a way that is both useful and entertaining. But there's no requirement that you read it in order. Feel free to dip into the rest of the chapters when you need to — to research how to deal with planning, writing chapters, making graphics, obtaining blurbs, marketing, or whatever's on your mind — as you set out on your own author journey.

The first section, Prepare, focuses on the crucial skill of making and executing a plan that will put you in the best position to succeed. I'll explain the different objectives people have in writing business books, how they can make their books memorable, the three ways you can get your book in print, how to structure your book's story, and how you can sell your book to traditional publishers with a book proposal, provided that's your preferred route to publication.

The second section, Research and Write, will walk you through everything you need to assemble the ingredients and bake them into a book. It includes tips on research, where to find case studies and stories, how to structure and plan chapters with a "fat outline," and how to write and improve prose (and graphics) to compel people to believe you and to keep on reading. I'll also talk about how to collaborate with editors, coauthors, and ghostwriters in a way that makes writing faster and more efficient, not just more troublesome.

Once you've completed a manuscript, you're not quite done. The process of turning words into actual books is mysterious to most authors, so I tackle that in the third section, Manuscript into Book. It deals with nuts-and-bolts topics like your book cover graphic, how to verify facts, copy editing, pagination, indexes, and, of course, footnotes. I'll also describe what's involved in self-publishing, if you decide to take that path to publication.

The final section, Success, details how to launch and promote your book, including how to leverage your friends and followers, how to generate publicity, and how to get blurbs (back-cover quotes). I'll also discuss some ways to make money from being a published author.

My aim is to answer every significant question you have about becoming a business book author. If you're worried about something, it ought to be in here — just check the index.

I don't know if I scared the crap out of you in this chapter, but I hope I did, at least a little. You should be greedy about what a book could do for you — I'll give you what you need to grasp that opportunity. And you should be fearful about the effort you could be wasting. Crafting the story of your book — and the stories *in* your book — could be the most rewarding thing you'll ever do. And it all starts with having a goal and a purpose, as I describe in Chapter 2.

Key takeaways

- People love and remember stories, so stories are central to successful business books.
- Five story-related qualities are central to the success of a book: audience, idea, case-study stories, a narrative thread, and promotion.
- Chapter 1 of your book must scare the crap out of the reader. There are two ways to do this: with fear and with greed.

Chapter 2

Why Write a Book?

Build a book that matters.

Laura Gassner Otting has had an amazing career. By age 22, she was working in Bill Clinton's White House on the volunteer national service program AmeriCorps. Then she got a job sourcing and hiring nonprofit executives. Eventually, she became frustrated with the way sourcing companies work, so she launched her own prosperous executive search agency — and sold it. She went on to develop a successful career as a public speaker.

In the process of all these changes, Laura started to recognize an idea called *consonance*. Consonance, as Laura defines it, is the concept that what you *do* must match who you *are* (or want to be). When you have consonance, you feel fulfilled because you know your work is part of a worthwhile quest, one you are invested in. Without it, you feel stuck, even if others looking on from outside would describe what you are doing as success. Allowing others to define your limits is what limits you.

So Laura decided to write a book about consonance: a book that tells the story of people who achieved it, how they did it, and what you need to do to find it in your own life. *Limitless: How to Ignore Everybody, Carve Your Own Path, and Live Your Best Life* (Ideapress Publishing, 2019), a bright yellow book featuring a hand-drawn infinity symbol on the front, quickly became a bestseller, debuting at number 2 on *The Washington Post* bestseller list, just behind Michelle Obama's memoir.

Limitless wasn't just a bestseller. It touched a lot of lives. More than 200 people have given it five-star reviews on Amazon. Here's an excerpt of a typical review, from SusanCW:

> I wasn't sure what to expect from *Limitless*, but I can tell you that it was exactly what I needed that I didn't know I needed. I knew that I wanted to dig deeper into *Limitless* when I found what might be my favorite sentence in the whole book (also that I want to plaster everywhere so I can see it every day) on page 4, "I encourage you to stop giving votes to the people in your life who shouldn't even have a voice." Never did I think that a book would cause the significant pivot and perspective shift that it did.

Limitless made so much of an impact that it got Laura a coveted segment on "Good Morning America," which she of course nailed. But it also caused what may be the most amazing instance of influence I've ever heard of.

Tara Diab is a friend of Laura's — they row crew together. It took Tara a while to figure out what she wanted to do with her life, but after stints as a not-that-great photographer and in her brother-in-law's flooring business, she started a company, Diab Custom Design, in the depths of a recession. Now she loves what she is doing. Diab Custom Design makes beautiful things, mostly from wood, and it is Tara's baby — she takes pride in every set of kitchen cabinets, armoire, or drawer handle, crafting them as elegantly as possible. Tara is tough as nails and rough as sandpaper, but the results of her woodworking are achingly beautiful.

Laura actually included parts of Tara's story in her book. Tara became intrigued. She consumed Laura's book, reading some and listening to the whole thing as an audiobook. She recognized herself and her ideals in the messages of *Limitless*. "You go for your dreams, you realize that what you're doing doesn't have to keep up with anybody else," she explained to me. "It is about building a life that matters in the world, no matter what you do."

A lot of people get inspired by great books. But Tara went further. She got a tattoo of *Limitless* on her left upper arm, complete with the infinity symbol.

This is not Tara's first tattoo. But it is in an important spot, especially when Tara is rowing crew. As she told me, "The *Limitless* tattoo, the placement of it is important. I can see it as I'm rowing; as I take my stroke, I come across my body with my left arm. Every stroke I take, I can see that tattoo."

To Tara, the tattoo symbolizes how each of us must be present in every single stroke we take, every moment of our days.

To Laura, though, the tattoo is something different — it indicates that she has reached her target. Someone has felt so strongly about Laura's book that she got it permanently inscribed on her body. Laura Gassner Otting was able to inspire someone to think differently. And that is more powerful than any bestseller list. It is the kind of thing that makes writing a book worthwhile.

Are you writing a book for the right reason?

There are already hundreds of thousands of business books in the world. What makes you think you ought to write one?

If all you want is to see your words in print . . . put this book down. Walk away. What I'm about to describe is more work than you want to put in.

If you think a book will be a business card for your business, I'm not the right person to help you. People don't read "business card" books, they pass them around like totems. It doesn't much matter what's in them. So they don't interest me (and realistically, they shouldn't interest you, either).

If you are putting your own goals first — goals like becoming famous, getting lots of new clients, increasing your speaking opportunities — you're thinking about it backward. Those are worthwhile things to wish for, certainly. But the book is not about you — people don't want to read about how great you are.

Instead, a book must be about what you know that no one else knows and how you can help people. *The goal of a business book is to help the reader succeed.* Think of the audience's goals first, and your goals second, and you're on the right track.

Effective business books reach their target because they are relevant and useful. Jay Baer and Daniel Lemin's *Talk Triggers* was useful to marketers. Laura Gassner Otting's *Limitless* is useful to people who feel stuck. They succeed if they make people recognize something new and act on it. All the benefits flow from that.

I know personally how exhilarating this is. My former colleague Charlene Li and I wrote a book called *Groundswell: Winning in a World Transformed by Social Technologies,* published in 2008 by Harvard Business Review Press. Groundswell sold 150,000 copies and was translated into a dozen languages. It became the essential manual for a whole generation of thinkers about marketing and social media. More than ten years have passed, and some of what was in *Groundswell* is now obsolete (need any tips on Myspace strategy?). But when I meet marketers and technology thinkers, they still tell me how we changed their thinking about social media, even now, more than a decade later. No one has a *Groundswell* tattoo so far as I know, but our ideas managed to move lots of minds in ways that still resonate.

In my work and interactions with hundreds of business authors, this is the commonality. Authors come in all types — female and male, shy and brash, funny and thoughtful, ambitious at the start of their careers or taking a victory lap at the end. But despite their diversity, they manifest a common goal: sharing what they have learned to help others succeed.

The learning they share may be practical (how to invest in real estate) or motivational (how to love yourself as you are). The learning may come from experience in their work, data they have access to, or interviews with people succeeding in the world. Regardless of how they know what they know, they are passionate about helping others with that knowledge.

Why people actually write business books

I wanted to know why authors write business books. So I asked them.

Between 2019 and 2022, I surveyed 242 nonfiction authors, nearly all of whom had written or were writing business books. Of these, 172 had completed and published a book, and 70 more were actively working on their first book.

When I asked them to identify their goals, the leading answer was "Share the knowledge I had," with 75% (see Figure 2-1). More than one in four authors said this was their primary goal. The results were similar for the authors who were not yet published — 84% of them were focused on sharing their knowledge.

Figure 2-1: Goals of published authors

Source: Bernoff.com author survey 2019-2022 (N=172 published authors)

"Review this list of possible goals people have when writing books. Which of these goals motivated you to write your first nonfiction book? Check all that apply."

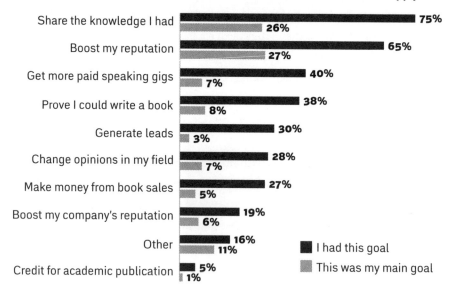

Among the published authors who had a goal of sharing their knowledge, 91% said they accomplished it. So it is, indeed, realistic to think that you can share knowledge and help people to become more successful, just as Jay and Daniel, Laura, and Charlene and I did.

Authors are not all altruists of course. Their second-most popular reason for writing a book was "To boost my reputation." But they know that their reputation as an author and an expert comes from the value inherent in their books. So "boost my reputation" effectively comes back once again to "share the knowledge I had."

I recognize that you, as an author, are not a charity. You want something for yourself from this book you're working on. While it's possible that you'll sell a million books and get rich, that's very unlikely. But the more realistic goals that authors have for themselves — to provide more visibility to their companies, to get a speaking career, to generate leads — all come back to a book that shares useful knowledge to help readers succeed. (I describe authors' best ways to monetize books in chapter 23).

If your book is successful — if it matters — it will come back to the factors I described in chapter 1: You had an idea that was relevant for your audience, you told stories that kept people engaged, the story of the book resonated with that audience, and you promoted your book's idea in a way that people related to. In other words, you shared that knowledge effectively, and it made a difference to the people who read it.

Don't be a sucker

Caveat scriptor — let the author beware.

Authors are dreamers. Unfortunately, everybody in publishing knows this. And because dreamers dream, they are vulnerable.

For example, here's a quote from one book that panders to author dreams:

"I want to give you easy access to that same accomplishment, freedom, and sense of self-worth [that I had]. [This book] is the map that will help you obtain any level of success you desire. . . ."[4]

This is typical. There are many, many websites and books you can read that will tell you: "Yes! You can do this! You *can* write a book. Realize your dreams to be a respected, bestselling author!"

That's just bullshit. Sure, you can get published. But writing a book to accomplish your goals takes a lot more work than dreaming. And because you are an author with a dream, you have a target on your back. Everyone wants to sell you something.

There are publishing services. Custom printing services. Book promotion services. Ghostwriters. Editors. Cover designers. Ebook formatters. Audiobook sound recordists. Speakers' bureaus. Experts in Facebook for authors, sizzle reels for authors, podcasting for authors, book tours for authors. If an author might need it, somebody is ready to sell it.

There are even people who will promise to manipulate your book onto a best-seller list, for tens of thousands of dollars, and with no actual guarantee of success.

Some of those services are worth paying for, and some are not — and

---

4   From *Published.: The Proven Path From Blank Page To 10,000 Copies Sold* (2016) by Chandler Bolt, p. 17.

distinguishing one from the other depends on your exact situation as an author.

It's very confusing. You may be tempted to connect with your accountant's Uncle Harry who wrote a novel about elves and published it himself. (Please don't.)

Authors are smart, but many, even those who've been through the process once or twice, have a lot to learn about what it takes to conceive, write, and publish a book and actually profit from it. Each author's path is different. And the book business is continually shifting, with new avenues of success opening up and others becoming harder to get access to.

You might think a bestselling author is automatically the best source of information on business book publishing. They're not. Why? Because of survivorship bias. A hundred people have tried what they tried. Ninety-nine failed. Why are you willing to listen to the one who got lucky? If you copy what they did, it won't necessarily work for you.

Why listen to me, then? Not because I got fortunate and sold a lot of one book. But because I've helped dozens of diverse authors to achieve their diverse sets of dreams — each on a different, personalized path. And I'm not here to sell you anything. You already bought my book — I just want you to have the best possible advice on this journey.

I will not sugarcoat things, and I will present as unbiased an account as possible. If you ought *not* to be an author, you'll be out no more than the cost of this book. My goal is to help you make good decisions and write and publish your book as effectively as possible.

Your book is more than a book

When people think about books, they tend think of little rectangular packages of bound paper pages. They think of shelves full of books in colorful dust jackets in bookstores. Or they may think of icons on their Kindle or iPad, each a promise of a neat package of insight.

But, after speaking with many, many authors, I know that these are not the ways that published authors think about their books. Yes, it feels good to hold a nice bound copy of all your insights in your hand and know, *I created this. I shared what I knew. It's all here.*

But as you embark on the journey of creating a book, don't limit yourself to thinking that way. Experienced authors know a book is more than that.

- **A book is you.** A book with your name on it is you. It is a physical (or digital) manifestation of who you are and what you believe. If it is brilliant, you are brilliant. If it is entertaining, you are entertaining. If it is helpful, you are helpful. And if it is poorly organized, repetitive, or wrong, it could reveal you as a weak-minded blowhard.

- **A book is the largest possible lump of content marketing.** Content marketing comes from useful or entertaining content intended to make people pay attention to you or trust your authority. A book is the weightiest way to make that point; it establishes you as an expert. People who read it and find it helpful may seek you out for help. People who know about it, even if they don't read it, will likely see it as reinforcing your authority.

- **A book is a block of your time and money.** A book requires many hours of research, writing, and rewriting. Even if you hire a ghostwriter, it demands that you pay attention to what belongs in it. It sucks up your money in the form of editorial resources, promotional expenses, lost opportunities, and, if you use a hybrid or custom publisher, actual out-of-pocket dollars.

- **A book is needy.** Even after it's written, a book needs feeding. It needs bylined articles, supporting blog posts, or sharable infographics. It needs speeches. It needs your time with journalists, reviewers, bloggers, and podcasters. Eventually, it needs updating. It gives — but it takes, too.

- **A book is an obsession.** Read any acknowledgments page, where the authors thank their families for putting up with how they became much less available while writing. A good book requires extra effort to find the best examples, identify supporting points, root out errors, and maintain a constant commitment to quality from start to finish. Unless you pay obsessive attention, it won't be as good as it needs to be.

Once you begin to think about a book this way, you begin to get a more realistic expectation of what a book demands — and what benefits it can deliver. And you're ready to get started.

If you help readers, they will respect you

Lots of people have business and motivational ideas. Few have earned the widespread respect their ideas ought to generate.

This is especially true for women and minorities. They have to work a little harder for their voices to be heard.

Take Melanie Deziel. She had a clever idea about how to do content marketing — a systematic way to break it down into ten areas of focus and ten content formats. The resulting grid of 100 possibilities makes it easy to generate content to drive interest in your products. She published her ideas in *The Content Fuel Framework: How to Generate Unlimited Story Ideas* (StoryFuel Press, 2020). And she turned that into a reputation for expertise in a hot field. She had an inflexible deadline — she completed the book just before giving birth to her first child. But as a result of all that work, she was in position to promote it and boost her business as she could turn her attention back to it.

Michael C. Bush is another entrepreneur who has boosted his research and consulting business with a book, as I will describe in more detail in chapter 10. Michael used his data-heavy book, *A Great Place to Work for All: Better for Business, Better for People, Better for the World* (Berrett-Koehler Publishers, 2018), to get attention that might otherwise be challenging to get for underrepresented people. As he explained it to me, "Black people have a lot of headwinds to face: bias, racism, access to capital. They are working hard to keep their heads above water in a way that isn't quite the same as the dominant [cultural] groups. When people are using so much energy just to survive, everybody loses. The key is to create organizations that have the best people on earth so that the complex problems in society can be addressed." For a deep thinker like Michael, being known as the author of a book on corporate culture adds credibility.

Another group that doesn't get sufficient consideration for visionary thinking consists of leaders outside the US/UK/Canada axis of business and management. I've worked with thinkers from countries like Sweden and Australia who've published books to gain broader recognition for their ideas — and to get respect that goes well beyond their home countries. A book in English, generating speaking engagements in the US, goes a long way toward turning local leadership into being part of the global conversation.

Writing a book is also a great way for young thinkers — people in their twenties or early thirties, for example — to get people to pay attention to their ideas, putting aside any preconceptions about youth.

For members of all these groups, a book can do what nothing else can easily do: gain them the respect their ideas deserve.

Let's get practical

The rest of this book is simply everything you need to know to write a business book that matters. My intention is to provide practical advice and, just as I am advising you to do, be useful.

There is no requirement that you read what follows in order. The next three chapters are about nailing down your idea and title, deciding on your publishing model, and planning: three essential challenges for every author. After that, you can dip into the chapters about researching, writing, and promoting based on what your biggest questions are right now.

Key takeaways

- The main reason authors write books is to share what they have learned.
- Lots of people want to take authors' money for all sorts of services, worthwhile or not. Author beware.
- Be aware that your book represents you in the world, and it will swallow a lot of your time, both while you write it and after you publish it. Books that matter require effort.
- Books can generate respect, especially for people in groups striving for recognition, such as young people, women, minorities, and business thinkers outside of North America.

Chapter 3

Great Ideas and Great Titles

Stand out in the reader's mind.

Charlene Li is pretty damn smart. I learned that from working with her as a colleague a decade ago, and I've continued to see it as I observed her success with the research and advisory company Altimeter, which she ran until recently as part of the consultancy Prophet.

When I noticed she was planning a book on disruption — perhaps the hottest topic in business thinking these days — I anticipated something special. How does a thinker like Charlene come up with ideas? It's a lot of work. Since most of us don't have a clear concept of what "working on an idea" looks like, let's take a look at how she came up with and refined this one.

First off — where does an idea come from?

In Charlene's case, she works regularly with big companies and their executives as they grapple with changes in technology. Naturally, they ask about disruption. What is it? How can you define it? How can a big, probably slow-moving company latch onto growth from it? How can executives get beyond the inertia of their own business to benefit from disruption? A lot has happened since the late Harvard Business School professor Clayton Christensen originally named and analyzed the phenomenon of disruption in 1997; people are seeking new insights.

In three years of public speaking on the topic of disruption, Charlene tried out several different definitions. Striving to serve audiences who wanted actual, useful strategic advice, she had to get beyond the clichés about how Blockbuster and RadioShack became obsolete and focus instead on success stories of big companies that had embraced disruption and succeeded.

This led her to examples like T-Mobile, which revolutionized the mobile carrier landscape with its "Un-carrier" strategy, and Adobe, which cannibalized its own business in a shift from packaged software to annual subscriptions.

From case studies like these and many conversations with executives, she came up with a new description of what it means to be a disruptive company:

Disruptive organizations focus relentlessly on the needs of future customers to drive their growth, lifting the strategy above departmental battles or technology disagreements.

This is both simple and counterintuitive. Focusing on future customers over present customers sounds simple — *but present customers are the ones generating the revenue.* Every customer experience and business management book says to give customers what they want. Charlene says that's fine, so long as it doesn't conflict with giving them what they *will* want — and that you have to focus on the future, sometimes even to the detriment of the present. That's easy to say, but very hard to do. (Charlene's book, of course, tells you how to do it.)

What's the right title for this book? What would *you* call it?

Halfway through writing it, Charlene had a good working title: *The Disruptor's Agenda.* That title made logical sense for a book about disruption strategy. But people she trusted were telling her that the proposed title seemed boring. A book this powerful needed something better than a boring title.

So Charlene came up with about eight different alternative titles, along with subtitles, and tested them in an online comparison tool with people similar to the corporate executives she was targeting as an audience.

In those tests, an alternative title floated to the top: *The Disruption Mindset.* Connecting that to her ideas demanded a subtitle that positioned the book as a research-based breakthrough. The full title of the book, published by Ideapress Publishing in 2019, is *The Disruption Mindset: Why Some Organizations Transform While Others Fail.*

That sounds like a big idea book. This book has already shaken up the business world, driven Charlene's speaking career, and generated the influence she needed with executives to be successful.

People with brilliant ideas often make it seem as if the idea came to them in a moment of inspiration. Charlene's experience is more common: Observe what people need, refine your thinking until you come up with something both simple and powerful, and work hard at getting just the right title for the book about that idea.

What makes for a book-worthy idea?

What is an idea?

Forget dictionary definitions. For an idea to be solid enough to base a book on, it has to have consequences. And it has to be surprising, but simple.

So here's my definition:

An idea is a previously unsuspected connection among concepts that leads to non-obvious consequences.

If you make that previously unsuspected connection, you can ask "Now that we know x, what does that mean?" And if the consequences are not obvious, you can write a book about it.

Charlene's previously unsuspected connection was that disruption is about focusing on future customers, not present customers — even if that means pivoting your business in a surprising direction. That's a big idea, and it has consequences for everything a company does.

Let's look at some other examples.

David Allison's book *We Are All the Same Age Now: Valuegraphics, The End of Demographic Stereotypes* (Lioncrest Publishing, 2018) posits that marketers should target consumers based on their values, rather than on whether they're a suburban mom or a millennial. David Epstein's *Range: Why Generalists Triumph in a Specialized World* (Riverhead Books, 2019) explains how the most successful people pursue and connect a diverse collection of expertise, rather than specializing in one area. Both are simple ideas, but with significant consequences for their audiences (marketers and workers, respectively).

The best ideas are simple, but significant. They must also have three other qualities: They must be new, big, and right (see Figure 3-1).

Figure 3-1: Ideas must be new, big, and right

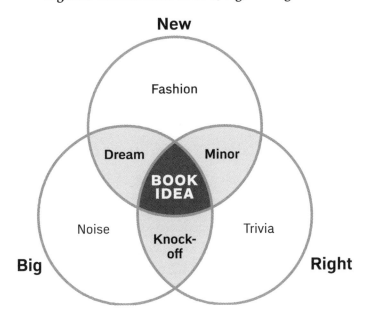

New ideas mark you as an original thinker

Here's an idea. I'll write a book about how you can take a business and scale it up rapidly, prioritizing growth over everything else. Sure! I could call it *Blitzscaling*.

Too bad Reid Hoffman and Chris Yeh already published that book in 2018.

It's virtually impossible to build a career on being known as the second, third, or tenth thinker to come up with an idea. To get attention for a book, you need to be first.

Obviously, you can't write the first book on confidence at work or email marketing or leadership or innovation. Regardless of what you are writing, someone has written about the *topic* before. But an original idea is a new twist on the topic, one that makes people see things in a new light. You need to be able to complete the sentence, "This will be the first book that . . ."

That's why Charlene Li can write a book on the well-trod ground of disruption — because her book is the first book built around the unifying idea of focusing on the future customer.

How do you get to new?

First, do research. Talk to people about your idea. Test it out. Observe how it matches reality. Push beyond the common clichés to new insights.

Research what other thinkers believe about your topic. Test your idea against theirs. What's different? Have you seen further into the future? Have you applied it globally? Have you come to a counterintuitive conclusion? Search relentlessly for that different angle that will set you apart.

Big ideas have consequences

Newness is not enough. New things come and go all the time — Facebook redesigns, fashion trends, fads. It's tough to write books about them; they're too small.

If you try to write a book about a small, simple idea, you'll run out of material. You'll repeat yourself. (We've all read those business books where every chapter seems like a rehash of the same stuff we read in chapter 1). Those books should just be a blog post.

For a real book, you need a *big* idea.

A big idea can still be limited to a specific field of study, like marketing, or direct marketing, or even email marketing. But it must be big enough to have facets and consequences worth writing about at length. It must create ripples. You can write a whole book about those facets, consequences, and ripples and then build a career off of your expertise in it. You'll never run out of material.

As I said in chapter 1, memorable business books are structured in the form of a narrative. The big idea and its consequences lead naturally to a narrative: Understand *this*, and then do *that*, and everything will be different.

What do big ideas look like? Here are three big books and a description of the ideas in them:

- *The Long Tail: Why the Future of Business is Selling Less of More* (Hyperion, 2006) by Chris Anderson. Online markets succeed by allowing millions of people to buy thousands of possible products, even if any given product only sells a few.

- *Atomic Habits: An Easy & Proven Way to Build Good Habits & Break Bad Ones* (Avery, 2018) by James Clear. The key to establishing good habits is to create a system that reinforces them.
- *Start with Why: How Great Leaders Inspire Everyone to Take Action* (Portfolio, 2009) by Simon Sinek. Great organizations move forward around a common purpose.

If you accept any one of these ideas, you have to think and act differently. You have to organize differently, plan differently, communicate differently. Start these books and a light goes off in your head — and you want to read the rest of the book to understand how to apply what you now realize.

How do you make your idea bigger?

Ask some questions without easy answers. How would this change things in the next five years? How might it apply to the small businesses that power the economy? What steps should members of my target audience take to address the idea? What types of people or companies will thrive, and which will wither? How could I measure the change?

These questions will inevitably lead you to a broader concept of your idea — one big enough to write a book about.

Right ideas stand the test of time

Simple, big, new ideas are great. But it doesn't make them accurate.

Here's an idea: Social media will make the world a better place. That's an attractive concept, but the evidence is mounting that it's just not true.

What's the penalty for being wrong? Plenty of wrong ideas get published every day. Wrong ideas can certainly spread and make you famous. The problem with wrong ideas is that eventually, they get proven wrong, and you lose your credibility.

So how do you make sure your idea is right?

You search for evidence, not just to confirm it, but to challenge it.

You put elements of the idea out there in the form of blog posts or tweets and see how people react.

You road-test the idea with clients or people you interview for the book and refine it to make it stronger.

One way to convince people ideas are right is with stories about people who learned about them or followed them and succeeded (or failed to follow them and flopped). If business books are made of stories, those stories should convince readers that the idea they're based on is right. (I talk about where to find these stories and how to tell them in chapter 9).

Another way to convince people that an idea is right is with research that surfaces data, statistics, analogies, and insights by respected thinkers. (For more tips on research to support or challenge your ideas, see chapter 10.)

Simple, new, big, and right combine to make an idea spread

Simple ideas are easy to repeat.

New ideas pique interest and attract attention.

Big ideas have far-reaching consequences.

Right ideas stand the test of time.

Combine all of these and you'll be able to build a solid book whose premise people are likely to understand, care about, and repeat. That's a formula for an idea that catches on.

(Incidentally, I do follow my own principles. The idea behind the book you're reading is simple: Successful business books are built around stories. This book is new: It's the first book to address the *modern* business book landscape, including new publishing and publicity models. It's big because it's a comprehensive treatment of everything that authors need to know. And it's right because I've road-tested it with a wide variety of authors and books.)

How to come up with a great title

There is no better way to launch your idea into the zeitgeist than to come up with an awesome book title. In your dreams, your book has an iconic title. You know, like *Lean In*. Or *The Tipping Point*. Or *Made to Stick*.

You are deluded.

And your delusion is leading you astray.

These books sold because of huge promotion (*Lean In*) and incredible ideas and writing. You think they are great titles; the truth is that they are good titles for great books.

Do you think a book called *Lean In* by John Paul Nobody would be successful? Or a book called *The Tipping Point* by Nevah Herdava? Not likely. Not unless they were fantastic books.

Here's the truth: Except in rare cases, titles don't sell books.

You might have come up with that kind of rare title — like *You Are a Badass* or *The 4-Hour Workweek*. If so, it probably came to you in a dream, or while you were writing. It's wrapped around the concept and the prospective reader's brain so tightly that no other title is possible.

But based on my experience with many authors, where you are is this: You have an idea, and maybe a proposal or part of a manuscript. You have tossed around a bunch of possible titles and subtitles. You are not overjoyed with any of them. You're looking at *Bad Blood* enviously and wondering if you can come up with a title that great.

Maybe this will help: The job of the book title is *not* to sell the book. People are not going to invest their time, which is more important than their money, in your book just based on the title.

The first job of the book title is to get someone who might be interested to want to know more about the book.

Start with your audience. If your audience is lawyers, the job of the book title is to get lawyers interested. *Tortious Interference* might be a good title for them, even if no one else knows what it means.

It matters if the audience is investors, or business strategists, or new college graduates, or salespeople. You need to speak their language.

If someone in that audience becomes interested, they will read the subtitle. The job of the subtitle is to make a promise about what the book will deliver. So a title that gets you to read the subtitle, and subsequently to become interested in the book and maybe buy it, is great.

The book title has a second job. It is a name for the book, a "handle." This is important for word of mouth and reviews.

Here's an example. I helped two authors with a book called *Data Leverage: Unlocking the Surprising Growth Potential of Data Partnerships* (Ward PLLC, 2018). It's about strategy for making money from the data your company has collected.

If you're somebody who deals with your company's data and you read this book, you might find it was just what you needed. And then when you were speaking with a professional friend who does the same thing at her business, you could say, "You should read *Data Leverage*. It's about making money with partnerships around data." And your friend will remember the name, since she wants to get leverage from her data.

Your prospective reader might read somebody else's Facebook post about the book. They might read a review on a blog. They might hear it mentioned in a LinkedIn video. They might read a review in a newspaper. They might see the name mentioned in a roundup of books about this topic. They might see it as a recommendation on Amazon because it is on a topic related to a book they were perusing. They might see the author give a speech about it.

Eventually, after a few repetitions of hearing about it or seeing it mentioned, they might become intrigued, read more about it, read the description on Amazon or Bookshop.org, and actually buy it.

This only works because these mentions connect the concept and the title in the potential reader's mind.

Consider some of the titles I've mentioned earlier and some others, and you see how this works.

Lean In = How women should do leadership.

You Are a Badass = Get over your fears and do your best work.

The Long Tail = An innovative theory about how things sell online.

The 4-Hour Workweek = Be successful with less effort.

Getting Things Done = Be more productive.

Atomic Habits = Establish good habits for powerful results.

The titles don't necessarily tell the whole story (what does "lean in" or "the long tail" mean without the context of the book?) But they connect *your audience* with your idea, they are catchy, and they become handles for that idea.

When you see Serena Williams' face, you think of incredible tennis talent. This is not because her face has anything to do with tennis, it is because by repeated association you think of tennis when you see it.

Similarly, with these books, after enough mentions, you associate the title with the concept.

Your title should intrigue, then connect with the idea. Unless you're really lucky, it's not going to explain the idea, but that is not the objective.

The objective is to intrigue and be a good handle for the idea as people talk about it.

Subtitles fill in the missing information

The subtitle, in conjunction with the title, should explain a little more. It should make a promise about what the book will deliver. This gives the prospective reader enough context to make a decision to read the book, or at least to consider reading it, so that successive mentions, or the flap copy, or an endorsement by Oprah Winfrey, or whatever else happens next can push them over the edge to buying the book.

Look at the full titles/subtitles of some of these books, and what they're telling you:

Lean In: Women, Work, and the Will to Lead

You Are a Badass: How to Stop Doubting Your Greatness and Start Living an Awesome Life

The Long Tail: Why the Future of Business Is Selling Less of More

The 4-Hour Workweek: Escape 9-5, Live Anywhere, and Join the New Rich

Getting Things Done: The Art of Stress-Free Productivity

Atomic Habits: An Easy & Proven Way to Build Good Habits & Break Bad Ones

The titles and subtitles might get you to the buy the book. But they're more likely to just move you down the path to buying, so something else can push you over the edge.

The title brainstorm

How do you come up with a great title? You could try banging your fists on your forehead until a title pops out, but that doesn't tend to work. (I've been there.)

You could also try crowdsourcing it. Go on Facebook or Twitter and describe your book and ask for suggestions. You will get a lot of stupid, misguided ideas. People will throw mud at each other's ideas. Or worse yet, they'll come to a mealy-mouthed compromise. I've seen this happen over and over: Crowdsourcing titles not only fails, it makes you hate yourself and all your friends.

What you need is a focused way to get the right words to come out of your own head, even if you don't know what they are.

I've done this about 40 times. What I learned is that you need exactly two people other than the author or authors.

One is a word person — someone with excellent facility with language. (In my brainstorms, this is me.)

The other is a person who will be a proxy for the audience. This must be a person that the author or authors trust, but who isn't overly familiar with the concept.

We all get together, and I ask the author to explain the concept to the audience proxy. I listen for words that sound original or unusual and then start writing them down in a shared document.

When you're looking for good words to use in a title, tap any word-related tools you can. Use a thesaurus like Thesaurus.com or WordHippo. Or paste ideas from your text into ChatGPT and ask it for some book title suggestions. Sometimes the words you're looking for are related to the words you've already got — these sorts of tools can help you find them.

I did a title brainstorm with the author Denise Lee Yohn for her second book. Denise is a branding expert, but in her work with companies, she had a fascinating insight: Brand and corporate culture are two sides of the same coin. Brand is the company's external image; culture is how it operates with its employees. Unless the two are in sync, the company cannot ultimately succeed. Her working title was *Bound to Thrive: Bond Your Brand & Culture to Build a Great Business,* but she wanted to do better.

Denise and her brand-building colleague Steve met with me by videoconference as she was planning her book. Denise explained her concept. And with the help of an online thesaurus, we started to play with words about two related elements connecting: Yin/yang. Lock/link. Bond. Mashup. Jazz. Duet. Harmony. Fusion.

When Steve suggested "Fusion," something clicked. This was the iconic term she was looking for.

A bit more work allowed us to fill in a subtitle that explained the meaning further: *Fusion: How Integrating Brand and Culture Powers the World's Greatest Companies.*

And that was the title of the book Denise sold to Nicholas Brealey Publishing, a division of the large publishing house Hachette, and published in 2018.

Making sure the playing field is clear

Before you fall in love with a title, you need to make sure you can own it. I don't mean literally. I mean in searches.

Go to Amazon.com and search the title. Before Denise's book was published, an Amazon search on "fusion" revealed that there was no popular business book with the same title. (While your book can share the same title as another book, it gets in the way of your branding.) A Google search on "fusion book" didn't reveal any other books squatting on the term, so we were good to go.

One book I was involved with included the acronym HERO — for "highly empowered and resourceful operative." We considered naming it *HEROes*. But there was an NBC television series with the same name, and we knew it would dominate all the searches. So we came up with a different name: *Empowered*.

The book needs a web address. But a common word like fusion is not going to be available as a dot-com — you'll have to find a workaround. Don't let the availability of a URL determine your choice of title; you can always pick a dot-net, or even a page on your existing site, like yoursite.com/booktitle.

Finally, it's a good idea to search your desired title in a trademark registry site like trademarkia.com. Even if someone has trademarked your title, you don't necessarily have a problem, because trademarks apply in limited domains, like food products or consulting. If there is a potential conflict, consult with an intellectual property attorney to ensure you're still in the clear.

To avoid title hell, decide on a title early

There are major benefits to nailing down your title before you get too far in the writing process. Once you've set the title, you can:

- Weave references to the title throughout the book.
- Reserve web domains, Twitter handles, Facebook Pages, and other branding elements and ensure they're available.
- Sell the book before it's written. Publishers recognize the value of a great title.
- Avoid roadblocks. A title settled early prevents publishers, colleagues, and, if you have them, managers from butting in with unwanted and ill-informed suggestions.
- Get to work on designing the cover. (You can't realistically make progress on the cover design until the title, subtitle, and all the other text elements on the cover are settled.)

What happens if you don't nail down the title early? You could end up in title hell.

In the case of one book I worked on, there was no consensus on the title even though the manuscript was nearly complete. I found myself attempting the acrobatic feat of getting my coauthor, each of our bosses, my CEO, the editor at my publisher, the editor's boss, and the head of the publishing operation to agree on a title. We settled for a compromise title that didn't help the book to succeed. It's far better to inspire everyone involved with a great title rather than getting them all to settle on a blandly acceptable one.

A great title inspires everyone involved with the book: authors, publishers, readers, booksellers, reviewers, and colleagues. That's way more effective than getting stuck in title hell.

Key takeaways

- The foundation of every book is a great idea.
- A book idea must be simple. It must also be new enough to stand out, big enough to support a book's worth of content, and right enough to be credible.
- A book title is a handle — it catches the eye, intrigues the mind, and promises more.
- A subtitle fleshes out the title with enough detail to describe what the book promises.
- Use a title brainstorm — including a creative word person and a sounding-board person representing the audience — to surface good title ideas.
- Search title ideas on Amazon and Google to make sure similar or prominent books aren't already using them.

Chapter 4

Publishing Models

Select a publishing path for speed, cost, or prestige.

P hil M. Jones knows *exactly* what he wants his books to do for his business. In different situations, at different points in his career as a speaker and consultant, that meant taking three different paths to publication — each with its own benefits and challenges.

Phil's expertise is in how people communicate in sales situations and generally. His big idea is that unless you use exactly the right words in any given situation, you won't get the desired result. As it says on the first page of his most successful book, "The worst time to think about the thing you are going to say is in the moment you are saying it."

Phil's started by putting his thoughts down in three small, self-published books through Lulu: *Toolbox, Magic Words,* and *PHILosophies.* Of these, *Magic Words* was the most significant. In a scant 44 pages, Phil laid out the basics of his method and created a content collection that he could use to promote or accompany the speeches he gave.

Phil loved the self-publishing model. "The biggest pro of self-publishing is the creative and editorial freedom. It's the fastest way to get to market, on your terms and on your own timescale."

But as Phil's business grew, he wanted to create a more finished-looking, professional package. He teamed up with the hybrid publisher Page Two. A hybrid publisher does pretty much what a traditional publisher does, but for hire, working for the author. The result is more of a partnership than you get with a traditional publisher. He retooled his content from *Magic Words,* invested around $20,000 in the process with Page Two, and came away with a beautifully produced book created with a high level of attention to detail.

The result was *Exactly What to Say: The Magic Words for Influence and Impact* (Page Two, 2018). Phil knew the new title would resonate because he'd piloted it in a Facebook group and in workshops; eventually, the word "exactly" became sort of a Phil M. Jones trademark, since it perfectly signifies his perspective on the power of specific words in specific contexts.

His marketing rollout, based on social media sharing and a massive podcast tour, was incredibly successful. It went on to sell 1.4 million copies and generate $2 million in book royalty revenue. Phil has also worked with Page Two to create dozens of custom editions for specific clients and situations, a project that demands a level of flexibility that no traditional publisher could ever come close to.

The success of *Exactly What to Say* attracted the attention of Wiley, a traditional publishing house. Phil negotiated a two-book deal with Wiley, scoring an advance of $25,000 per book. That deal generated two hardbacks: *Exactly How to Sell: The Sales Guide for Non-Sales Professionals* (Wiley, 2018) and *Exactly Where to Start: The Practical Guide to Turn Your BIG Idea into Reality* (Wiley, 2018). Together with his Page Two book, these three books create a trilogy of Phil's "exactly" content, which gives him flexibility to create book packages to align with his various speeches and workshops.

Traditional publishers have far more leverage with the bookstore channel. For example, Wiley was able to secure placement in the window of Barnes & Noble's Fifth Avenue store in New York for each of the two books it published for Phil. But traditional publishing is not a "drop off the manuscript and forget it" kind of deal, as much as authors would like it to be. Phil found he needed to pay close attention to identifying and correcting errors in page layout. He also found the publisher unable to get books to a launch event he planned in London, and he ended up carrying stacks of books in his checked luggage. And just as with the hybrid published book, Phil personally took most of the responsibility for book marketing and publicity.

Phil's an in-demand speaker now. Control and speed trump whatever clout the traditional publishers could bring — which is why his next book is far more likely to be published with a hybrid publisher. But that's Phil. Your situation is probably different. Which means you have an important decision to make.

Consider three publishing models

As Phil's story demonstrates, business and other nonfiction authors now have three main options for publishing a book. Each has a different schedule, generates different costs, and delivers a different end product, delivered through different channels. Because the economics and schedules of these methods are so diverse, it's smart to identify the right publishing model *before* you put a huge amount of effort into the book. That's why I'm covering this in chapter 4, rather than leaving it to the end of the book.

These are the three publishing options (see Figure 4-1):[5]

1. **Traditional.** Develop a proposal, pitch traditional publishers, and publish with a traditional publishing house. This is the model we all grew up hearing about, but it's no longer the only realistic way for a business author to get to market. It's the only method that pays you up front, but it's also the slowest. Among the published authors I surveyed, 46% used traditional publishers.

2. **Hybrid.** Hybrid publishers operate much like a traditional publishing house and generate a similar product, but the economics are different. In a hybrid publishing deal, you pay the publisher to do the work for you, and you, the author, are the customer. This method requires the greatest investment, but it can pay off if you sell a lot of books. About 21% of the authors in my survey used hybrid publishers.

---

5 Most books with publishing advice for authors are published by people with a vested interest in one of these methods. For example, Tucker Max and Zach Obront's *The Scribe Method: The Best Way to Write and Publish Your Non-Fiction Book* is an excellent primer, but you need to keep in mind that it was written by the founder of Scribe Media, a company that offers hybrid publishing services. Chandler Bolt's *Published.* makes it sound like creating a book is easy, and sure enough he runs an operation that helps people with self-publishing. You can learn a lot from these books, but recognize the bias based on how their authors make money.

Figure 4-1: Publishing models of published authors

Source: Bernoff.com author survey 2019-2022 (N=172 published authors)

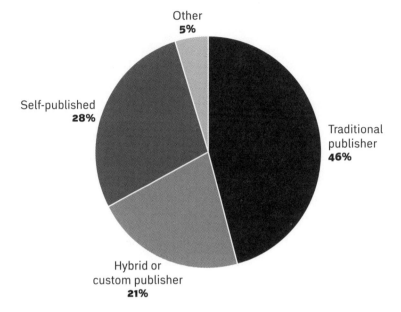

3.   **Self-published.** With suppliers like Amazon Kindle Direct Publishing and IngramSpark, you can launch a book on your own. The result is usually a print-on-demand book — a book that's actually printed one-off each time someone orders it. This method is the cheapest and the fastest to market, but it requires the author to do more of the work. It generates less impact and has more limited distribution. Self-publishing was the choice of 28% of the authors in my survey.

Before I get into describing the differences in these models, consider one thing they all have in common: *You* have to do most of the work. That means you, the author, need to conceive the idea, do the research, write the text (or hire and supervise a ghostwriter), and ride herd on it throughout the publishing process to make sure no errors creep in. And regardless of what you may hear or believe about publishers, you're still better off hiring your own developmental editor and preparing to do most of your own promotion, because publishers just don't do nearly as much of that work as they used to.

Even so, the three models are very different, both in economics and in how long they take. So let's walk through a detailed comparison.

Traditional publishing has the highest impact but longest time to market

The traditional publishing market underwent a significant contraction around the time of the Great Recession in 2008. The market for business books has since stabilized, but getting a book into print with a traditional publisher is not easy.

Traditional publishers bring a valuable set of assets to a business book author. Perhaps the most important is their relationship with bookstores, which in the US include Barnes & Noble and the airport bookstore chain Hudson News. Publishers have sales forces that call on the buyers from these stores and represent their entire collections of books. And publishers have the best ability to sell book rights overseas, licensing translations to Asian and European publishers, and distributing English editions to places like the UK, Australia, and India.

Even with all the major shifts in the publishing world and the advent of various self-publishing options, the imprimatur of a major publisher carries some weight. An imprint such as HarperCollins Publishers, Harvard Business Review Press, McGraw Hill Education, Random House, or Portfolio implies an endorsement by a highly selective editorial team that chooses manuscripts and authors carefully and rejects most applicants. Book reviewers at major publications are more likely to review books from these major publishers.

And of course, traditional publishers provide a financial incentive that other publications do not: They usually pay advances. An advance is a series of cash payments (often paid in three or four installments on specific milestones: signing a contract, delivering an acceptable manuscript, publication, and afterward) that the author keeps, regardless of how the book does. Among authors in my survey who used traditional publishers, the median advance was $17,500, but 23% of those authors got advances of $100,000 or more. Note that if the book sells well enough that the accumulated per-book royalty exceeds the advance payments, then the author will receive additional royalties as well — this is called "earning out the advance."

What's not to like? Well, first off, you don't just submit a manuscript and get accepted. To get a traditional publishing contract, you'll need to create an extensive and detailed book proposal, as I describe in the next chapter. Your proposal needs to describe not just how you will research and write the book, but also how you will market it. These days, publishers are as interested in your marketing plan and "author platform" — that is, speaking, social media, newsletters, and other channels you have to reach potential readers — as they are in your idea.

Then you need to get that proposal in front of publishers. Regrettably, publishing runs like an exclusive club, and you are probably not a member. I hear it all the time from authors. "I don't know anybody in publishing. How am I going to get anybody to look at my book idea?"

Editors are most likely to consider books from people they've published before. They'll consider a book represented by a reputable book agent, but agents are no more receptive to unsolicited pitches than publishers are.

Wail and scream all you want about how unfair this is, but you have to understand why it is the way it is: The chance of a publishable proposal coming in unsolicited (into the "slush pile") is very low. Editors and agents protect their time by focusing on the projects most likely to be worth publishing.

If you're not in that club, you need to network like a demon and tap the friends of your friends who are published authors to get introductions to publishers and agents.

Those introductions might be able to get you a publisher. Natalie Nixon, a creativity strategist and CEO of her business Figure 8 Thinking, is a good example. The first proposal for her book *The Creativity Leap: Unleash Curiosity, Improvisation, and Intuition at Work* read more like a dissertation. She despaired of getting published; as she described it to me, "I felt like publishing was this stone castle, and I was trying to climb it with a long nail manicure and stilettos." But based on some wise advice, she revised the proposal to be shorter and less academic and sent it to several professional friends. One of those was Joseph Pine, coauthor of the bestselling book *The Experience Economy: Competing for Customer Time, Attention, and Money* (Harvard Business Review Press, 1999). Joseph forwarded the proposal to three of his friends including Neil Maillet, the VP of editorial at Berrett-Koehler Publishers, an author-centric independent publisher focused on social, financial, and environmental sustainability. Berrett-Koehler offered Natalie a publishing deal and, after a very supportive and author-centric experience, published Natalie's book in 2020.

The other path to publishers is through an agent. A book agent makes recommendations on your proposal, then manages the process of pitching it to acquiring editors — and any decent agent has a long list and knows exactly who is buying what at any given time. The agent can solicit bids from multiple publishers at once and get them bidding against each other, and that makes it likely that you'll get the best possible offer. That's a tricky process, so you're really better off with an agent handling it than trying to do it yourself. (Note that while an agent can work with multiple publishers to get a bid, you cannot sell your book with more than one agent at a time, because the agent becomes your exclusive representative.)

In exchange for the agent's essential work, they take 15% of any advance and any subsequent royalties.

Of course, it's not easy to get the agent's attention, either. My agent Katherine Flynn says that she might pick up one unsolicited proposal per year from general inquiries, and one or two a month from recommendations from her previous clients. Even if you come recommended by a friend, your chances of the agent saying yes are only about one in ten and, of course, the agent can make no guarantee that publishers will bid on your proposal.

Assuming you have the connections, what kinds of books are publishers buying? Hollis Heimbouch, VP and Publisher at the Harper Business imprint of HarperCollins Publishers and publisher of some of the most influential books of the last 20 years, says she's looking for "New ideas, as well as old ideas packaged in new, exciting, contemporary ways." The ideas are crucial, but the writing makes a big difference as well. "What has changed over time is the demand by readers for business books that are actually engaging and entertaining to read," she says. "It used to be that you could write a really dry tome, the dryer the better, and that would be a good business book . . . but you can't get away with that anymore." Citing what she calls "The Malcolm Gladwell Effect," she says, "There must be lots of interesting stories from all over. People expect them to be entertaining and fun."

Wiley publishes more business books than any other publisher, which is why I was particularly interested in what Richard Narramore, executive editor there, had to say. He described his ideal book as one that can be a definitive book on a given topic. And, like other publishers, he is increasingly looking for authors who can, through their platforms, speaking, or sales forces at their companies, have a reasonable chance of selling 10,000 to 20,000 books. Publishers are counting on you to do most of the selling and marketing. As the agent Katherine Flynn states, "The publisher is making a calculation of whether the author can sell books on their own — the platform description is that important."

If you get that dream offer and take it, you'll have to accept a few realities. One is that traditional publishing is slow. Once you accept a publisher's offer, unless you're writing about something hugely timely and perishable, you can expect to wait 15 to 18 months before publication. (Richard Narramore says that Wiley is an exception; once your book manuscript is ready, he says he can get it on the shelf within six months.) If you're in a hurry, a traditional publisher may not be the best option.

And be realistic about what publishers do and don't do. They don't do developmental editing — they expect you to deliver a manuscript that's in publishable shape (so you may have to hire your own editor). They don't check facts. They supply copy editing for grammar, lay the pages out, design a cover, manufacture and warehouse and distribute physical books, and format ebooks for Kindle or Apple Books. They work with bookstore chains. They contact all the usual outlets for reviews or excerpts. Beyond that, the book marketing is your job and that includes getting endorsements for the back cover.

One quick tip: A lot of the money in book sales these days is in audiobooks. If you can possibly do so, retain the audiobook rights and work directly with Audible for distribution. Of course, publishers aren't stupid — they know there's money in audio, too, so many of them insist on audio rights in any publishing contract.

While traditional publishing pays advances in the tens of thousands of dollars, sometimes more than $100,000, you'll have to put up with the barriers to acceptance, the delays in publication, and wrangling with the publisher over control of the content. If that doesn't sound ideal to you, consider hybrid publishing or self-publishing instead.

Hybrid publishing enables control at a cost

What if you could hire your own publisher? That's the concept behind hybrid publishing.

There was at one time something a little embarrassing about the idea of paying your publisher. People called publishers that worked for hire "vanity presses," and the implication was that you were only printing up copies because you were in love with your own prose.

Things have come a long way since then. Greenleaf Book Group, established in 1997, has published 35 *New York Times* and *Wall Street Journal* bestsellers. And now there are a variety of excellent alternatives for those who want to hire a publisher on their own. Today, publishers for hire that adhere to high editorial and ethical standards are known as hybrid publishers. As Naren Aryal, publisher and founder of Amplify Publishing Group, my publisher for the book you are now reading, put it, "Back when hybrid publishing emerged as viable, there was a bias perpetuated by agents, [traditional] publishers, book buyers for bookstores, and other publishing industry gatekeepers." That bias has faded; Naren would tell you that it's gone altogether.

As an author hoping to work with a hybrid publisher, you still have to submit a limited proposal. That's because hybrid publishers don't want to waste time with authors who aren't actually able to complete a book and accomplish their goals, even if they can pay. But hybrid publishers accept all sorts of proposals that wouldn't necessarily attract a traditional publisher. The traditional publisher asks, "Can we make money on this book?" The hybrid publisher asks, instead, "Can we help the author to be successful with this?"

There's a big difference in the responsiveness of hybrid publishers. For a traditional publisher, the customer (that is, the entity that pays them) is the bookstore. For a hybrid publisher, it's the author. When you, the author, are the customer, you get treated far better, and you have ultimate control of the content that gets published. In my survey of authors, 86% of those with hybrid publishers said their publisher did a good job, compared with only 54% of those with traditional publishers.

I personally experienced this with *The Age of Intent: Using Artificial Intelligence to Deliver a Superior Customer Experience* (Amplify, 2019), a book that I ghostwrote for P.V. Kannan, the CEO of the Silicon Valley company [24]7.ai. Our hybrid publisher was Amplify. Luckily for us, P.V. was connected with the well-known columnist for *The New York Times,* Thomas L. Friedman, author of *The World is Flat.* Through that connection, we got Mr. Friedman to look at the book. He then surprised us all and published a column in *The New York Times* prominently mentioning the book — but three months before the publication date!

The New York Times column linked to the book's page on the publisher's site. Given that it was three months until the book was due to come out, the page just said, "Coming Soon." When I found out about the column at 6 a.m. Eastern time, I knew we were missing an enormous opportunity. So I emailed and messaged Naren at Amplify and begged him to fix the page so we could take advantage of all the traffic from the *Times* article to generate sales. Sure enough, somebody in his organization fixed it by 6:30 a.m. that same morning — including adding a link to pre-order the book on Amazon. That's a level of service you could never get from a traditional publisher, but when you're the customer, hybrid book publishers like Naren go out of their way to make your experience as effective as possible.

Hybrid publishers do all the same work as traditional publishers: copy editing, page layout, ebook preparation, manufacturing, and distribution into bookstore channels. Many have sales reps that call on bookstore buyers. You pay for all of that, including manufacturing the books, which is where most of the expense comes from. The up-front cost varies between $12,000 and $50,000, depending on all the different services you use. The median amount that hybrid published authors in my survey spent to create their books was $28,000 (See Table 4-1).

Books produced by quality hybrid publishers are typically of equal quality to books produced by traditional publishers, both in the quality of the content and the quality of the manufactured product. In addition to *The Age of Intent,* I've worked on books for several other hybrid publishers, and, in each case, my coauthors and I were pleased with the result.

However, Jane Friedman, a prominent publishing industry consultant and *Publishers Weekly* columnist who has done detailed analysis comparing paths to publication, advises caution. As she points out, "There are countless predators calling themselves hybrids, and the average person who's new to the publishing industry cannot possibly filter out the good from the bad. . . . No one is policing the term 'hybrid,' and it's not realistic to tell authors that hybrids work out great if you can only find a 'good' one. There is no qualified, vetted list of hybrids anywhere. So we have to live with the messy reality that some hybrids are predators and warn authors accordingly."

Table 4-1: Spending to create books by published authors
Source: Bernoff.com author survey 2019-2022

	Traditionally published authors (N=79)	Hybrid published authors (N=37)	Self-published authors (N=48)
Median out-of-pocket spending to create book	$3,000	$28,000	$4,500
Proportion that spent at least $10,000	32%	78%	35%
Proportion that spent at least $50,000	13%	30%	10%

I can personally vouch for all the hybrid publishers I've mentioned in this book. But if you select a different one, make sure you get references from other authors you trust who had a positive experience, because you'll be spending a significant amount of money to work with them.

If the books you publish with a hybrid publisher sell, you can make much of your money back, because the per-book royalty for hybrid publishers is typically much higher than for traditional publishers. One place where you come out ahead is on author copies. You'll be paying the manufactured price, which is far less than traditional publishers' author discounts, and you're free to sell the books for whatever price you want. Publishers like Ideapress Publishing and Amplify will set up a portal so you can sell books from your own site, often clearing a profit of $10 or $15 per unit. If you sell more than 5,000 units across both retail outlets and your own site, you'll be very likely to make back your up-front investment with the hybrid publisher. And if you sell a lot more than that, you can make a much higher profit on sales, as Phil M. Jones did with his book published by Page Two.

Quality hybrid publishers are not all the same. For example, Rohit Bhargava, the publisher of Ideapress Publishing and himself an author of eight books, takes a personal interest in and works one-on-one with his authors as a peer — including developmental editing when it's needed. As he puts it, "We aim to be author-centric and put control back into the author's hands. Our editors, proofreaders, and cover designers are generally people who formerly worked at big publishing companies and are now freelancers." With this level of attention, Rohit only puts out ten to 12 books a year; several of those, like Laura Gassner Otting's *Limitless*, have gone on to become national bestsellers. (Rohit's Ideapress Publishing also published Charlene Li's *The Disruption Mindset*, the book I mentioned at the start of the previous chapter.)

Phil M. Jones' publisher Page Two, based in Toronto, is another hands-on hybrid publishing operation that's growing rapidly. It puts some books into distribution and some remain available only through Amazon, depending on the author's goals. As its cofounder Trena White explained, "One of the things that we do well is we are relentlessly focused on market and audience. How to position this book for the audience — that is baked into our sales and marketing thinking, baked into the editing, into the design, it's part of every conversation we have. When you ask about what our editorial process looks like, that's a really critical part of it."

Trena's description of Page Two's experience with Phil M. Jones' book shows how flexible this model can be. "Phil's *Exactly What to Say* started as print-on-demand with a fast timeline. Once it started to snowball, we put it into the full book trade [bookstore distribution]. Now it is selling through brick-and-mortar bookstores and Hudson stores [in airports]." You'll never see that evolution with a traditional publisher, because traditional publishers have little interest in books that don't sell in bookstores right away.

Wonderwell, a smaller nonfiction publisher started by Maggie Langrick, takes an even more intensive approach, coaching authors every step of the way. And she expects even more diversity in publishing models. "I think we will see an increasing fragmentation of models and of pathways to market," she told me. "As always, quality will rise to the top. There has already been a gigantic explosion in the number of titles, but that doesn't mean people are reading more. As the market matures, we will see hybrid publishing continue to gain prominence as a viable third option, an alternative to the two dominant models [traditional and self-publishing]."

Two companies I haven't mentioned are large players here. One is Scribe Media, founded by Tucker Max as Book in a Box, which is now publishing 500 titles per year. It runs seminars for authors and walks them through a process. It also offers ghostwriting services, books assembled from author dictation, and other services at a variety of models and prices, from a bare-bones process that generates a Kindle Direct Publishing print-on-demand title to a highly edited book in full distribution. Tucker has even posted video excerpts from his author training for free on scribemedia.com. As you might expect from a company with an output this large, the quality of the content is quite variable, but Scribe has delivered excellent results for talented authors like Jay Acunzo, a prominent expert in podcasting and content creation.

The other company you may run into is Forbes Books, formerly known as Advantage Media Group. *Forbes* has set this company up to cater directly to thought leaders and is even setting up a speaker's bureau. It focuses on a process it calls "authority marketing." According to its book *Authority Marketing: Your Blueprint to Build Thought Leadership That Grows Business, Attracts Opportunity, and Makes Competition Irrelevant,* "Authority = Expertise x Celebrity." As you might expect with a focus like that, its services are notably more expensive, with an investment of around $55,000 to $65,000 in the book itself and $5,000 to $10,000 per month for an "authority marketing program."

Does hybrid publishing make sense for you? It will allow you to get a book out in eight to ten months, far less than most traditional publishing options. You'll have a publishing partner who's much more responsive. But you'll have to pay up front, and that's not easy for many authors. And you'll still have to do most of the book marketing and promotion, just as you would with a traditional publisher.

If this description of hybrid publishing interests you, I recommend that you plan out just how the book will pay off for you — by generating leads, increasing speaking engagements, or as a tool for your sales team — and modeling how those benefits will compare with publishing costs. Pitch several hybrid publishers and choose a partner carefully, based in part on how much editorial guidance you need and whether the publisher has published books in the same category as yours. The good news is, since you'll be hiring the partner, you get to interview them ahead of time and get a handle on the costs and services that matter to you.

Self-publishing is fast and cheap, but takes more effort

Who needs a publisher when you can publish a book yourself? That sounds like a great concept, but if you talk to people who've done it, you'll see it's a lot of work.

One of the most successful self-published business authors is Shel Israel. Unlike Phil M. Jones, Shel started writing and publishing books in the traditional way. His first book, with Robert Scoble, was the groundbreaking *Naked Conversations: How Blogs are Changing the Way Businesses Talk with Customers* (Wiley, 2006). It was pretty much the first business book to talk about social media, and it sold 100,000 copies. But while it made Shel and Robert into international speakers — and Shel a hot commodity in the book publishing world — it didn't generate a windfall of cash directly from publishing.

Shel stuck with traditional publisher Portfolio for his second book, *Twitterville: How Businesses Can Thrive in the New Global Neighborhoods,* but the experience left a bad taste in his mouth. He had pitched and written the book as a series of many case studies, and it's an amazing piece of work; he actually predicted the Arab Spring before it happened. But Shel told me that an editor at Portfolio attempted to tack on a "how-to" chapter and sneak it into the book at the last minute. After that, Shel vowed not to work with traditional publishers again — he just didn't want to give up control of the content.

What followed were a series of popular self-published books: *Lethal Generosity* on his own and *Age of Context* and *The Fourth Transformation* with coauthor Robert Scoble. Those last two sold about 50,000 copies each — not nearly as many as Shel and Robert's first book, but enviable totals nonetheless. And because of how Amazon's self-publishing revenue splits work, those books generated more than $200,000 each in book sales revenue alone, not including the speaking and sponsorship opportunities they opened up.

As Shel learned, to publish your own books on Amazon takes a bit of extra effort. Amazon's self-publishing platform, formerly known as Amazon CreateSpace, is now called Kindle Direct Publishing (KDP). (Don't let the name confuse you — it's for printed books, not just ebooks.) If you're going to go forward with self-publishing, you're much better off with a content or developmental editor. (Shel has used various editors on his books, including hiring me to help on *The Fourth Transformation.*) You also need to line up a copy editor, a cover designer, and someone to do page layout and prepare the book for ebook format.

"The quality of talent that I can find is great and is also affordable," Shel says. "Talent that used to belong to publishers is now easily outsourced. My book covers come from a guy in the Philippines."

If you don't fancy managing all those details, there are plenty of book packagers that will take care of all of them — but of course, that adds cost. One outfit I've seen do a pretty decent job is Gatekeeper Press, which as of this writing will turn your manuscript into a print-on-demand paperback book for around $4,000.

Working with a self-publishing process has some significant advantages. In the case of *The Fourth Transformation,* Shel and Robert's original plan was to publish it in February of 2017, but they needed some advance copies for an event the previous December. The two authors, their page layout freelancer Shawn Welch, and I figured out that things were going well enough that we could complete the book well ahead of the original plan, so we moved the publication date from February back to December. For a traditional or hybrid publisher, moving the publication date two months earlier is a heretical notion; for us, it was an easy decision that solved a problem.

Obviously, there are drawbacks to self-publishing. The result is typically a print-on-demand paperback, a product actually manufactured by a specialized binding machine at the moment a customer orders it. The quality is close to, but not identical to, an actual manufactured book. And you're operating without guardrails, so there are a lot of ways to fail. You need a cover designer you can trust. You need to write your own marketing copy for the Amazon site. You want to be sure the internal layout looks professional — avoid margins that are too small or too large, type that's out of proportion, or blocks of text in a sans-serif font, for example. It's easy to make changes at the last minute, but conversely, it's also easy to inadvertently introduce errors.

If you go straight to Kindle Direct Publishing, you give up the possibility of carrying the book in bookstores. The book will be available only through Amazon.com. (If it sells well enough, though, you might get an offer from a publisher to republish it in traditional form — but you might turn that offer down, since you'll be making a high royalty rate on every copy you sell.)

Amazon is not the only self-publishing channel — some authors prefer to work through IngramSpark. IngramSpark can create print-on-demand hardbacks with jackets, not just paperbacks, and enables distribution to bookstores through Ingram, a major book distributor. According to IngramSpark director and co-founder Robin Cutler, IngramSpark is also reaching out to libraries and book-sellers, including independent bookstores. Starting with IngramSpark may be a better option if you've got a local bookstore connection who wants to carry the book, or if you imagine you will sell well enough to get Barnes & Noble's attention. But remember that being *available* to the bookstore channel is not the same as being carried *in* the channel, since the bookstore won't carry a book unless there's evidence it's going to sell.

It's much harder to create a big, successful book through these self-publishing channels, simply because they're not available in as many places. If you have a major social media presence, like Shel Israel and his coauthor Robert Scoble, you may be able to make up for that. And if your objective is just to have a book published for a niche audience, you may find self-publishing sufficient to fill that need. Or you may just cherish the flexibility it gives you, as Shel did.

Key takeaways

- The three main publishing models are traditional, hybrid, and self-pub-lishing. You should pick one and pursue it before you get too far with your book project.
- Traditional publishers deliver more prestige and pay advances, but typ-ically take 15 to 18 months to publish — and you'll need an agent and a proposal to get their attention.
- Hybrid publishers can complete a quality book in less than a year, but you'll have to pay tens of thousands of dollars up front to publish your book.
- Self-publishing is fast, but the results are less impressive, and you typi-cally need to source and manage a team of freelancers to complete your book. If you work directly with Amazon, your book won't be available in any other channels.
- Regardless of the model you select, expect to hire your own developmental editor and do most of your own book promotion.

Chapter 5

Book Proposals That Sell

Secure a publishing deal with a sexy proposal.

Stefan Falk is one of the world's most insightful management and productivity experts. But most people have never heard of him.

Stefan studied psychology under the renowned expert Mihaly Csikszentmihalyi. His work has been cited by leading business authors, including Daniel Pink. He has worked with, coached, and trained more than 4,000 senior leaders across 60 organizations in North America and Europe and driven corporate transformation efforts with a total value north of $2 billion. He was one of the main trainers for partners and staff at McKinsey & Company, the world's most influential management consulting company.

When the time came to put his ideas into a book, Stefan knew he'd have a wealth of ideas to write about. But because most of his work with clients was confidential, his name was unlikely to be familiar to editors and publishers. His only previous book had been published in his original native language, Swedish.

His objective was to get his hard-nosed, firmly logical, psychology-based ideas on productivity and management as much visibility as possible — which meant pitching and winning over a major publisher, despite his relative anonymity.

And that demanded a killer proposal.

Stefan's proposal featured a solid and counterintuitive central idea — by focusing on exciting outcomes in your work, you can develop intrinsic motivation, learn to enjoy your work, and be more productive. His proposal featured a detailed table of contents featuring about 40 short chapters on everything from time budgeting to journaling to managing anxiety. He included endorsements from authors including Daniel Pink and business leaders like Forrester CEO George Colony. His sample chapters demonstrated bite-sized insights, incisive examples, and sparkling clarity of writing. And despite his lack of social media presence and limited number of recent publications, he included a clever way to prove he could, indeed, promote his book successfully — with bulk book purchases from some of his clients.

Stefan worried that no agent or publisher would pick up his book. I was convinced otherwise — his content was unique and strong, and his proposal showed it off in a highly differentiated way. So we made a sort of bet. I reduced the consulting bill for the work I'd done to help him craft the proposal. In exchange, I would get a share of potential revenues from any book advance. I was betting on his proposal to succeed. He was convinced he'd saved money because the proposal would fail.

In the end, I referred him to my agent, Katherine Flynn, of the prestigious agency Kneerim & Williams. She accepted his proposal and shopped it to publishers. The result was a six-figure advance from a major publisher. (I won the bet — but of course, he won the chance to publish his book.)

Stefan's book *Intrinsic Motivation: Learn to Love your Work and Succeed as Never Before* was published by St. Martin's Press in 2023. And he'll get his chance to influence a whole generation of managers and professionals.

How to write a great proposal

Stefan's success — and the reason he lost his bet with me — came from having a good agent and a terrific proposal. So, what does it take to write a book proposal that will get agents to take notice and traditional publishers to bid on your book?

The audience for proposals is editors and publishers — a little different from the audience for your book, which is readers. The work required to create a complete proposal is about 20% of the work required to do a full book manuscript, but none of that work is wasted: You'll use everything you put into the proposal when you're writing and promoting your book anyway.

The key elements in the proposal are the same essential story-related ingredients for success I described in chapter 1: defining your audience, describing your idea, listing the stories you will tell, defining the narrative thread of the book, and detailing your promotional plan. The title and subtitle are also essential. Publishers want to see that you're a disciplined thinker and writer, and the proposal is a way to make sure that you've done your homework.

Should you write the full manuscript first, before doing the proposal? No! There are two reasons why. First, why complete the manuscript when you can do less work and shop the proposal to get an advance that will fund you to do the rest of the writing? And second, the agent and then, eventually, the publisher may read the proposal and request changes. It's a lot easier to revise the proposal and then write the book knowing what changes they want, rather than having to revise a whole book that you've already written.

Even if it's too late and you've already written the whole book, you'll need to add the other parts of the proposal, such as a description of the main ideas and a promotional plan. A full manuscript is not a substitute for a proposal.

I've created an online resource that may be helpful to you here. Go to wobs.co/BBBBproposal and you can download the actual book proposal that I created to pitch my previous book, *Writing Without Bullshit*. This proposal includes all the parts I'm about to describe, and with the help of my agent, it generated multiple offers from publishers including the one I accepted from Harper Business for a six-figure book advance. The content is proprietary, but feel free to copy the framework as you craft your own proposal.

Table 5-1 lists the main parts of the proposal and what it takes to make them successful. The rest of this chapter includes details on each part.

Table 5-1: Elements of a book proposal

Proposal element	What it does	How it persuades editors	How to do it
Title and subtitle	Creates a memorable handle for the book	Intrigues editor right up front	Brainstorm (see chapter 3)
Opening of book	Introduces book in a fascinating way	Shows your talent; sucks editor in further	Tell the best story
Main ideas	Shows the ideas that make the book worth reading	Convinces editor that you have something worth saying	Develop a simple, new, big, right idea (see chapter 3)
Market and differentiation	Defines audience and explains what sets this book apart	Helps editor estimate sales	Position against similar successful books
List of comparable titles	Lists other books in your general field for comparison purposes	Defines where your book fits in the market	Describe similar books and how yours is different
Detailed table of contents	Lays out what each chapter will cover	Shows you've thought the book through	Expose the storyline of the book (see chapter 6)
Author biography	Explains why you are the authority	Editors invest in authors, not just books	Describe your most impressive accomplishments
Platform and promotion plan	Describes how you will promote the book	Shows editor your promotional resources	List specific assets and plans (see chapter 21)
Sample chapter	Shows what a typical chapter will include	Proves you can write in an effective and fascinating way	Research and write it (see chapters 9, 10, and 11)

Title and subtitle

The only thing on the first page of your proposal should be "A proposal for" plus the title, subtitle, and your name. More than anything else, a great title gets your proposal read. Without it, even if you sell the proposal, you'll end up arguing titles with the editor, and nobody wants to be in title hell.

Opening passage of the book

Others may tell you to start with an "Overview." I disagree. Start with the same text you will use to open your book. Don't start by talking to the editor about how great your book is. Start by writing directly to the reader. The editor will get the message if your writing is excellent.

For example, here's the start of Stefan's proposal for *Intrinsic Motivation:*

> It's time we start to enjoy our work.
>
> In America, the most advanced economy in the world, 80 percent of the working population say that they suffer from stress, and 50 percent say they really need help managing their stress. The cost of work-related illness and stress rose from $200 billion in 1999 to nearly $300 billion in 2015.
>
> So what's going on? To feel good, be productive, and feel optimistic about personal and professional life, we humans have evolved a huge need for control and predictability in our personal and professional lives. We want to feel that we understand what is happening around us, that we can influence what happens, and that we have a reliable insight into what is happening tomorrow and in the future. And we want to know we are not wasting our time and brain power on worthless corporate tasks that have very little to do with the organization's success.

Anyone reading that wants to know what comes next. Stefan has sucked in the reader — who in this case is the acquisitions editor at a publishing house.

Here's another approach. This is the start of the proposal for Mitch Lowe's autobiographical business book *Watch and Learn: How I Turned Hollywood*

Upside Down with Netflix, Redbox, and MoviePass — Lessons in Disruption (Hachette Go, 2022):

I was there for all of it. The total disruption of the movie business. I not only had a ringside seat, I made a lot of it happen. The arrogance of the entertainment executives was epic. In the end, all my colleagues and I had going for us was intuition, perseverance, and an unerring sense of what the viewing customer really wanted — a sense, I might add, that the very people who sold and distributed those movies either lacked, or just were too shortsighted to care about.

The stories I could tell . . . well, that's why this book exists. To tell those fascinating stories. But there's more to it than that. I want you to understand how we got from movie and TV shows released and controlled rigidly by the huge studios to a world where we can stream whatever we want on our big screens at home, sitting on the couch with popcorn we made ourselves or watching your smartphone while waiting at a bus stop. I want you to know what it took to disrupt a huge and hidebound business — and the lessons you can draw from that story for your own quixotic adventures, whether that means upending uninspired management at your company or disrupting whatever business domain you have your dreams set on.

What's in this book? I'll show you how I went from a high-school dropout smuggling cheap money into Eastern Europe and transporting used Mercedes sedans to Damascus, to the owner of a chain of video stores. I'll explain how as the "video guy" who knew the rental business, I joined up with Reed Hastings and Marc Randolph to found Netflix, a nationwide company that built a tight monthly relationship with movie renters when everyone else thought you could only do that with expensive stores on Main Street in every town. I'll show you how, in my quest to demonstrate that I could manage things at a big company, I got McDonalds to invest in a DVD rental kiosk, and how we spun that out to create Redbox, the DVD rental business that's outlived Blockbuster and all the rest. And finally, I'll explain how I tried to remake the theatrical exhibition business with MoviePass, a monthly subscription to the movies that, even as it failed, still managed to change the way theaters operate, a change that is even now reverberating in the COVID era.

What should you do? Start with a story. Start with some marketing copy. Start conversationally and get quickly to your main point, as Stefan does. But whatever you do, fascinate the proposal's reader quickly.

Main ideas

As I described in chapter 2, your book needs a differentiated idea. The idea should be simple, big, new, and provably right. Here is where you describe that idea. If you have a graphic that neatly encapsulates the idea, use it here.

As with all other parts of the proposal, write this section as you would describe the idea in the book, rather than pitching the acquisitions editor. That editor will catch on quickly if your description of the idea is compelling.

Market and differentiation

Tell who will buy the book. Explain how many people there are like that (people who do content marketing, for example, or people with psoriasis).

More importantly, tell why your book is different or better. Complete the sentence that begins, "This is the first book that . . ." Bullet points work great in this section ("four reasons that this book will stand out"). It's also helpful to position yourself against competing books.

List of comparable titles

List five to ten books already out there in your field ("comps") and how your book will compare to them. There are three reasons to include comps in your proposal.

1. Show you know your market and demonstrate your knowledge of what other books are available.
2. Show that similar books are selling well.
3. Show that your book is differentiated from other books in its market.

For each book, describe the positives (whether it sold well, for example) as well as how your book will approach the market in a way that is unique and different from that book.

Publishers you pitch will already know some things about your general market (say, leadership books or books about being a new parent). In part, they read your list of comps to see if you see the market in the way they already do, or differently. But they will also use your list to educate themselves about the details of your specific market (say, leadership for millennials) that they didn't previously know.

Nobody in publishing wants to take a chance on a book that's completely different from everything else, so there are always some sort of comps. What sorts of books are "similar" enough to include?

- **Similar topic.** If you wrote a book on content marketing, what other content marketing books are there?
- **Similar audience.** If you're targeting Gen Z job seekers, what other books are there for Gen Zers hoping to make a professional impression?
- **Similar appeal.** If you're writing a memoir of your life as a woman in start-ups, what other books are memoirs of women in challenging professional settings?
- **Similar format.** This applies only if your format is unusual. If your book is a book of cartoons about corporate politics, what other similar cartoon books are there? If you have a book of data visualizations in color with elements identified and called out, what other books feature color illustrations with callouts?

If a book in your field made a particular impression on you, include it as well.

Detailed table of contents

This is where you convince the editor that you've actually thought this book thing through. Spend some time compiling and arranging the content you think you will include. For each chapter, imagine you're explaining to a friend: "This is what's in this chapter." And, as I describe in the next chapter, make sure your chapters, taken together, form a narrative.

For each chapter, tell us what's in it and how many pages long it is (and I know you haven't written it yet — just estimate). Describe those chapters. What case studies will they include? What points will they make? I find this works best if you include a series of sentences or phrases for each chapter. For example, here's the description of chapter 7 in the proposal for my book with Charlene Li, *Groundswell*.

> **Chapter 7. Energizing the groundswell** (24 pages, 1 diagram, 1 chart). What is energizing? Energizing the base and Social Technographics. The value of an energized customer. Techniques for energizing enthusiasts. Case study: eBags: energizing with ratings and reviews. Benefits of ratings and reviews. ROI of reviews. Case study: Lego — energizing an existing community. The ROI of energizing a community. Energizing the groundswell: what it means for your company.

Author biography

Tell us who you are — "about the author." Prove that you are not only the one to write this book, but the one who would be best at promoting it as well. Explain to the editor why you're a good investment. Your professional bio is just a starting point here — rewrite and expand it, listing your impressive speaking engagements, places that you're quoted, awards you've won, and accomplishments you have. Include items that would impress general readers and editors, not potential employers; this isn't a résumé or CV, it's a promotional bio.

Platform and promotion plan

This is both the hardest part of most proposals to write and the most important. Your ability to promote — and to sell — books is crucial to convincing publishers that you'll be worth investing in.

Please refer to the detailed set of suggestions in chapter 21 as you think through all the elements of your promotion. Then describe your author platform, listing every possible asset you have, including:

- Social media followings.
- Regular places that you publish content, such as columns, blogs, or podcasts, with the size of your audience.
- Places you have been quoted.
- Speaking opportunities, both past places you've spoken and places you've identified for the future.
- Connections you have to prominent people and how they may help.
- People you expect to provide endorsements. It's even better if you can get the actual endorsements, pre-publication, and include them in the proposal. (That's what Stefan did, and it was quite a persuasive list.)
- Publicity or marketing staff you intend to hire. If your company has a publicity staff, describe what they can do. If you are going to hire an outside publicist, name the firm that you're working with.
- Other staff at your company that can help, such as sales staff if they will be helping distribute the book. (See chapter 8 for more ways to leverage staff at your company to help.)

This is not a complete list. You may have unique assets that others would never think of. In Stefan's case, he was able to convince some of his clients to make bulk book purchases. This made up in part for his lack of social media accounts.

This section is far more persuasive if it includes assets you already have, rather than assets you plan to build. "I will start and grow a YouTube channel" is not something that will impress an editor. "I already have a YouTube channel that has accumulated 250,000 views" will. Actual promotional assets, even if small, are more persuasive than potential assets of any size.

If you have a publicist or publicity team already in place, get their help with this. They're used to thinking about promotion and can likely think of assets you don't realize you have.

Sample chapter

Submit a representative chapter (not chapter 1). And put the same level of effort into it that you would into an actual published chapter — include case studies and graphics if appropriate, show that you've done stellar research, and get an editor to help you make sure the writing sparkles.

Which chapter should you include? The one that's easiest to create with research and interviews you've already completed.

This is of similar importance to the promotional plan. If it's good, you'll win over the editor. If it's flawed, it's a huge red flag. So get help to make sure it's fantastic.

Is it okay to exaggerate in your proposal?

Yes. But don't lie.

You will be writing about the future. For example, you will be describing interviews you have not yet conducted and publicity plans you have not yet put in place. Here's my rule of thumb:

> *In a book proposal, describe what you actually did and what you plan to do. Describe it as if it is actually happening. But don't make up things that you cannot, will not, or are unlikely to do.*

Don't make up implausible crap ("I was president of Yale University from 1991 to 1996.") Publishers are not dumb; they *will* check. And never lie in your bio — that's an unforgivable sin.

The publisher wants to see the quality of your thinking. But they aren't interested in flights of fantasy. If you can show what you will do and it sounds great, that will impress. That takes some imagination. But it's not a deliberately made-up fantasy. I'm hoping that, as a smart writer with integrity, you can tell the difference.

Your proposal *is* you as far as publishers are concerned

Agents and publishers will judge you based solely on the proposal. Leave nothing out that would help the book. Include everything that makes you look good. And get editorial help to ensure it is flawless.

With so much included in them, excellent proposals often run 25 to 45 pages.

It can take up to a month for agents to respond to your queries, another month to finalize the proposal, and another month for publishers to submit bids and respond to requests to improve those bids. So it may take a total of up to three months from when you start pitching agents to when you have a possible deal. (And as I described in the last chapter, another 15 to 18 months to get the book published after you have a deal.)

Publishers will offer "term sheets" that describe the details of the deal. You and your agent (if you have one) will use those to decide which offer to take, or who to ask to up their bids. Once you settle on terms, you have a deal. While a term sheet is not binding, publishers never go back on them (barring the author getting caught doing something criminal or unethical), as that would ruin their reputation in future deals. Even so, it may take the publisher's legal department two or three months to complete the final contract.

Your agent is helpful even after the proposal is accepted

Once you've got a publisher, you'll be working with their team on everything from editorial content to publicity. If you have an agent who made the deal happen, they bow out until you start to get advance checks (which flow through the agent to you). But the agent is always there to help. If the publisher is behaving strangely or dragging their feet, go back to the agent and ask for advice or help in getting the publisher to move forward.

Key takeaways

- If you are pitching traditional publishers, you'll need a book proposal, which may run to 25 pages or more.
- Your proposal must include multiple parts, including main ideas, market and differentiation, comparable titles, detailed table of contents, promotional plan, and sample chapter. Every piece of it must be flawless. The promotional plan and the sample chapter are crucial.

Chapter 6

Book as Narrative

Structure your chapters to tell a story.

A consultant — whose name I'm not at liberty to share — was planning a book on a trendy business topic. His knowledge was vast, covering all sorts of aspects of his topic. He had organized those insights into a detailed table of contents spanning 13 chapters over eight pages.

The book would be a comprehensive perspective on his topic. It was neatly organized, because he'd classified all of his knowledge precisely.

And it was likely to fail.

Why?

Because he had organized the content the way it was classified in his head. That might seem logical for an expert in the field, like him, but it did not provide a path into the knowledge for a naive reader. It did not create a story worth following, remembering, and sharing. And that's what makes readers keep reading — and what makes a business book successful.

Organize your book into chapters with the reader question method

Of the published authors in my author survey, 47% found it challenging to organize their book content. Other than getting time to write, it was authors' main writing challenge (see Figure 6-1).

Figure 6-1: Book writing challenges

Source: Bernoff.com author survey 2019-2022 (N=172 published authors)

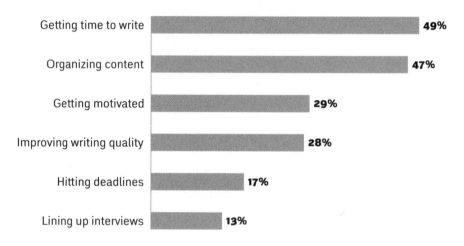

"Which of the following were the biggest challenges in writing your book? Check all that apply."

Getting time to write	49%
Organizing content	47%
Getting motivated	29%
Improving writing quality	28%
Hitting deadlines	17%
Lining up interviews	13%

When it comes to organizing your book content, don't think about writing a book. Think about writing a series of chapters that form a story — because, as I pointed out in chapter 1, business books are stories. Each chapter flows into the next to create a through line: the book's narrative. Once you've determined the narrative sequence of the chapters, you can concentrate on the manageable writing task of writing the chapters one at a time.

How should you think about those chapters? Use the *reader question method*.

Each chapter in a business book should be an organized collection of knowledge that answers a specific question that your audience has. That's why the consultant

I just described couldn't get the organization of his book right. He was thinking in terms of what he had to say, not what questions his readers needed to answer.

In chapter 1, I asked you to think about your audience. Think of a specific person that fits your description. If your book is for people starting a new job, think about, say, Charles, who just got a new job at IBM.

What does that reader want to know?

Each chapter should answer a question that a reader would be asking.

If the questions for each chapter combine to tell a story, your book will be easy to follow and will draw readers in. If not, you need to rethink the structure of the content you're sharing.

Thinking carefully about those reader questions comes down to three things: size, sequence, and structure.

Choose a chapter size

Is your book going to have long or short chapters?

Let's do a little basic math. A typical business book is 45,000 to 75,000 words. A typical business book chapter is 1,500 to 8,000 words.

It's best if the chapters are of relatively consistent size — it's awkward if a 2,000-word chapter follows an 8,000-word chapter.

So you might have 11 relatively large chapters of 6,000 words each. Or you could have 25 smaller chapters of about 2,000 words each. Both are valid ways to divide your book into chapters, but each requires a different approach.

To determine the right chapter size, consider the size of the questions the chapters will answer. Your book could include long chapters that answer big questions, like "Why is this important?" or "How will this concept affect my career?" Or it could include shorter chapters that answer smaller questions, like "What sort of emails should I include in my marketing plan?"

Figure out right now if your book is a collection of small pieces of advice or a smaller number of larger topics. Then you'll know what size chapters to work on.

Sequence chapters into a story

After you've settled the chapter size query, think about *sequence*.

If you're writing a book that describes a narrative in chronological order —
like a memoir, a biography, or a narrative of an event — then the order of your
chapters is obvious. But for books about concepts, you need a better organizational structure.

The questions in a typical book storyline follow a sequence something like this:

- "Why is this idea important?" (That's the "scare-the-crap-out-of-you"
  question.)
- "What are the elements of this idea?" (For example, five main principles,
  seven steps.)
- "How can I understand the elements of this idea more clearly?" (For
  example, chapters on each of the principles.)
- "How will that change things that matter to me?" (For example, advice
  on how to change how you work, what strategies you will adopt, or how
  you measure success.)
- "What are the broader consequences of my following this advice?" (What
  are the nonobvious consequences of what you described?)

How do you create and sequence that list of questions? Start by brainstorming
a set of potential questions that your reader wants to know about. Then narrow
it down to the questions for which you have enough content to fill a good-sized
chapter. Avoid questions that are too small, or too focused on your own knowledge, or that presume that your reader already thinks the way that you do.

Then sequence the questions into a deepening dialogue you might have with
a reader.

Let's look at an example. Evangelos Simoudis is an expert on the future of transportation — how trends like electric vehicles and autonomous cars will change how
people get around. He wrote a book called *Transportation Transformation: How
Autonomous Mobility Will Fuel New Value Chains* (Corporate Innovators LLC,
2020). Given his encyclopedic knowledge of the topic, he could have organized his
insights in any number of ways. But in the end, he created a sequence that followed
a logical series of questions that his reader — an executive or decision-maker in

a car company, a mobility company like Uber, or a local or national government — might ask. Here are the big questions that his chapters answer, one question per chapter:

1. How is consumer transportation changing, and why should I care?
2. What's the current state of consumer transportation?
3. What's the future for carmakers?
4. What's the future for mobility services like Uber?
5. What will the new value chains look like?
6. How will municipal governments — cities — participate in this future?
7. What is the value of data in the new value chains?
8. What are the business models for the new value chains?
9. What risks will we face on the way to this future?
10. How should we think about this future?

Notice how each question is large enough to deserve a whole chapter of analysis, but self-contained enough to answer a single question. Also notice how each question leads to the next; once you know what the current state is, for example, it's logical to ask what will happen in the future.

Your book is a conversation with a reader that starts with a big question and broadens out into elements of the solution. That's a sequence that will keep people reading to the end.

Make your table of contents reflect the structure of your ideas

Once you've determined the *size* and *sequence* of your reader questions (and the chapters that will answer them), you can go further. You can get the resulting table of contents to reflect the *structure* of your content.

For example, here is the table of contents for Denise Lee Yohn's popular marketing book *What Great Brands Do: The Seven Brand-Building Principles that Separate the Best from the Rest* (Jossey-Bass, 2014).

Introduction
1. Great Brands Start Inside
2. Great Brands Avoid Selling Products
3. Great Brands Ignore Trends
4. Great Brands Don't Chase Customers
5. Great Brands Sweat the Small Stuff
6. Great Brands Commit and Stay Committed
7. Great Brands Never Have to "Give Back"
8. The Eighth Principle: Brand as Business

The whole point of Denise's book is the seven principles. She hammers that home in the table of contents, with seven chapters whose titles are the principles themselves. A misguided editor might suggest deleting the apparently redundant "Great Brands" at the start of each chapter title and just naming the chapters "Start Inside," "Avoid Selling Products," "Ignore Trends," and so on. But that would obscure the simple parallelism and the chance these titles have to reinforce that they're all what great brands need to do. If you want to build a great brand, this book's table of contents is seducing you. (The eighth chapter, which breaks the pattern, just reinforces that the principles are what matter here.)

Here's one more example. In 2016, I published a book about writing within corporate environments, titled *Writing Without Bullshit: Boost Your Career by Saying What You Mean* (Harper Business, 2016). I used 24 short chapters to tell people how to write better. And I organized them into four larger parts that answered these broad questions:

1. Why is it crucial for professionals to improve their business writing?
2. What specifically should you change in your writing?
3. How can you change your writing process to help you to write better?
4. How do these changes affect common formats like email and reports?

To increase the parallelism and reflect the structure, I made each chapter title into a short command directed at the reader. And I made each part title start with "change" to emphasize what I was asking the reader to do differently. You can see the resulting table of contents in Table 6-1:

Table 6-1: Table of contents for **Writing Without Bullshit**

With this structure, readers opening the book to the table of contents — or seeing it online — would see a well-organized description of exactly what questions I'd be answering, like "How can I write shorter documents?", "How can I use numbers wisely?", and "How can I collaborate effectively?".

A beautiful table of contents does two powerful things. It organizes your work of research and writing into chunks that you can tackle, with a clear idea of how they fit into the storyline of the book as a whole. And it communicates that elegant organization to the reader, making the book appear more accessible and valuable.

Working on the table of contents forces you to think about your book's organization before you delve deeply into the writing. And as I'll show in the next chapter, that's an essential way to make your work on the book as productive as possible.

Key takeaways

- Organize your book according to the reader question method, using each chapter to answer a big question your target readers have.
- Match the size of the chapters to the size of the questions.
- Sequence the questions so that they form a storyline.
- Reveal the elegance of your book's structure in the table of contents.

Chapter 7

The Book Plan

Be a planner, not a pantser.

My friend was in pain. "I'm 78,000 words into my next 60,000-word book," she shared. And I knew just what she meant. She'd written and written and written some more and come up with a big, tangled ball of spaghetti. Now she had to figure out what was in there and untangle it.

She was not alone. In my author survey, 55% of authors said that their process consisted of "writing, rewriting, and research all mixed together."

In my experience, there are two kinds of authors. Planners meticulously plan what they're going to research and write before they start writing. Pantsers (think "seat-of-the-pants" writers) start writing and see where things go.[6]

It's tempting to start writing by, well, writing. But setting out to write without a plan is hugely wasteful. Nonfiction writers who plan first have significant advantages.

Pantsers like my friend often end up with masses of prose that don't cohere. They duplicate material in some places and have holes in other places. That's not

---

6 I've borrowed these terms from a common description of two types of fiction writers: plotters and pantsers. See https://wobs.co/BBBBpantser.

surprising. If you started building a house by just hammering boards together, you might find that you've got twice as many bedrooms as you need, and the bathroom is in the wrong place. Planners avoid these problems because it's a lot easier to spot gaps and overlaps in a detailed outline of the book than in a collection of lumps of text. They can figure out the best place for each case study, insight, and statistic.

Planners can plan the research they'll need to fill each chapter and make it fascinating and believable. Given the lead time necessary for some types of research, such as surveys and case studies, you're a lot better off if you know and plan for what you will need ahead of time.

Planners can also fix structural problems more easily, because a plan is easier to modify than a mass of prose. The plan has the advantage that you can see it all at once, and therefore rearrange it without a lot of difficulty. That's a lot more effective than taking a partially written manuscript and just moving hunks of it around in hopes that you'll fix the issue you've identified.

And if you're working from a plan, it's a lot easier to figure out your context when you resume your book project after a pause.

Even if you have pantser tendencies, there are two places you must have a plan. You need it in an extended table of contents — which is basically, a book plan — to show publishers how well constructed and comprehensive your book will be in a book proposal. And if you have a coauthor, you'll need a plan so you both know which parts of the book you're working on and how they will fit together. Making a plan and following it could cut your total writing time in half.

What is a book plan and how can you create one?

A book plan is basically a blueprint for what you're going to put into the book. If you did the work I described in the previous chapter, you have the basis for it: a table of contents.

The best tool for book planning is a spreadsheet. If formulas and math terrify you, fear not — there is almost no calculation in the spreadsheet I'm going to describe. It's just a way to classify everything you need to do.

I recommend using Google Sheets, because it allows you to easily get access to your plan from any computer, tablet, or phone. It's especially useful if you are collaborating with a coauthor, editor, or ghostwriter, because you and your collaborators can all work from the same file accessible from a single web link. (If you prefer Microsoft Excel to Google Sheets, feel free to use that instead.)

The main sheet in your planning spreadsheet is a list of chapters and content. For example, Table 7-1 shows the headings and the first four rows for the starting chapters of this book.

Your planning spreadsheet doesn't need to look exactly like this. But you'll want to have chapter numbers and titles, as well as the reader questions you produced in the last chapter. I like to add columns to keep track of ideas, case studies, and data.

When you're ready to start writing, you can add another column to this: the deadline for completing the chapter draft.

You can use more sheets in the same spreadsheet to track other tasks. For example, it's helpful to use another sheet to track outreach to potential interview targets. Table 7-2 shows what that might look like (I've redacted the email addresses for privacy).

You can put anything else you're tracking in additional sheets in this file. I have a sheet to track blog posts I've written (with links) and chapters that they're relevant for. I have one for a list of graphics. As I get closer to the end of the process, I add a sheet to keep track of fact verification (see chapter 16).

Once the writing is underway, I add a word count column to the primary sheet and use it to compute an estimate of the total final word count. (That's the only math formula in the whole spreadsheet.)

In this Google Sheet it's easy to reorder chapters, keep track of how I'm doing on completing the book, and track progress on any other tasks required.

There's one other reason to use a planning sheet this way: psychology. It's easy to get depressed about your progress if you're not actually writing. But with a planning sheet, you can see how you're making progress on organizing chapters, identifying content for them, and lining up interviews. You're doing crucial work on the book, even if you're not typing text yet.

This is the right way to plan a book, and it's a lot more efficient than churning out prose without a clear idea where it's going to fit.

Table 7-1: Excerpt of the book plan for **Build a Better Business Book**

Ch	Title	Subtitle	Reader question	Ideas	Case studies
1	Business books are stories	To engage readers, tell a story.	What is the most important factor in a business book's success?	• Business books are stories • Audience/ideas/stories/narrative/promotion • Scare the crap out of you • Fear and greed	Jay Baer Dan Bricklin
2	Why write a book?	Build a book that matters.	Why should I write a book?	• Help the reader succeed • Authors are suckers • Books are more than just books • Books create respect	Laura Gassner Otting Melanie Deziel Michael C. Bush
3	Ideas and titles	Stand out in the reader's mind.	How can I choose a good title?	• Definition of a book-worthy idea • Simple/big/new/right • Title brainstorm • Title hell	Charlene Li Denise Lee Yohn
4	Publishing models	Select a publishing path for speed, cost, or prestige.	What are the main ways to get published?	• Traditional publishing • Book agents • Hybrid publishing • Self-publishing	Phil M. Jones Shel Israel

Table 7-2: Tracking interviews with a Google Sheet

Name	Role	Email	Source	Priority	Status
Charlene Li	Author		Client	4	5 done
Robin Cutler	Publisher		Research	5	5 done
Katherine Flynn	Agent		Agent	4	5 done
Clay Hebert	Editor		Network	5	5 done
Jay Baer	Author		Network	4	5 done
James Fell	Author		Facebook group	4	5 done
Tom Webster	Author		Idea Dev	4	2.5 messaged
Chandler Bolt	Publisher		Expert	4	2.5 emailed
Richard Narramore	Publisher		Network	5	2.5 emailed
Bryan Eisenberg	Author		Facebook group	1	2 emailed
Greg Satell	Author		Facebook group	1	2 emailed
Mike Ganino	Author		Facebook group	1	2 emailed
Mitch Joel	Author		Facebook group	4	2 emailed
Neen James	Author		Facebook group	3	2 emailed
Elizabeth Marshall	Author		Facebook group	1	1 poked
Michael Bungay Stanier	Author		Facebook group	1	1 poked

Planning and writing are not mutually exclusive

Does this advice mean you can't write anything until you have a plan? No!

Writing is an important way of developing ideas. Even as you're planning, you can be doing writing that's integral to the planning process.

Write a "treatment" for your book — a one page description of what's in it. Or write the flap copy. These bits help develop ideas.

Write up case study stories about people you interview. They're fun to write and will motivate you. And once you've written them, you can slot them into the plan you're working on.

Write chapter 1. That will help you feel like you're off to a good start.

Or write a sample chapter. This helps you create a template for the rest of the chapters.

All of those activities will exercise your writing muscles and help you stay excited about the project.

But don't just write and write. You'll write yourself into a corner. You'll get frustrated. You'll feel blocked. And you might even end up with 76,000 words written on your 60,000-word book, wondering where — and whether — those words even belong in the final manuscript.

Key takeaways

- Don't just write. Plan first. Be a planner, not a pantser.
- A Google Sheet is a great way to plan and organize the chapters in your book. You can use it to track other book tasks, too, like interviews that you're lining up.

Chapter 8

The Employee Author

Make your book support your job — and vice versa.

In 2010, Jeff Fromm was senior vice president and chief growth officer at Barkley, a marketing agency. And he was obsessed with millennials.

At the time, the youngest of the millennials was 14. (The oldest was 29.) The suggestion that marketers should pivot to target millennials, originally from his business partner Brad Hanna, was controversial. But convinced that becoming the agency best known for understanding millennials would benefit Barkley, Jeff did everything he could to build momentum for the idea.

He soon convinced management to back him as he explored the concept. Then he convinced Boston Consulting Group to fund a joint study with Barkley on what drove millennials and how brands could tap into that. Next came a Barkley-run conference on marketing to millennials, with a plan to write a book on the topic and solidify the agency's reputation for millennial insights. The conference, ShareLikeBuy, took off, generating a nice profit with coproducers including *Time* magazine and *National Geographic*.

To say his plan worked would be an understatement. Jeff's book with coauthor Christie Garton, *Marketing to Millennials: Reach the Largest and Most Influential Generation of Consumers Ever*, was published in 2013 by AMACOM, the publishing arm of the American Marketing Association. It was the first solid book published on millennial marketing. Jeff told me it created "gravitas" for the agency and "put them on the map." Along with the millennial marketing event, it put Jeff and Barkley squarely at the center of one of the hottest marketing trends of the decade. Barkley's business grew. Jeff got more than 500 speaking requests. And he went on to write four more books (so far): *Millennials with Kids, Marketing to Gen Z,* and two books in a series called *The Purpose Advantage.*

Crucially, Jeff and his employer Barkley continue to have a great relationship; as he says, "We were umbilically attached." That was no accident; the book and the business it helped create were the result of a well-planned partnership. Barkley reserved time for Jeff to work on the book as part of his job. While Barkley retained the copyright and book revenues, Jeff was able to keep some of the speaking fees. "I was happy to give them the book rights, since they were happy to give me the time [and compensation] to work on it," he explains. "If it sold 100,000 copies, I knew the speaking fees and direct business impacts would be there. It was not a big debate, since there was strong alignment between my goals and those of the business."

If you're working in a company, Jeff and Barkley's win-win partnership, based on mutual support and transparency, may be a template for you. But plan carefully. Because unless you and your employer see eye-to-eye on your authoring plans, you're sure to have a lot bumpier and more contentious ride than Jeff did.

The challenge of writing a book while working at a company

While many authors are independent consultants, public speakers, or heads of their own small organizations, many others are in larger organizations. Their experiences are decidedly mixed. Of the 74 published authors in my survey that were working in companies, 43% responded that their company was "an integral part of my writing and book promotion; we were partners" (see Figure 8-1). The rest wrote in various degrees of discomfort, describing their companies as partly helpful, tolerant, indifferent, or in a few cases, actually hostile.

Figure 8-1: Attitudes of companies toward employee authors

Source: Bernoff.com author survey 2019-2022

(N=74 published authors who worked for companies)

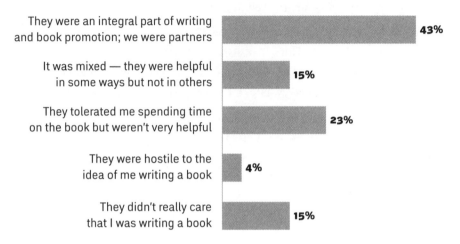

"Was your company or organization supportive as you wrote and publicized the book?"

They were an integral part of writing and book promotion; we were partners — **43%**

It was mixed — they were helpful in some ways but not in others — **15%**

They tolerated me spending time on the book but weren't very helpful — **23%**

They were hostile to the idea of me writing a book — **4%**

They didn't really care that I was writing a book — **15%**

In the worst cases, there can actually be legal trouble. Dan Lyons wrote a tell-all book called *Disrupted: My Misadventure in the Start-Up Bubble* (Hachette Books, 2016) about his experience at the marketing services company HubSpot. (Because of an oversight, HubSpot had never required Dan to sign any contracts regarding intellectual property or confidentiality with respect to his experience at the company.) By the time the book deal was in place, Dan had left HubSpot. But HubSpot's leaders became so concerned about what might be in the book that they reportedly undertook some questionable tactics to try to get a peek at an advance copy of the manuscript.[7] They were later forced to publicly respond to the book's scathing portrayals of HubSpot's workplace and tactics.

Challenges don't usually look quite that contentious. Usually, it's just a bit of discomfort internally as authors become well-know. Dan Pontefract wrote

---

7   The *Boston Globe* published a series of stories about company executives' efforts to get a look at the manuscript. As a result, several of those executives were fired or sanctioned for violating the company's code of business conduct and ethics. See https://wobs.co/BBBBlyons.

his first book on culture change, *Flat Army: Creating a Connected and Engaged Organization* (Wiley, 2013) when he was working as chief learning officer at the telecom company Telus. But he left Telus after his speaking career took off. "You can't always be a truly authentic business book writer when you're in the employ of a $14 billion company," he explains. Some of his managers had questioned some of what he wrote, even though it was factual and wasn't airing the company's dirty laundry.

Or consider the experience of Vince Molinaro, author of *The New York Times* bestselling book, *The Leadership Contract: The Fine Print of Becoming an Accountable Leader* (Wiley, 2017). He wrote this book, and several others, when he was part of three consulting firms.

His employment agreements stipulated that he'd own all the intellectual property (IP) created from books he was working on. In turn, the company benefited from the revenue generated from all the seminars and consulting services based on the books. It was a win-win relationship.

However, a subtle unease began to grow with the success of his books. "The real challenge I found in being an employee was the unease within these organizations as my brand grew in the market. My sense is they feared my brand would eclipse the company brand. So there was a healthy tension in the relationship; they wanted what I brought but only to a point."

Vince continues, "This is a reality for any thought leader working within a large consulting firm and the challenges they may face."

Vince is back to running his own company and no longer has to worry about tensions with his managers.

Even in very large organizations, there may be room for negotiation. The high-profile advertising agency executive Rishad Tobaccowala had risen to become Chief Growth Officer after several successful decades at the global agency Publicis Groupe. When he decided he wanted to write a book, he began a very open set of discussions with Maurice Lévy, the executive chairman of Publicis and his longtime boss. He agreed to give Publicis a year of advance warning and after that, to work for more than a year on the book for 50% of his time, at a reduced salary. The reduced salary reflected his reduced time on agency business — and the agreement established that because the book was created on his own time, he would retain the rights to the content. Publicis agreed because he and the company had had such a productive relationship for so long. "My basic belief is that if you don't have trusted relationships with the people at the top, it's not going to work," he says. Rishad was careful not to use any of Publicis' IP or company materials in his research.

The result was Rishad's first book, *Restoring the Soul of Business: Staying Human in the Age of Data* (HarperCollins Leadership, 2020). Publicis chairman Maurice Lévy publicly endorsed it. "I was open with them, not doing it on the side," he explains. "I said, 'If I am going to do this, I am going to be serious.' And when the book is out, I want to be an advisor to the company, not an employee. Speaking and writing is my next career."

Prepare to negotiate with your bosses

If you're a company employee and you don't plan how your book will change the relationship with your company, almost anything could happen. Unplanned outcomes could be bad for your career, bad for your book, or both.

Unless you plan an ambush as Dan Lyons did, you're much better off talking to your managers. You'll have to convince them that the time and effort you will invest in the book is going to pay off for them to a greater extent than if you just keep doing your job the way you do now. (Since authors are often creative and effective problem solvers, they're often in positions where they're already contributing significantly to the company's revenues.) Prepare some talking points about how the success of the book will benefit both the company and you, and be prepared to explain those benefits, repeatedly, to different managers within the company.

Here are some issues you should negotiate with your managers:

- **Settle who owns the IP.** When I worked at Forrester, my contract specified that Forrester owned all IP that I created. This was appropriate: They were paying me to come up with ideas for clients. It also meant that they owned the copyright on the books I wrote. You can still succeed if your company owns the IP (as Jeff Fromm and I both did), but only if the book is a corporate priority. Regarding your own IP situation, check your contract carefully and consult a lawyer. If ownership of IP is not in your contract, you'll still want to be careful about when and how you create your book. For example, although Christian J. Ward created his 2018 book *Data Leverage: Unlocking the Surprising Growth Potential of Data Partnerships* while he was at a company called Yext, he did all his writing on the ferry going back and forth to work, using a different computer from the one he used at work. This (as well as the terms of his employment contract) ensured that he could retain ownership of the book's content.

- **Agree on financial issues.** Who gets any advance or royalties? Who gets the revenue if you get a speech? If you license content to others? If you run a workshop? As I describe in Chapters 22 and 23, books generate revenue in all sorts of ways, many of which your company may want to get in on. It's best to try to create a win-win outcome: Visualize revenue streams, develop a plan with your managers, and determine how you'll share the results. While it's possible that you'll be able to create an entirely independent business that your employer is not even involved in, that's rarely going to work out as nicely in practice as you may be fantasizing.

- **Negotiate time to write.** Jeff Fromm's managers allowed him time to write. Rishad Tobaccowala's did, too, but he had to reduce his salary, because he wanted to retain all the rights to the book. Don't imagine that writing a book while working full time will be easy. When Charlene Li and I wrote *Groundswell* together, I got time set aside to do that, but Charlene didn't. While I did most of the writing, she told me that the effort of collaborating on a book while working full time as an analyst was one of the hardest things she ever did. One possible workaround is to take a sabbatical and use the time to write; it's worth investigating if such an arrangement is possible with your employer.

- **Line up corporate resources, especially promotion.** The question here is not whether the company will *let* you write a book, but whether they will *help* you make it successful. While writing, you may be able to access resources like editorial reviews, groups that conduct or analyze surveys, smart colleagues who can help brainstorm ideas, or coworkers' recommendations and contacts for people to interview and case study subjects. There may be design resources you can use to create graphics within your book. Even more valuable is promotional help. Work with the company's PR and marketing teams on outreach to media; web marketing; advertising; content marketing through blogs, podcasts, newsletters, or social media; and speeches at company events. Recognize how valuable it is to work collaboratively *with* the company, rather than attempting to do everything yourself or invest your own money to hire publicity and marketing help. (Review chapter 21 for more ideas on how the company can help with your book launch.)

- **Quote your colleagues (and get quotes from their contacts).** People will be jealous. It helps to find a few internal experts, pick their brains, and quote them in the book. This simple ego-stroking tactic improves the book, reduces jealousy, and costs nothing. Another way to involve colleagues is to tap their networks for back-cover "blurb" quotes. If your vice president of marketing is close friends with Gary Vaynerchuk, Daniel Pink, or Mark Cuban, maybe you can get a sweet endorsement.

- **Limit internal reviewers.** Once people know you're working on a book, they'll become curious — and curiosity often turns into meddling. While you're writing, people will want to review drafts (probably not on a schedule that's convenient to you), provide advice on how the cover should look, and explain why they have a better title than the one you came up with. For every useful suggestion, there will be a dozen that are just annoying and time-consuming. Instead, I recommend keeping the list of reviewers as short as possible (typically, just two or three people including your boss) and requiring those who do review content to give feedback on a clear deadline.

- **Use the manuscript to create internal enthusiasm.** My advice on reviewers changes completely once the manuscript is locked down. You can inexpensively create bound versions of the text at a copy shop or get advanced reader copies from your publisher. Distribute these internally to anyone who can help you. The objective here is not to get feedback, but to get people on board to help you promote the book throughout the company and with its clients.

- **Connect with sales.** Your company's sales team is likely to be pleased with the book, because sending out copies is a smart way to connect with clients. If the book become part of your company's marketing, you may even need administrative resources to deal with distributing and mailing out all those copies. The sales team may expect you to get on the phone with selected clients to demonstrate your capabilities; given the help that the company is providing to boost your book, that's the least you can do.

- **Be generous with signed copies.** Signed books are a great way to thank the coworkers who helped you along the way. Get their addresses and plan to send personally signed copies to each one.

Plan for the inevitable: the day you leave the company

It's unlikely you'll be at the company forever. What happens when you leave? Who gets custody of the book?

Ideally, of course, you'll own everything you created and can continue promoting it without interruption. But your company would much prefer that if you created a book while there, that it gets the benefit of that content. That's why you need to carefully check your contractual situation regarding intellectual property and competitive activity.

For example, when Charlene Li left Forrester within a year after *Groundswell* was published, she had to leave the book content behind, because it belonged to the company, not to her. She had to rebuild her own data, research, and content from scratch, since the book still belonged to Forrester.

Be aware of noncompete agreements. Setting up your own shingle as a consultant on your area of expertise is not going to thrill your bosses — and you may be contractually prohibited for a period of six months or more, depending on your contract and the laws in your state.

If your book is successful, your visibility will rise. This is likely to benefit both your company and you, provided you can still find ways to work together. Having created a successful book will improve your negotiating leverage with the company, as well as your status if you decide to leave. And even if your company still owns the book, you'll always be the author whose name is on the cover.

Key takeaways

- If you're an employee of a company, don't write a book in secret. Negotiate with your bosses about the book.
- Settle contentious issues like who owns the intellectual property and who gets revenues from book advances and speeches.
- Books can aid the company's visibility as well as your own. See if you can get help from the company's editorial, design, promotional, and sales resources.
- Get a clear perspective on what will happen to the book and the IP from it when you eventually leave the company.

PART II

RESEARCH AND WRITE

Chapter 9

Case Studies and Stories

To compel readers, find and write about people.

Scott Stratten's a pretty interesting guy. He's "an award-winning keynote speaker known for his energy, passion, knowledge, humor, and man-bun." Yeah, it actually says that in the biography on his website unmarketing.com. And if you've ever talked to him, you know that's exactly what he's like.

UnMarketing is a phenomenon. It started with the book *UnMarketing: Stop Marketing. Start Engaging* (Wiley, 2010), which was a huge bestseller, since revised for several new editions. Scott and his wife and business partner, Alison, turned that into a robust and lucrative business, with speeches for Scott, a popular podcast, and five more books. The prose in his books sparkles and the ideas are startling and resonant. But the stories are the fuel that UnMarketing runs on.

Like the story of Joshie the giraffe.

Chris Hurn's family had stayed at The Ritz-Carlton in Amelia Island, Florida. Upon returning home, they discovered that Joshie, the beloved stuffed giraffe that Chris' son slept with every night, was missing. Every parent knows what a disaster that is. So Chris told a white lie — he said that Joshie was on an extended vacation at Amelia Island. And the next day, Chris called The Ritz and desperately begged them to look for Joshie.

As it turned out, Joshie had gotten stuck in the laundry. The Ritz sent him back by overnight package. And what a package it was — since it included photos of Joshie lounging by the pool in sunglasses, hanging out with some other stuffed animals, getting a massage with cucumbers on his eyes, and generally having a great time at the resort.

Chris' son was happy. Chris was impressed. He wrote about how impressed he was in HuffPost. The story of how awesome customer service was at The Ritz spread like mad — a story for the ages, documented with photos on page 4 at the very start of Scott and Alison Stratten's book *UnSelling: The New Customer Experience* (Wiley, 2014).

Scott and Alison build everything they do around stories. The *UnMarketing* book has 60 stories in it. In *UnBranding: 100 Branding Lessons for the Age of Disruption* (Wiley, 2017), Alison and Scott brag about the number of stories right in the subtitle. Like Goodwell, the company that audits, not your company's finances, but whether it treats employees with respect. And ADT Canada, the security company so cringeworthy that it made a video of its own boilerplate of a newsletter, scrolling by with music in the background, and shared it with customers as a Christmas message.

Stories are why Scott and Alison's books are worth reading, why they are persuasive, and why, above all, they are entertaining. After all, if you can't laugh at people who are bumbling marketers like ADT Canada — and marvel at people who are awesome at it, like The Ritz-Carlton on Amelia Island — why bother reading about marketing at all?

Where do all those stories come from?

Alison and Scott are always on the lookout for stories and case studies. As Scott told me, "The main part of our job is research. We spend the most hours of the day reading stories and sharing with each other. Did you see this, we ask? We sort of keep a running list."

They may call it a list, but I call it a pipeline. The interesting stories end up on their podcast. The best of those end up in a book. And the most resonant ones in the books end up in Scott's speeches.

Of course, the best research includes primary interviews. That's why, for *UnSelling,* Scott and Alison reached out to Scott Harrison, the amazing founder of charity: water, as well as Carey Smith, founder of the ceiling fan company

Big Ass Fans. Both found radically different ways to sell, and Alison and Scott were able to tell their stories based on firsthand conversations.

Scott and Alison Stratten tell stories for a living, and businesspeople eat up their insights. What Scott does on stage, nobody else can do. But collecting stories? Anybody can do that.

Business books are about people and stories

When I completed my first book proposal — for a book on the future of television — I sent it to the legendary agent John Taylor "Ike" Williams. The book proposal was full of groundbreaking ideas about how the industry of TV was about to change completely. But Ike was unimpressed. "This is not a book," he said. "It reads like a research report."

Since I wrote research reports for a living, I guess I should have expected that.

"Let me tell you something," Ike told me. "You may be very smart. But you need to know that business books are about people, and stories. There are no people and stories in your proposal. So I can't sell it."

It's too bad that book was never pitched properly or published, or you might know me now as the guy who predicted the TV streaming revolution. But I sure took Ike's words to heart. And he was, fundamentally, right. Business books are about people and stories.

In this chapter, I'll explain how to find stories, how to conduct interviews, and how to write about stories to keep your book interesting.

How to find stories

Stories are all around you. You just need to train yourself to notice. That's what Alison and Scott Stratten are good at — and what you can be good at, too.

Where will your stories come from? Here are some ideas:

- **Your own experience.** Obviously, if it happened to you, you're set. But unless your book is a memoir, first-person stories can get tedious. Readers are automatically skeptical, and we can only hear so much about the author's own heroic deeds.

- **Your clients' experience.** The best case studies come from your best contacts, especially if they've done something iconic. Clients who trust your counsel will also likely trust you with their stories. This is why authors whose companies have a lot of clients have an edge. If your clients are publicity-shy, you can offer to tell their story with the name changed.

- **Case studies from vendors.** Who sells technology or services in the area you're looking in? Check out their press releases, case studies, and white papers — even if they compete with you. But don't stop with writing up what's in their releases. In these accounts, you'll often find the names and positions of the people who did great work. Reach out to them and mention where you read about them; if they've gone on the record already, they're likely to be willing to talk about their work.

- **Stories told online.** You can find these if you use Google intelligently. I used this technique for a book I ghostwrote about chatbots: I searched "customer service chatbots," "intelligent agents," and "virtual agents." Then I looked for article and blog titles like "The 10 best corporate chatbot applications." You will often need to follow links in articles to other articles or stories; the story you seek may be three or four links away. It's not a requirement, but you can often increase the yield of this kind of research by hiring an experienced researcher.

- **Books.** You can often find stories in other people's business books. You can quote one or two, with attribution. Don't overdo this, or your reader will wonder why they're reading a book full of other authors' stories.

- **Watchfulness and networking.** Once you're attuned to what kind of stories you're looking for, you'll start to pick up examples all around you. Check your daily news feeds in the trade publications you follow. Go to conferences and attend relevant sessions. Go to networking breakfasts. If you live every day with your antennae alert to what you're looking for, you're likely to find it.

- **Trusted friends.** You probably have five to ten mentors or colleagues who do the same kind of work you do; often they're former coworkers with whom you share a trusted bond. Email them and tell them what kind of stories you're looking for. It's easier to interview people if your friend has already recommended you.

- **Your social network.** I've sourced stories with Twitter, Facebook, and LinkedIn: I just tell folks what I'm looking for, and ideas pour in. Most of these ideas will be useless, but if you get 20 suggestions and can only use two, that's two stories you didn't have before. Your friends' referrals will make these people more open to being interviewed.

- **Hypotheticals.** Sometimes you just have to make things up. So you tell the story of Sally, who tried everything to pitch her business, but then figured out the problem was in how her website presented her. Or Fred, who could never get his sales calls returned until he found the secret formula for making the connection. So long as you make it clear that Sally and Fred are composites, not real people, you can plug holes in your book with hypothetical stories.

Of course, finding stories is not the same as telling stories. If you want your stories to resonate, I suggest adopting two core principles.

First, whenever possible, interview actual participants and tell their stories from their perspective. A firsthand interview generates a better narrative than a secondhand story cribbed from somewhere else, because you'll be able to ask just the right questions to make the story rich and illustrative.

Second, pursue variety. A mix of your own stories, your clients' stories, stories found online, and hypotheticals will come across as fresh and interesting. If it's all about your experience, or all hypothetical, or all copied from a few sources, your book will feel stale and lack credibility. Seek diversity in industries as well; unless your book is about financial services, it shouldn't all be banking stories. While it's challenging, if you possibly can, pursue geographical diversity, too; if you have stories from China and Germany and Brazil along with US stories, you expand your market.

And one more thing. Keep close track of the contact information for everyone you interview. You'll be recontacting them at the final fact verification stage, as I describe in chapter 16.

How to get and conduct interviews

Since firsthand interviews generate the best stories, how do you get somebody who's done awesome work to go on the record with you? Here are four steps that will get you there:

Step 1. Find the right person to interview

That's not always the CEO. Even if you're writing about marketing, it may not be the CMO. But you want the highest-level person who can tell the whole story.

Existing articles and blog posts are an excellent resource for identifying interview targets — see who's quoted in an article or vendor case study, and reach out to that individual.

Step 2: Get an introduction, most likely through the PR department

How do you get this executive to speak with you? You probably don't even have their email address. Even if you do, they're less likely to respond to a random email. You could message them through LinkedIn, but many won't respond to random inquiries that way, either.

To get an introduction, go through the company's public relations department, because it's their job to help executives get coverage.

So how do you find the PR contact? You could find a PR page on the company's site and pick the PR contact that seems best. But the easiest thing to do is to find a company press release in the general area you're writing about and find the PR contact's email or phone number there.

Step 3: Write a brief, personalized, and persuasive pitch email

Your pitch should include a subject line that says exactly what you want (an interview with the target executive). And it should include the following elements:

- The PR contact's name in the body of the email (showing you did your homework and will treat them as an important connection).
- What you're seeking (say, a 45-minute phone interview). Be up front about the length of the interview; your PR person is going to have to represent what you want and why and how much time it's going to take.
- A short description of what interests you, with a link. For example, "I saw [target name]'s comments in [article or vendor case study], and I'm very interested in how they accomplished that. That company is one of the few who have [accomplishment], and I'd love to write about that in my book."
- Information about your book and your background. How many books have you written? How long have you been researching this? Who is your publisher? You want to assure the PR person that the visibility you are providing is going to be worth the executive's effort.
- A polite closing, including a deadline. "If you can get back to me in the next ten days, that would be very helpful." Don't give more than two or three weeks, or your request will be forgotten.

The main thrust of this email is "I know about the company's accomplishments, I plan to write positive things, I have experience, and I have a publisher." The other crucial element is to treat the PR person as a valuable professional. PR people get dumped on by media all day long. If you're nice to them, they're more likely to respond.

Step 4. Conduct the interview cordially but professionally

After some back and forth with PR and, possibly, the executive's admin, you'll get your time on the phone.

If they ask for questions ahead of time, send a few but say those are typical of what you're asking. Don't send a complete list.

If they ask for final approval of the text, don't grant that. (Otherwise, they'll try to make your case study sound like a puff piece.) Instead, agree to allow them to review the final text for accuracy. (Language is crucial: *review*, not *approve*.)

Then conduct the interview. Tell them this is an on-the-record interview, and that you'll share the results when the book is nearing completion so they can check facts and quotes for accuracy.

If you said it would take 40 minutes, take less than 40 minutes. Start with easy questions and go to harder ones. Sound as fascinated as you can about what they're doing. Take careful notes or record the interview. Go in with a plan about what you're going to find out, but be prepared to go in whatever directions seem most productive. But don't leave anything out.

You're unlikely to get a follow-up interview, and asking for one marks you as an amateur. If you need some little fact — well, you have the PR contact's name and you made friends with them, so they can track down that little detail.

How to write a case study

Having completed the interview, you can now write up the case study as a short story vignette. Fundamentally, all case studies are pretty similar. "John (or whatever the person's name is) comes from an interesting background. At his company, he had a problem. He tried this. It didn't work. He tried that. It didn't work. Then he realized something important and tried something new. It worked. It paid off for John professionally and personally. And here's what you can learn from that."

That has all the elements of a story: a protagonist, a problem, some twists, a resolution, and a happy ending (or sometimes, a sad ending).

What does that look like? One of the best case studies I ever read was written by Harley Manning, a customer experience expert at Forrester, for *Outside In:*

The Power of Putting Customers at the Center of Your Business (New Harvest, 2012). Here's the whole thing:

> Kevin Peters sat alone in his car in the rain, watching the entrance of an Office Depot store. He was wearing a baseball cap and a well-worn pair of jeans.
>
> Over the course of the last half hour, he'd watched one customer after another emerge from the store. None of them carried a shopping bag. On their way out, they walked past an Office Depot employee leaning against a wall under the awning, smoking a cigarette out of the rain.
>
> Kevin was torn. On the one hand, he didn't want anyone to know he was there. As the president of Office Depot's North American retail division, he'd come to this parking lot in New Jersey on a gray, dreary day to get a firsthand look at how customers experienced one of his stores.
>
> His method, already followed at dozens of other locations, was to observe customers coming and going, then enter, walk the aisles, and talk to customers about whether they were finding what they needed and how they liked the store in general.
>
> The success of each visit hinged on the store manager not knowing he was there. Kevin wanted to see the store as a customer on a shopping trip, not as an executive on an inspection tour. But this situation was too much. Frustrated customers were leaving without products while one of his employees not only ignored them but laid down a cloud of tobacco smoke for them to walk through on their way out the door. Should he blow his cover by telling the manager to get his slacking employee back in the store to help shoppers?
>
> Kevin made a decision: This couldn't stand. There was no way he was going to sit idly by and watch his business erode one customer at a time. He abandoned his undercover plans, got out of his car, and walked into the store on a new mission.
>
> Because he'd planned to go incognito, Kevin hadn't bothered to find out the name of the store manager. But he knew that every retail location has a stanchion near the front of the store with a picture of the manager and, right under it, this service promise: "If you are not satisfied with your

shopping experience, please see me or another manager on duty." Kevin walked over to the stanchion, looked up to see what the store manager looked like — and found a picture of the smoking employee outside.

When he tells this story you can see very real pain in Kevin's face and hear it in his voice. "The darn store manager! The person with whom we trusted our customer relationship." He pauses and repeats, "The person with whom we trusted our customer relationship."

This passage appears at the very start of Harley's book with his coauthor, Kerry Bodine. Just after this, they introduce the concept of customer experience and how it makes a crucial difference to companies like Office Depot — and how complex it is to analyze and improve. (That's why it needs a whole book to explain it.)

Notice a few things about Harley's case study. It's short: fewer than 500 words. It gives you an idea of what matters to its protagonist, Kevin Peters, without belaboring the point. It has telling details — the rain, the smoking employee — so you can put yourself in the protagonist's shoes. And it has a little bit of drama. In this case, it doesn't really have an ending, but later in the book you get to find out just how Kevin Peters identified and then solved the problems at Office Depot, ironically with the help of the smoking store manager.

You may or may not be as talented as Harley is at telling business stories, but don't worry too much about it — even an imperfectly told business story is compelling. Readers want to hear about people like them solving problems like the ones they have. They enjoy reading stories like the story of Kevin Peters, so long as they have a point.

We are all programmed since birth to read stories, remember stories, and retell stories. So find out the stories of people like your readers, track them down, interview them, and explain what they learned — and what your readers can learn from their experience. That's a great way to make sure you're writing a business book that matters.

Key takeaways

- Stories and case studies are essential. The best business books include plenty of them.
- You can track down business stories from news articles, press releases, and personal contacts. Mix up different kinds of stories to keep your book interesting.
- To get firsthand interviews, it helps to go through a company's public relations department and write a carefully worded email about the interview you're seeking.
- Case study stories should be short, feature a sympathetic protagonist, include telling details, and deliver a point that's relevant to the ideas in your book.

Chapter 10

Research and Data

Assemble evidence to prove your case.

Michael C. Bush, CEO of the company Great Place to Work, has made research into a competitive advantage for his company. His book shows off his methods.

Michael's company surveys employees about their experiences at work: whether they feel respected, are treated honestly and fairly, and believe the company cares for them as employees and people. His surveys measure diverse company attributes including values, innovation, financial growth, leadership effectiveness, maximizing human potential, and trust. His team and he have proven that companies that do those things consistently at a high level are far more innovative, and their businesses outperform the S&P 500 by a factor of three to one.

Michael's survey research fuels *Fortune*'s "100 Best Places to Work" list. His book *A Great Place to Work for All: Better for Business. Better for people. Better for the World* (Berrett-Koehler, 2018) explains the methodology and exhorts companies to improve their performance on his metrics to attract, retain, and motivate an inclusive workforce. The book has become a crucial tool for showcasing his proprietary research for potential clients.

Some companies buy hundreds of copies of the book to go along with retaining Michael to speak to their organizations. And his sales team uses the book to open doors with potential clients. As Michael told me, "The book has given us clarity and credibility because we defined 'For All' before the racial and discriminatory injustices that occurred during the pandemic. When the need for Diversity, Equity, Inclusion, and Belonging became clearer, we had a research-based road map just a click away."

You need research to be credible

Research is the process of finding facts and information that will inform and support the concepts in your book. And while you may not need research at the level that Michael C. Bush's company collects it, you do need it, because business books that matter are *built* on research. As Scott and Alison Stratten, the bestselling authors whom I profiled in the previous chapter, told me, "The main part of our job is research."

Research is how you assemble compelling evidence. The proof of your ideas must come from somewhere outside your own head; otherwise, you're just rambling on about what you imagine to be true, which is hardly convincing. Among the published authors I surveyed, 84% listed some form of research beyond their own experience — such as surveys, interviews, or web research — as a primary source of content in their books

The best books include evidence from two kinds of research: primary research that no one has seen before to reveal new insights and secondary research assembled from published sources to fill in and broaden the base of proof in the book.

In my survey of authors, the most popular source of content in their books was their own personal experience. But most authors cited other sources such as web research, interviews, and data they collected (see Figure 10-1). They knew that a book based solely on their personal experience was less credible.

Figure 10-1: Data sources of published authors

Source: Bernoff.com author survey 2019-2022 (N=172 published authors)

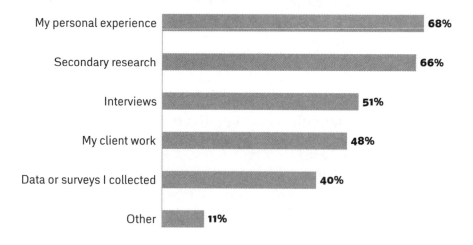

"What are your primary sources of content for the book? Check all that apply."

My personal experience	68%
Secondary research	66%
Interviews	51%
My client work	48%
Data or surveys I collected	40%
Other	11%

Make the most of primary research

Primary research is new information that you gathered and published for the first time. It's a powerful way to differentiate and promote your book, but it can be costly and time-consuming to collect.

The simplest way to gather primary research is to interview people with something relevant to say about your topic. Those interviews should include people who've done what you're writing about (fended off a cyberattack, run an accounting department, written code in Python, or innovated at a start-up company, for example). They may also include other experts in your field or companies that sell services to your readers.

The advice I shared in the last chapter on gathering case studies applies to these types of interviews as well: Identify people from news articles or your own interactions with them, approach them respectfully, tap corporate PR to make contact, interview them for new insights, and quote them directly in your writing.

You may be worried that quoting other experts or vendors will diminish your expertise. In fact, the reverse is true. Smart people who quote other smart people appear more knowledgeable, not less. You will be communicating that you're in touch with the whole market. And since it's your book, you still get the last word, because you can comment on what these other experts have told you.

Data is even more valuable than interviews. There's nothing like statistics to inform and support your conclusions.

You can hire survey firms to help you design surveys, identify a group of people to survey, and analyze the results, as Michael C. Bush's company does. This can cost tens of thousands of dollars, but it gives you access to data that no one else has, which will make your book more valuable and credible.

Not everyone can invest in research at this level. But nearly everyone can do simpler research cheaply with tools like SurveyMonkey, which, as I write this, costs just $39 a month for up to 15,000 responses per year. With little more than basic survey skills, you can design and field simple surveys yourself. And you can perform the base-level analysis with simple tools like Microsoft Excel or Google Sheets.

Who should you survey? The quickest and simplest answer is "people like your target audience." If you're writing a book on careers in software development, survey software developers; if you're writing about investment strategy for Gen Z, survey Gen Z investors. (For this book, of course, I surveyed business authors.) Finding people willing to take your surveys can be expensive, but if your business has clients, you can often use them as a base for your survey. If you can gather data from at least 150 people, your statistics will be credible at a basic level.

Primary research also includes analysis of data other than surveys. For example, Seth Stephens-Davidowitz's book *Everybody Lies: Big Data, New Data, and What the Internet Can Tell Us About Who We Really Are* (Dey Street Books, 2018) analyzes revealing data collected by Google and Pornhub about what people are looking for online. (Among other unexpected insights, he shows that searches for gay porn are just as popular in conservative states as in liberal ones.) Diane Hessan's book *Our Common Ground: Insights from Four Years of Listening to American Voters* (RealClear Publishing, 2021) reveals proprietary information gleaned from her conversations and emails with a panel of 500 voters.

It's certainly possible to write a business book without primary research. You could write based completely on your own experience and your work with clients, for example. But unless you're writing a memoir, quoting only from your own experience makes it easy for readers to be skeptical of every point you're trying to make.

Secondary research requires judgment

Secondary research nuggets you can find in other sources will add significantly to the authority of what you are writing. And for the most part, secondary research is free. Your job is to identify what sources are worth quoting and cite them appropriately.

What sorts of nuggets are we talking about? Statistics. Quotes from prominent experts. Survey results from surveys conducted by large research organizations. Stories about people doing whatever your book is about, published in case studies and articles. Analogies and metaphors.

When you're writing a book — or even considering writing one — you should constantly look out for these research nuggets. If something you read seems like a good metaphor for an argument you're making, bookmark it. If you hear a business story or case study that applies, bookmark it. It's the same with statistics you read or quotes that seem relevant. Keep a file of such useful information in a tool like Evernote or Scrivener, as I describe in chapter 12.

Of course, waiting around for good stuff to appear isn't sufficient. You also need to go out and get it.

Here, you're likely thinking, "Great, I already know how to use Google." But unless you want to waste a lot of time swimming through irrelevant material — or worse yet, quote people and stats that are full of crap — Google is just the beginning of your secondary research.

Emily Riley, CEO of Riley Strategic, is an expert on the best research strategies for business content. She was an analyst at both JupiterResearch and Forrester, where she was briefly a colleague of mine. And she did much of the research for a book I ghostwrote, *Marketing to the Entitled Consumer: How to Turn Unreasonable Expectations into Lasting Relationships* (Amplify, 2018). I was impressed at how she was able to efficiently surface the most relevant and authoritative nuggets.

"Google is your friend and your enemy," Emily says. "It's like boiling the ocean." You need to start with a wide variety of searches on different and related terms, such as "AI," "artificial intelligence," and "machine learning." Then narrow it down to fit what you're working on, for example, "Machine learning financial services," "Machine learning risks," or "Machine learning security breaches."

Don't just assume you can use anything you find. As Emily says, "Once you start to see the bigger picture, you need to think about how to categorize what you find as real and good research, random opinion, or a rehash of a rehash."

Judgment is crucial here. Content with little credibility often surfaces in searches like this, such as posts from random "contributors" on Forbes.com or writers on HuffPost, sites that exercise little editorial judgment in what they publish. If you cite content from such sources, you're communicating to readers that you don't care about the accuracy of what you write. Your judgment is crucial; otherwise, you're just rehashing Google searches they could do themselves.

Don't stop at the first mention of a statistic or quote, either. Often the sources you find will have a link to their own sources. You may have to click through two or three articles to find the original data or quote. That's the only way to verify that what you're quoting originally came from a reputable and dependable source.

Look for gold-standard research without bias. If content comes from Harvard Business School, Northwestern University's Kellogg School of Management, The Wharton School of the University of Pennsylvania, Stanford Graduate School of Business, the MIT Sloan School of Management, or a similar business school source, it's less likely to be biased. Look also for research from major consultancies and research companies such as Accenture, Bain & Company, Boston Consulting Group, Deloitte, Ernst & Young (EY), Forrester, Gartner, IDC, or McKinsey & Company. The Pew Research Center, a respected nonpartisan research organization that publishes major consumer surveys, is a great source.

Carefully scrutinize the sample quoted in any research study. As Emily quipped, "Maybe they say '80% of respondents view AI as dangerous,' but it's a survey of 200 truck drivers — who might reasonably expect AI-driven trucks to be taking their jobs." The best studies are more recent, have larger samples, and come from unbiased organizations.

Be especially wary of consumer surveys, because respondents rarely think deeply about their answers, so, as Emily describes it, "consumers contradict themselves regularly."

Surveys of businesspeople are often quite small, perhaps a few hundred people, but they can still be revealing. And don't worry too much about quoting people you compete with; insight is insight, regardless of where you find it.

You can find more than statistics and surveys, of course. Search the name of the industry and a trend (such as "online banking") along with the words "case study." And check out the blog posts and press releases of vendors in your industry. As I described in the previous chapter, you can follow up with your own interviews to find out what's really going on with these folks.

Here are three more tips on how to find research tidbits.

First, check out Google Scholar, where searches will often unearth academic studies that can buttress the points you're making.

Second, scour Wikipedia articles for links to credible sources. Please don't *quote* Wikipedia, because the text there is contributed by random people, and there's no guarantee that the facts you're reading are true. Instead, review content in the linked *sources* at the bottom of the Wikipedia page. Even if Wikipedia itself isn't dependable, it's an excellent compendium of links to potentially dependable primary sources.

And third, read other people's books. If an author has written about the same space you're describing, you can quote them or check out and potentially cite some of the same examples and statistics they've unearthed. And contact them, too: Most authors love to be interviewed about their books.

Avoid inadvertent plagiarism

I know you would never plagiarize the work of another author. No reputable author ever would.

Except that authors do this — accidentally — all the time.

Look what happened with Jill Abramson, former executive editor of *The New York Times*, who published a book on media called *Merchants of Truth: The Business of News and the Fight for Facts* (Simon & Schuster, 2019). Soon after it was published, Vice News correspondent Michael C. Moynihan tweeted about a bunch of passages that were nearly identical in the book and in other published works, in some cases with no attribution. Writer Ian Frisch complained of seven instances where Jill had copied his prose closely. And Jill paid the price: Days after the publication of her book, it had 74% one-star reviews on Amazon, a terrible performance for a major nonfiction book.

In an interview on Vox, Jill defended herself. She told Sean Illing, "This was completely unintentional. I mean, I have 70 pages of footnotes and I tried to credit everyone's work as best I can. What we're talking about here are sets of facts that I borrowed; obviously, the language is too close in some cases, but I'm not lifting original ideas. Again, I wish I had got the citation right, but it's not an intentional theft or taking someone's original ideas — it's just the facts. But I'm owning it and I'm disappointed in myself for these mistakes."[8]

It's clear to me what happened here. The author (or her research assistant) was not fastidious with the research. Material from other sources was dumped into the text without noting that it came from elsewhere. Then Jill or her researcher forgot what she had done, polished some of the prose, and published it, stripped of its source. That's not evil, but it is sloppy.

It is extremely easy to make this same mistake as you do research. The time to fix it is not when you are writing, it is when you are compiling information. Every piece of information you obtain from research needs to come along with a source, and that source must stay with the information through every draft. The easiest way to do this is to include a link in the text you're writing or revising. One of my blog's readers, Paul Stregevsky, had a good suggestion: he marks direct quotes he's working on by putting the text in color, and only removes the color when he has picked out what he wants to quote and identified the source appropriately.

At the end of the publishing process, when you're creating footnotes (as I describe in chapter 16), you'll be glad you were fastidious about your sources.

Research makes all the difference in differentiating a business book that matters from a hack job. Putting effort into research will pay off — and that includes carefully and fastidiously keeping track of sources. And having collected all that information, you're finally ready to write a chapter, a process I'll describe next.

---

8   "'I made mistakes': Jill Abramson responds to plagiarism charges around her new book," by Sean Illing, Vox News, February 8, 2019. See https://wobs.co/BBBBabramson.

Key takeaways

- Primary research, including interviews and surveys, is expensive and time-consuming, but it creates unique value in your writing.
- Secondary research can bolster your arguments. Get adept not just at searching out statistics, quotes, and case studies, but also at selecting the most credible sources to quote.
- Keep track of sources fastidiously to avoid inadvertent plagiarism.

Chapter 11

Drafting Chapters

Use a fat outline to move beyond writer's block.

Fotini Iconomopoulos' childhood nickname was "the negotiator." She has turned that skill into a career, advising corporations, training people, and giving speeches on the art and skill of negotiation. Her reputation spread to HarperCollins Publishers, generating a query: Could she write a negotiation book?

When Fotini faces off with an audience, she feels confident and assured because she knows her topic; she knows how to persuade people, one-on-one or in groups. But having agreed to write a book, Fotini found herself face-to-face with her most formidable adversary: the blank page.

She described writing chapters as "a soul-crushing experience." "I never expected it to be this hard," she told me. "If you ask me to talk about negotiation, I can riff about it for hours. But as soon as I am sitting down at a computer, a lot of imposter syndrome creeps in. There is a mental barrier that makes me not want to put things on paper."

Fotini muscled through the resistance. She had to escape her house; she and her laptop became a regular fixture at her local coffee shop. "At some point, you write something, even if it is absolutely garbage," she said. "I ripped apart the middle of the book at least three times and started over. I didn't know what to write next."

Eventually, with help from her editor at HarperCollins and an outside editor, she pummeled the text into shape. Her well-written, useful, and entertaining book is called *Say Less, Get More: Unconventional Negotiation Techniques to Get What You Want* (HarperCollins, 2021).

Looking back, Fotini recognizes what it would have taken to more easily win the negotiation with the blank page. "I made a mistake," she says, "not fleshing out the skeleton of the book before I started writing."

The cure for writer's block

I don't believe in writer's block.

Oh, I know writers get blocked. I've seen it a thousand times. Writer's block stalks the online author communities I frequent like the specter of the red death.

I just don't believe writers understand where it comes from.

The reason you can't write is because you don't know what to write. And you don't know what to write because you don't know what job the chapter is supposed to do, and you don't have a plan for how to make the chapter do that.

The blank page has very few suggestions. So you type, delete, type, delete, type, delete, cry, and feel like a fraud.

It's a lie. You are not a fraud, any more than Fotini Iconomopoulos, renowned negotiation expert and advisor to powerful corporate executives, is. You just did things in the wrong order. When it's time to write a chapter, you need to write from a plan, not the seat of your pants. The easier path from research and ideas to beautifully written page has a couple of essential stops in the middle: the chapter objective and the fat outline.

Create a chapter objective

Before writing a chapter, consider what you're trying to accomplish. Every chapter has a job to do.

In chapter 6, I suggested a way to do this: the reader question method. Each chapter should answer a question for the reader. Get that question up in front of you now. If your thinking about the chapter has evolved since you originally planned it, revise that question accordingly.

You may feel blocked, but you can certainly write one question that won't even be in the actual text of the book.

For example, in Fotini's book, chapter 5 is called "Why Power Matters." It answers the question: "How does the power balance between parties affect negotiation strategy?"

Having crafted a question like that, writing becomes a simpler task: *Answer the question.* You may not be ready to write, but you're one step closer to knowing what to write.

What's next? Create a reader objective. I've cribbed the concept of behavioral objectives from educational theory. Just as a teacher should be able to describe the skill a student will learn from a lesson, you must describe what your reader will learn from your chapter. What do you want the reader to know and be able to do after they've read your chapter?

This objective is the answer to the reader question for the chapter. Write the objective in this form: "After reading this chapter, you will . . ."

Here's how this might look in Fotini's case:

After reading chapter 5, you will be able to assess the power balance between yourself and your negotiation partner — and maximize your own power to improve your negotiating position.

Behavioral objectives should be measurable. You could ask a reader who read Fotini's chapter 5: "In your upcoming negotiation, what power do you have, and what power does your opponent have? What are you going to do to maximize your own power here?" You could then listen to the reader's answers and determine if the reader had actually learned what they were supposed to from reading the chapter.

Objectives are a little harder to write than questions because they depend on the expert content you've assembled. If you get stuck, go back and look at all the research you did (and keep it handy, because you'll need it for the next step along the way to writing). But objectives are still short and far easier to craft than actual prose going into the book.

If you're finding it challenging to write the objective for a chapter, imagine the reader sitting across from you. Start the imaginary conversation by restating the reader question: "So, you want to know . . ." Then say "I can help. When we're done, you'll be able to do this." And what comes after that is the objective.

Now you're almost ready to write without pain. All you need is a fat outline.

Write a fat outline

As I mentioned in Chapter 6, after getting time to write, authors say that organizing content is their biggest writing challenge. A fat outline is the solution to the challenge of organizing a chapter.

In contrast to the outlines we all learned in school — which are effortless to write, skeletal, and useless — a fat outline has real substance to it. It's basically a list of all the bits and pieces that will make up the chapter, in the order in which they'll appear. Fat outlines are relatively easy to create, and essential to easing the task of writing.

The first step in creating the fat outline is to assemble all the ingredients that belong in your chapter. There are five basic elements of which all business book chapters are constructed:

- **Ideas and frameworks.** These are the concepts you want to explain — things worth defining and describing. They often have a structure (for example, five steps, three parts, or a hierarchy). You may have graphics that illustrate them.
- **Stories (case studies and examples).** This includes full case studies with an introduction, narrative, and conclusion, as well as simpler examples that might just be a paragraph or a sentence about what somebody or some company did and the result.
- **Argumentation (reasoning).** This is text where you make your case for something. For example, in this book I have continually made the case that it's better to be a planner than a pantser. To convince you, I needed to show logically that one path is better than the other.
- **Proof points (data, quotes, citations).** The proof points are the fruits of all the research I described in the previous chapter: the statistics, charts, events, quotations, and other bits of evidence that you so painstakingly collected to support your arguments.

- **Advice (how-tos).** People are reading your book to be better at something. This is where you tell them how to do that.

Based on all the research you did and all the knowledge you've assembled so far, you've got a collection of this stuff, either in the form of research notes and interviews or perhaps as a partly formed idea or three in your head or something you wrote before. Now is the time to collect it all.

Open a document — Microsoft Word, Google Docs, or whatever you usually write in. And dump what you've got for this chapter into it, including all five elements. To keep the size manageable, don't dump entire hunks of research, just put a sentence or two to remind you of what you have. Don't worry about sentence fragments or grammar — this is just a set of notes that no reader will ever see.

Now arrange the bits to form a story. That might sound challenging, but it's not as hard as you might think. For example, this is one typical way to arrange a chapter:

Here's a story of someone facing a problem (case study). You can learn from what they learned (main idea). Here are the elements of that idea (framework). Here's why that idea is valid and convincing (argumentation, supported by proof points). Taken together, here's what that all means (idea, restated as conclusion). And here is what you should do about it (advice).

Replace each of those sentences with actual content you've conceived, collected, or plan to create, and you have a fat outline: a blueprint for the chapter. For a longer chapter, you may have multiple sets of ideas, arguments with proof points, and advice, or even additional case studies, but the fat outline is still going to be just a page or two. Assembling it won't be difficult or time-consuming.

Let's look at Fotini's chapter 5 on power, the one for which we identified the reader question and the objective earlier. She didn't write a fat outline — remember her struggling in that coffee shop — but if she had written one, what might it have looked like? Like this:

- Power fuels your negotiations. Power gives you options. [idea]
- 2 types of power: actual power and perceived power. [framework]
- Manufacturer dependent on retailer example. Mfr collects data to improve negotiating position/power. Preso showing brand loyalty makes replacement a problem [case study]

- Power/recharge battery analogy. Full battery means more time on My Side v. Our Side [argumentation with proof point]
- You can choose to use power now or later. Benefits of choosing not to use power. Challenges of failing to use power [advice]
- Types of power, promise to explain more [transition to next chp]

That's a typical fat outline. Here are a few things about it that you might notice:

- It's short. You can scribble down one of these in just a few minutes.
- It's not hard to create. It's as if you were sitting down next to a reader in a bar, and you said, "Hey, here's the story of this chapter, here's what it's about. First of all . . ." and continued from there.
- It's informal. Nobody cares about language, spelling, or cryptic things that only you understand. Since this plan is only for you, you can include anything that reminds you of what the pieces mean, including pasted-in graphics, small chunks of prose, or links to web content you've researched. (The bits shown here in brackets aren't required — I've only included them to illustrate this example.)
- It's easy to play around with and rearrange, just a matter of moving a few scraps of text here or there, or adding or deleting a few things.
- It reminds you of what pieces you have so you won't forget anything when it's time to write.
- It puts things in a logical order that you can turn into a storyline when you write.

Taken together, these qualities mean that making a fat outline is a *low-stakes, low-stress activity*. You can whip one up in 30 minutes. And it's pretty much immune to writer's block, because writing down little notes and moving them around doesn't tap into the "people will be reading this, what if it sucks" anxiety of imposter syndrome. If writers have trouble with a fat outline, it's probably because they don't have enough material; recognizing that is the first step to solving it, by doing more research.

I have one more tip about the fat outline and the chapter that will emerge from it. Your temptation will be to start with an introduction of the idea. That's what

Fotini did, for example, and that's a solid way to write. But consider starting with a case study, plunging people immediately into a narrative. People love stories. They will absolutely read that story to find out what happened. And after the story, in the glow of the story's happy (or tragic) ending, your reader is primed to believe virtually anything you say. This is where you tie the story to your main idea ("What can you learn from this? That *[introduce main idea here]*.") Romanced by the story, the reader then falls for your idea, and your chapter is off and running.

It's not a coincidence that nearly every chapter in the book you are currently reading starts with a story.

Now write the chapter

Nonfiction writers who are stuck or blocked usually just don't know what to write. But you just solved that problem. Your fat outline divides your writing task into bite-sized pieces. Each scrap or item in the fat outline becomes a hunk of content in the chapter.

So "just write" is no longer terrifying.

If you followed my tip from the previous section, you'll start by writing up a case study. Writing stories is fun — all writers are storytellers at heart. So that will get you off to a good start.

Then tie the story to the main idea of your chapter. Your idea is fascinating and powerful, so feel that power and boldly tell readers what they need to know.

Next write the rest of the bits you've mapped out in the fat outline. This is easier because you've divided the chapter into tractable tasks. If you have 45 minutes, write out an argument. Or take an hour or two and write a section summarizing secondary research. You don't even have to write these pieces in order. You can just flesh out the fat outline into text, and you'll have written a draft of a chapter. And don't worry too much about whether each word and sentence is perfect; you can always improve them in the next stage of revision.

The fat outline is a scaffolding to guide and support you, but you don't have to slavishly follow it. You might decide to put things in a different order than the outline suggests or add or delete sections. Nobody will know you didn't exactly follow the outline. It's just there as an aid to getting words down on the page.

And remember, you have many more tools than sentences and paragraphs. Fiction is typically just written as a set of paragraphs, but nonfiction often has a more interesting visual structure to it. You can divide the chapter up into pieces with section headings and subheadings. Bulleted lists make sets of items easier to scan. Numbered lists are quite helpful for sets of instructions. You can use graphics to illuminate concepts and sidebars to hold interesting concepts that aren't integral to the main storyline of the chapter. You can even quote whole paragraphs of other work (with appropriate credit and permission, of course) if they help make your case. A chapter written with these types of elements will be more approachable on the page and more palatable to readers.

It's less stressful to write by mixing up these elements; it creates a chapter that is more interesting to read as well.

What to do if you insist on just writing

What I've just described is the easiest way to write a nonfiction book chapter. But it's not the only way.

You may be a devotee of the "butt-in-seat" school of writing that says that you must bang out a bunch of text every morning, evening, or weekend.

You may feel like you're not "writing" if you're researching or creating a fat outline.

Or you may be reading this already having batted out many hunks of prose, which are now lying around your hard drive, mocking you (much like my author from chapter 7 who was 76,000 words into a 60,000-word book).

Some people just work things out by writing. If that's you, I'm not going to judge you. But how do you turn what you wrote into chapters?

Well, first take inventory of what you wrote. Make a list of bits that you have. (If you use a tool like Scrivener, as I'll describe in the next chapter, it can help with this.)

Now reconsider your chapters. Go ahead and make a fat outline of a chapter you're planning using the notes you have about the bits you already created. Arrange the descriptions of the bits into a story.

And then grab the pieces you wrote and arrange them in a chapter that matches that story, fixing the text and transitions to make it hang together properly.

To some people, that "write, then plan, then rewrite" method feels more natural than my recommended sequence of "plan, research, outline, write." For example, it aligns with Anne Lamott's "shitty first draft" method as described in her writing book *Bird by Bird: Some Instructions on Writing and Life.* And it's been beloved by pantsers since time immemorial.

Unless you're great at conceiving whole chapters in your head, you'll end up doing the same organizational work either way. I just think it's easier — and less subject to writer's block — to create a fat outline before you begin writing.

A last-ditch cure for writer's block

Sometimes, even if you've done all the preparation I've described, you may still find yourself staring at a blinking cursor and feeling stuck.

Here's a simple tip that nearly always seems to work in these situations.

Open a new document. Visualize somebody in your audience who really needs to hear what you have to say. Then type this:

"Look, stupid."

Then start typing what comes into your mind next. What do they really need to hear? What do you want to unload? What do people just not understand?

Keep going as long as you can. Build arguments. Make good points. Support your evidence. Tell that stupid (actually, ignorant) person what you know, what they really need to know.

Based on my experience, this will unblock the blocked. It doesn't generate the most beautiful, well-organized prose, but it does shake loose things worth saying.

Obviously, your audience isn't stupid. So why does this work?

It gets you riled up and emotional. When you're blocked, that works better than logic to unblock you.

It focuses you on the audience. Thinking about what you want to say to an audience is a good place to start.

It is conversational. It generates conversational writing, which tends to flow better than other stilted forms of writing. Everyone can speak — and if you can speak, this method helps you go from speaking to writing.

It's always easier to edit roughly created work than to start creating it in the first place. But now that I've unblocked you, please don't publish what you wrote this way. While this method generates action, it does not generate the best prose.

To fix it, first delete the "Look, stupid." You don't want to insult the audience, after all. Then examine what you wrote. Which ideas and phrases are worth saving? What organization would suit them best? Revise your yawp into actual well-structured prose.

Can a robot write your book?

As I was completing this book, a new writing tool emerged: ChatGPT. This AI-enabled writing tool produces decent prose, good enough that many colleges are worried that students will use it to write their essays for them.

If you find writing a chore, should you just delegate it to an AI tool?

It's not a good idea. There are three big reasons.

First, your book has a unique tone that reflects how you express yourself. You don't sound like a robot (I hope). Robot-generated text won't sound like you.

Second, AI-generated text is soulless. It's even and boring. Since business books are stories, they should sound like stories. That takes a little drama, which AI text generators lack.

And finally, ChatGPT and other AI text generation tools don't know the difference between truth and random stuff they find on the internet. That means the text they write tends to include inaccuracies. Business writers don't lie. So they shouldn't use tools that don't understand what truth is.

A note about your last chapter

First chapters are different. You need to scare the crap out of the reader, as I described in my own chapter 1.

Last chapters are different, too. They tend to terrify writers. "I already said everything I had to say," they tell me. "What do I put at the end?"

There is no reason to be afraid of last chapters because of a simple fact: Readers who lost faith in your book partway through have already given up and will never read your last chapter, while readers who you retained through the first 50,000 words now believe in you, so they will buy just about anything you put in the last chapter.

Here's a technique I recommend for creating a rousing last chapter. It's based on a powerful concept that my former employer, Forrester, uses to end its research reports, called "What it means."

Identify five to ten of your friends or colleagues who are interested in your idea. Set up a 60-minute meeting (a virtual meeting is fine) to brainstorm ideas about your book.

Designate one person to take notes. You may also want to record the meeting.

Start the meeting by describing the main conclusions of your book in five minutes. It is essential that you do this quickly. Just hit on the main points.

Then ask your assembled colleagues questions like, "If I'm right about all of that, what would it mean? How would it change the economics of industries? The way we hire people? Future trends? Opportunities for start-ups?" (Your particular set of questions will vary based on the topic of your book.)

Listen to their ideas, reflect them back, extend them, and take them further. Your participants will inevitably riff off of each other's ideas.

If someone in the meeting is being quiet, ask them by name if they have any ideas. Often the shy people are hiding some wacky idea that is really interesting.

At the end of 60 minutes, you'll have a nice collection of unusual, counterintuitive consequences of your main idea. You can mold those into a chapter that shows the power of your idea and where it might go. And you don't have to be quite so rigorous in backing up these ideas as you were in the previous chapters, because this is the last chapter, and your readers who reach it are already grooving on what you wrote in the rest of the book.

Key takeaways

- Writer's block is the result of failing to have a plan before writing.
- Before you start a chapter, determine a chapter objective: After reading this chapter, what will the reader know or be able to do?
- Then arrange your ideas, stories, arguments, proof points, and advice into a fat outline that tells a story.
- Finally, turn the bits in the outline into prose. Break up the text with sub-heads, lists, graphics, and the like, not just paragraph after paragraph.
- If all else fails, type "Look, stupid" and keep writing to see if that opens the sluices.
- To write the last chapter, brainstorm ideas about the consequences of the book's main concept.

Chapter 12

Writing and Planning Tools

Master tools to use time wisely.

Did you know that Tesla CEO Elon Musk, LinkedIn founder Reid Hoffman, and Silicon Valley venture capital luminary Peter Thiel all launched their careers at the same company?

That company is PayPal; many prominent Silicon Valley entrepreneurs first crossed paths there during its early years. Author Jimmy Soni tells that story in his hot-selling book *The Founders: The Story of PayPal and the Entrepreneurs Who Shaped Silicon Valley* (Simon & Schuster, 2022).

The Founders is a massive undertaking, weaving vast amounts of research into a multi-character epic with a sweep reminiscent of a swords-and-dragons miniseries. In the end, Jimmy had to manage half a million words of raw material from hundreds of original interviews along with countless bits of historical content culled from the web and from other books.

That takes more than skill and meticulous organization. It takes a system — and specialized writing and research tools. Here's how he did it.

Jimmy started with all that raw material as a file collection across multiple folders in Google Drive, including content culled from the web, links, insights he had come up with, and interviews that he recorded and then transcribed with a tool called Otter.ai. (Jimmy's a bit paranoid about losing content, so a file collection saved in the cloud creates peace of mind.) He tracked every scrap of content, including dates, names of subjects, and links to source material, in several Google Sheets spreadsheets.

After years of collecting research material, Jimmy pulled it together in a $49 writing tool called Scrivener, which he describes this way: "It's as if somebody sent Microsoft Word to the gym and it came back all souped up." Scrivener's design makes it efficient to collect, manage, and combine bits of prose. He identified and sorted the raw material from Google Drive and put the cleaned-up pieces that could be useful into Scrivener. For example, if he had 20 useful quotes about Elon Musk's college experience, all those quotes would go into a single folder in Scrivener.

Since *The Founders* is a chronological narrative, Jimmy organized his Scrivener research content into folders by year, with subfolders for topics within those years. That organization allowed him to see where he had sufficient source material for a chapter, and where he didn't, or as he put it, "what was undercooked and what was overcooked."

Jimmy also depended on another Scrivener feature: its progressive word count tracking. He was determined to produce 1,000 words of completed writing per day. Scrivener kept track of the writing streak, which kept Jimmy motivated — a crucial psychological tool for a book that turned out to be 496 pages long.

Scrivener also enabled discipline about sources and endnotes, an essential quality for a book that included 100 pages of endnotes. "Given the people I was writing about, I had to make sure I was citing and sourcing and referencing things right," he recalls. He also hired a rigorous fact-checker who depended on Scrivener's meticulous source tracking as well as Jimmy's Google Drive folders.

As I write this, *The Founders* has more than 500 Amazon reviews, an amazing performance for a historical book in its first year of publication. Jimmy is now a major author, and major authors use professional tools.

Professional tools enable rigor and efficiency

The lesson of *The Founders* is not that you must use Scrivener and Google Sheets. Every author is different and every book process is different. You probably don't have 500,000 words of source material to wrangle.

The lesson is that you must have a disciplined process. For authors who are planners, professional tools allow you to manage your writing progress in a disciplined way. And for the pantsers — well, if you're generating scraps of writing here and there, you'll certainly want some way to keep track of all the pieces so you can pull them together into a book that's coherent enough to be worth reading.

If the tools you currently use are efficient and comfortable for you, stick with them. On the other hand, if you worry about spending time dejectedly sorting through content and assembling it into a compelling story, perhaps better tools will help you manage effectively. Either way, I hope you'll get some useful ideas from what I'm about to describe: how you can use inexpensive and common tools like Google Sheets, Microsoft Word, Scrivener, and Evernote to create an efficient writing process.

This advice is particularly important if you have coauthors or editors that you're working with — because you'll have to agree on process and tools before you get going. (For more detail on collaborating efficiently, see chapter 14.)

Organize content in the cloud

Organize your research with a folder structure in the cloud. I use Google Drive, but it's likely you can replicate a lot of what I'm going to describe in cloud storage from Microsoft, Apple, or other vendors. Be sure your system automatically replicates files and directories between your computer and the cloud, so you'll have automatic backups of everything you create, accessible from any computer or device. If you work for a company but want to retain personal ownership of your content, never access your book content from work computers (unless your company explicitly permits you to use work devices for your own projects).

I organize folders by content type within a master book folder, with one subfolder for chapter drafts, another for interview notes and transcripts, and another for research I've collected. If you're creating a book proposal to pitch publishers, create a folder for that, too.

One geeky little technique may make all the difference in your efficiency: file naming. Authors who name their chapter files "Chapter 1," "Chapter 2," and so on regret it later when they're surrounded by vaguely named files desperately seeking the chapter and version they stored last week. Remember, you aren't the only one looking at your file names: Your editor and reviewers won't be able to easily identify what is in the file "Chapter 1" in the midst of all their other files.

Instead, use a filename that looks like this: *BBBB Ch 07 Planning v1 jb.docx*. In this file name, "BBBB" tells you what book it belongs to (in this case, *Build a Better Business Book)*, Ch 07 is the chapter number, "Planning" is the chapter topic, "v1" means "first draft," and "jb" is the author's initials. Use two-digit chapter numbers like "07", and you can easily sort the chapters in order with an alphabetical listing. A name like "Planning" makes it easier to keep track of content, especially if you end up renumbering the chapters. Finally, if you're passing around documents between collaborators and editors, the author's initials help you keep track of who created which version.

Use spreadsheets to plan and track your work

You may not have nearly as much content to track as Jimmy Soni did. But unless you're the unusual writer who can write a book from the first word to last, keeping the whole thing in your head, you certainly need to track what you're working on.

Create a single Google Sheets spreadsheet for tracking and use sheets within it to track different parts of the project. You could use any other spreadsheet software for this, including Microsoft Excel or Airtable, but a Google Sheets spreadsheet is simple, easy to manage, free, saves all updates automatically, and is accessible from the same web link on any device.

Within this spreadsheet, the most valuable and necessary sheet is the chapter tracking sheet that I described in chapter 7 (see Table 7-1). Include columns for chapter number, chapter title, and draft status (fat outline complete, draft 1 complete, and so on). Add columns listing the case studies, graphics, and ideas or frameworks, too. And include a word count column. Then you can sum up the word count in your completed drafts and estimate how long the book will be. (If you've written four 5,000-word chapters and have 12 more planned, you're on track for an overlong word count of 80,000 words, a clue that you've got some editing to do.) And use additional sheets to track interviews and case studies with links to files, as I described in chapter 7. Use this tool to identify chapters with too many possible case studies and figure out which could be repurposed for chapters that have none.

You can also use Google Sheets to create an idea map: a sheet with all your main ideas and concepts listed down the side and your chapters listed across the top. Use shading or put x's in cells to show which ideas are in which chapters. For example, Table 12-1 shows a portion of the idea map for my previous book, *Writing Without Bullshit: Boost Your Career by Saying What You Mean.*

In a well-structured book, most ideas are described in detail in only one chapter, but a few key ideas are covered throughout. For example, *Writing Without Bullshit* includes the central concept of The Iron Imperative, which is that you should treat the reader's time as more valuable than your own. As you can see from the fourth concept row in the Google Sheets spreadsheet, it's mentioned in nearly every chapter. But the curse of knowledge is only in the chapter on jargon, chapter 7.

If your idea map is a randomly scattered collection of lots of ideas mentioned in lots of chapters, you've got an organizational problem. Your reader will find it far easier to consume ideas that you introduce, describe, and explore in a single chapter rather than all over the manuscript. In your next editorial pass, consider combining all the passages referring to one idea into one place rather than spreading them across multiple chapters.

Google Docs and Microsoft Word both have benefits as writing tools

What tool should you write with? Whatever tool you feel most comfortable composing and editing in. Most publishers and book formatters will expect a manuscript in Microsoft Word, but it's easy enough to copy and paste content from Google Docs into a Word document.

Table 12-1: Excerpt from idea map for Writing Without Bullshit

Black blocks indicate major ideas, grey blocks are ideas described in passing

Concepts	1	2	3	4	5	6	7	8	9	10	11	12	13	14	15
Writing teachers		█			▒										
Poor work training		█													
Say what you mean	█	▒		█											
Iron Imperative	█	▒	▒			▒	▒		▒	▒		▒	▒	▒	
Meaning Ratio	█							▒							
Bullshit definition	█	▒													
Learning is awkward	█														
Reading on screens		█													
Lack of editing		█													
Practical writing			█												
Fear			█												
Write shorter				█											
Imagine words cost $10				█											
Graphics					▒										
Don't bury the lede					▒										
Inductive writing						█									
Front-load					▒	█						▒			
Email			▒			█									
Rewrite title each draft						█							█	█	
Email subject lines						█									
Passive voice					▒		█								
Passive 5R's							█								
Jargon							█								
Curse of knowledge							█								
Insider bias							█								
Visualize audience							█		▒				▒		
Jargon used properly							█								
Weasel words				▒	▒			█							

Microsoft Word has significant benefits, including more formatting options and features for tracking references. It's most useful for writing processes where you want a single, completed document for each chapter, because Word files are easy to save and email, and there's no worry that someone (including you) will make edits to a draft that you consider complete. When it's time to read and revise edits from your editor, you'll find that Word's track changes features are superior to those in Google Docs. In my author survey, 61% of published authors said their primary writing tool was Microsoft Word.

But Google Docs has its devotees. I used it on one project where I was ghost-writing chapters for a pair of coauthors. When the chapter was ready to review, I sent the link to the coauthors, and they used Suggesting Mode to make edits and add comments — and comment on each other's comments. This worked well because we had a disciplined process. (See chapter 14 for more collaboration tips.) Of the published authors in my survey, 16% primarily used Google Docs.

You can write in Scrivener, as Jimmy Soni did, but it's better for collecting ideas and scraps of prose than it is at formatting content.

If you're used to writing in a tool like Google Docs or Microsoft Word, please keep in mind that you're now an author, not just a writer. Your finished content will go to page layout professionals at a publisher or a self-publishing service, so your manuscript is not just text; it actually functions as a set of instructions on how to transform the text into pages. To ease that process:

- Don't use two spaces after periods or other end-of-sentence punctuation. The layout people will have to strip those out, which can lead to errors.
- Don't use tabs or extra spaces to space out content on a line.
- Don't use blank lines to separate paragraphs. Instead, format your normal text so that each paragraph has extras space after it. (You may also choose to format your text with double-spaced lines, which makes it easier to read and review. The page layout pros will ignore the double spacing.)
- Avoid using words in ALL CAPS, **bold type**, or <u>underlines</u> for emphasis. They mark you as an amateur. Book authors use *italics* (and sparingly).
- Use styles to mark headings (Heading 1 for chapter titles, Heading 2 for section heads, and Heading 3 for subsections). This tells the page layout

people how to style and format your headings. Avoid marking headings with bold type or underlines, which are ambiguous.

- Use styles for bulleted and numbered lists, not hyphens or asterisks. Restart the numbering on each numbered list.
- Put graphics in place for position only. Send high-resolution graphics files along separately. (See the next chapter for more on graphics.)
- Be careful with tables. Complex tables are hard to format and tend to get scrambled in ebook formatting. Tables work best if they have only a few columns and few enough rows that they can easily fit on one page.
- Manage endnotes carefully. Microsoft Word does better with notes than Google Docs. For more on footnotes and endnotes, see chapter 16.

Evernote and Scrivener

Most authors will find common writing tools like Microsoft Word and Google Docs sufficient. But among my author friends like Jimmy Soni, Scrivener is developing an enthusiastic following. It's best for writers who assemble books organically from bits and pieces they've collected and written.

Evernote is another tool beloved by many authors. It's a system that allows you to collect and tag content you find online, allowing you to easily assemble, say, everything you have on Emmanuel Macron and figure out how to organize it.

Roger Dooley embraces Evernote for research. He's the author of *Friction: The Untapped Force That Can Be Your Most Powerful Advantage* (McGraw-Hill, 2019), recognized by *Strategy+Business* as one of the top business books of 2019. To prepare that book, he created a "notebook" within Evernote and dumped everything relevant into it. As he told me, "I might be researching a book for a few years before I am actively working on it."

His notebook included snippets from online articles, links to web pages, bits of PDFs, and even photos of book pages. Evernote makes them easy to add with browser extensions or apps from any device where you happen to spot something useful. (For books, Roger sometimes buys the Kindle version and saves a screen capture of relevant passages in Evernote.) Evernote optionally strips out ads and extraneous content from web pages, saving only the text and photos along with the original URL for reference. You can tag saved content with keywords to make searching easier.

Even the free version of Evernote is powerful and useful, but the professional version, at $9.99 per month, can hold up to 20 gigabytes of monthly uploads, more than you'll ever need, and it has features to make it easier for multiple people to share and contribute to a notebook.

Kate O'Neill, author of *Tech Humanist: How You Can Make Technology Better for Business and Better for Humans* (2018), uses Evernote and Scrivener together. And some authors like Phil Simon, author of 14 business books, have started to embrace a relatively new tool called Notion.

Among the published authors in my survey, 12% said Scrivener was the writing and research tool they used most, and 4% said Evernote was. Most authors are still counting on Microsoft Word or Google Docs for most of the work they do.

Use the tools that work for you

I can't tell you exactly what tools will be best for you because I don't know your writing process, workflow, and relationship with collaborators.

But I can tell you that just banging on the keyboard and hoping your research and writing will spontaneously assemble into a book is not going to work.

If you want to spend more time on productive activities, do what professional authors do: Subscribe to the tools that fit your work best, use them to plan and do research, and employ them consistently as you craft your book. The more time you spend on productive book work — and the less time on haplessly searching for scattered bits of content — the higher your chances of crafting your content into a compelling narrative.

Key takeaways

- Organize your content in a cloud-based file system like Google Drive; track it with a spreadsheet like Google Sheets.
- Whether you use Microsoft Word or Google Docs for writing, use styles and formatting effectively to communicate your intentions to the people laying out your book pages.
- Professional tools like Scrivener, Evernote, and Notion can help you manage research and content as you assemble your book.

Chapter 13

Graphics and Cartoons

Use well-designed graphics to enhance understanding.

E vangelos Simoudis, Ph.D., is one of the world's foremost experts on the future of transportation.

As you might imagine, this is a highly complex topic. Among other things, his analysis includes predictions about electric vehicles, autonomous driving, business models for transportation, ride services companies like Uber, car manufacturers, vehicle technology, car buying and leasing, government regulation, roads, and the movement of freight.

Evangelos analyzes all of this in his comprehensive 80,000-word book *Transportation Transformation: How Autonomous Mobility Will Fuel New Value Chains* (Corporate Innovators LLC, 2020). But for readers to find value in all this analysis in the automotive, technology, and government sectors, they need a way to visualize the changes Evangelos describes. So along with the text, Evangelos created a slew of diagrams: 36 in total. These diagrams show everything from paths for future business models to interactions among car companies, technology companies, and governments. They make the complexity of the subject comprehensible.

Some of Evangelos' diagrams started as PowerPoint slides, but most of them were hand drawings on paper. They were far from book ready. So Evangelos hired two graphic artists, Ad'm DiBiaso and Jens Kueter, to turn the diagrams into quality graphics for insertion into the book. Ad'm and Jens did far more that turn hand drawings into pretty pictures. They created a visual language for Evangelos' ideas, including a set of common icons, conventions for placement of those icons and arrows to represent concepts, and typographical rules for the text in the diagrams.

For example, see Figure 13-1, a foundational diagram from Evangelos' chapter 1 that shows the main elements of the mobility business model.

Figure 13-1: Mobility Business Model
from *Transportation Transformation*
Diagram reproduced with permission of Evangelos Simoudis

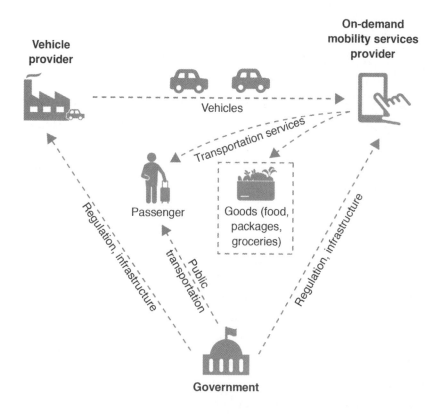

Creating and managing the diagrams and their relationship to the concepts in the text became a significant part of the work of completing the book. The author, illustrators, and I employed a rigorous process to ensure consistency as the manuscript neared completion and maintained it as Evangelos' publishing partner turned the text and graphics into a book.

When the time came to design the book cover, the cover artist adapted the same visual language that was in the diagrams. The arrangement of the icons on the cover reflected the depth and sophistication of the analysis in the book.

Transportation Transformation received praise from the kind of people that Evangelos wanted to influence: senior executives at Toyota, Hyundai, the Renault-Nissan-Mitsubishi Alliance, Avis, and McKinsey & Company. It burnished his reputation in the auto industry and all the other parts of the transportation sector. Those diagrams — and the thought behind them — were essential to Evangelos' path to success.

Graphics take extra care, but they're worth it

Graphics reveal insight. If you've got an iconic idea with any structure to it, a graphic will help cement it in the mind of the reader. If you've got data, you need charts. And if, like Evangelos, you have complex topics to explain, diagrams can help a lot.

But graphics have a price — and I don't just mean paying designers like Ad'm and Jens. Authors tend to underestimate the challenge, delay, and cost that comes with graphics. If you're going to use graphics, you need to be prepared.

If anything is going to trip up the production stages of your book, it's probably a graphic. And that's going to drive you (and your publisher) bonkers. That doesn't mean you shouldn't use graphics, because often they're exactly what you need to clarify a concept. It does mean you must be prepared, with a realistic idea of the time, cost, and pitfalls involved in doing graphics right.

Types of graphics and the artists that create them

These are the basic types of graphics that can enhance business books:

- Diagrams to illustrate concepts (like Figure 13-1)
- Data charts (pie charts, bar charts, and line graphs, for example)
- Photos
- Illustrations
- Cartoons

You need the graphics to look great, not least because you are likely to repurpose them for use in your speeches. Unless you are as good at design as you are at writing — a very unusual combination — don't create the graphics yourself. Extreme talent with PowerPoint or Keynote doesn't count; preparing graphics for print requires more than moving boxes and arrows around on display slides.

You need to find the right designer or artist. A graphic artist who does a great job with conceptual diagrams and bar charts is unlikely to be the same person who creates beautiful drawings or illustrations. And cartoonists are an entirely different category.

How do you find the right partner? If you work for a company that has a graphics department, you may find the right talent there. (Make sure they're experienced at formatting graphics for print books, not just for online viewing.) And if you see graphics in a book that look like they match your style, contact the author and get a referral to the artist. As Evangelos' graphic artist Ad'm puts it, "Try to find a designer who thinks along the same wavelength as you do."

One crucial type of graphic is the iconic graphic that illustrates your basic concept. Jens, Evangelos' other designer, suggests you first ask yourself questions: "Does this add to my point? What can I do to make this simple? What can I do to make this clear?" His process for this involves starting by stripping the graphic down to the basic shape, say a pyramid or a set of steps, keeping it as simple as possible. Once that's done, add back a little text, use different grey shades, or include a few icons as visual clues. This generates a better iconic graphic than taking something complex and just trying to make it look nice.

Embrace an orderly design process

Text is easy. Anyone can write it; anyone can edit it. As a result, it's easy for authors, collaborators, and editors to share it back and forth in a disciplined process.

Graphics require a different level of communication, and people who are talented with pictures are often not as good with conversation. So as an author, communicating what you want to a designer is mostly your responsibility.

For diagrams, the creation process is usually some version of the following:

1. The author scribbles an idea on a whiteboard or paper and takes a picture of it, or alternatively, roughs something out in PowerPoint or another drawing program.
2. The author sends this sketch to the designer, along with some notes, and sometimes, has a conversation about what the picture is supposed to represent.
3. The designer creates something.
4. The author is unhappy. Typical criticisms include "You missed the point," "This is ugly," or "This is just exactly the same as what I sent you, I was looking for an improvement."
5. The designer revises the picture.
6. Repeat steps 4 and 5 a bunch of times until the author grudgingly accepts the graphic as "done."
7. The author or some reviewer has an incredible insight about the graphic, which requires going back to step 5, or maybe even step 1, and starting again.

For data charts, the process starts with a set of numbers, but is otherwise similar. If you have a bunch of data graphics, take the time to work with your designers to develop a consistent and clear visual language for them. As Jens told me, consistency is key and it's crucial to make sure that the graphics are telling the truth about the data, not distorting it. "Keep the scale the same through all of them," he advises. "Use consistent labeling, label elements directly when possible, and keep colors [or shades of grey] simple."

Graphics can be expensive, but working with an inexperienced designer who doesn't understand your ideas or how printing works will ultimately cost you even more. A simple bar chart might cost $100, while a complex diagram with a dozen parts could cost $500 or $1,000. And that iconic graphic? If it's brilliant, it's not likely to be cheap — and why would you be a cheapskate about something that important?

Consider cartoons to perk up an intense topic

If your writing is completely serious, like Evangelos', you probably don't want to insert visual jokes into the text. But if a little levity would perk up an otherwise ponderous topic, consider working with a cartoonist.

There is a small class of business cartoonists who will allow you to license existing work. In Nick Worth and Dave Frankland's book, *Marketing to the Entitled Consumer: How to Turn Unreasonable Expectations into Lasting Relationships* (Amplify, 2018), which I ghostwrote, we licensed revealing and ironic cartoons to start each chapter from Tom Fishburne, the artist behind Marketoonist. Another resource for cartoons is ad-agency guy turned artist Hugh MacLeod, the principal behind Gapingvoid, who creates acerbic illustrations that might add just the right level of smartassiness to your manuscript.

You can also work directly with a cartoonist to illustrate your concepts. For Stefan Falk's book *Intrinsic Motivation,* which I wrote about in chapter 5, we brainstormed cartoons with Mark Anderson of Andertoons and put several of them into the ultimately successful book proposal.[9] Figure 13-2 shows one.

For this process, Mark the cartoonist would read chapters, both of us would come up with potential gags, we'd get on a Zoom call and collaborate, and if we liked something, he'd sketch it out. The thing that amazed me most is the speed with which we could do gags. We could conceive and vet a dozen in an hour. Either an idea is funny, or you tweak it to be funnier, or you dump it and come up with another one. As a cartoonist, Mark knows the tropes (the psychiatrist's couch, the meeting in the conference room, the sales chart, and, for some reason, dogs) and he also has a unique way of taking a concept and turning it in an utterly unexpected direction.

---

9   Surprisingly, Stefan's publisher bought the proposal with the cartoons in it, but Stefan and the publisher didn't end up using them in the published book.

Figure 13-2: Cartoon by Mark Anderson for *Intrinsic Motivation*
Reproduced with permission of Stefan Falk

Dog goals.

I was surprised by the reasonable cost of cartoons. For the Marketoonist cartoons for Nick and Dave's book, we licensed ten existing cartoons for $5,200. And for Stefan's book, we generated 38 custom cartoons for about $2,000.

Technical tips for graphics

Many things can go wrong in the production process for graphics. Here are some tips that will help your graphics look great once they're actually printed. (This advice aligns with the tips on how to maintain the quality of your book during the publisher's production process in chapter 17.)

- **Don't expect the publisher to make your graphics.** Most publishers expect you or an artist you've contracted with to deliver publishable, high-quality graphics. If you force them to re-render your graphics for print, they'll charge you for it.

- **Deliver graphics files separately from text.** While you can paste graphics into Microsoft Word files, that's not the best way to get them to your publisher. Package them up as a separate set of files or online folder and send or share them with the publisher along with the manuscript. The versions of graphics pasted within the text are "for position only," and will show the publisher where you want them to be displayed in the text.

- **Name and number graphics carefully and consistently.** Number graphics sequentially either in the whole book ("Figure 11") or by chapter ("Figure 3-6"). Make sure that the filenames of your graphics files match the references in the text, including numbers and, optionally, words that describe the graphic. Include the captions for the graphics *within the book text*, not in the graphic.

- **Don't send tables as graphics.** Include tables in running text, and let the publisher render them in the final pages.

- **Don't send color graphics; avoid subtle grey scales.** If your book, like most business books, is in black and white, then make sure your graphics files are not in color; otherwise, the results will be poor. And make sure any grey scales — for example, for different bars in a bar chart — are in highly contrasting shades, because most printing processes don't make it easy to distinguish subtle differences in shading.

- **Use the highest resolution format possible.** For charts and diagrams, EPS files are best, since they'll be printed at the highest resolution. If you have to send a bitmap file — such as a photo or screen capture — use the highest resolution file possible. TIFF is often the best formatting choice for such files.

- **Have your designer create separate versions for display slides.** While color doesn't work in black-and-white printing processes, it's essential in the slides that may accompany a speech. When the graphics are final and off to the publisher, have the designer generate a second set in a vector format like EPS. This will enable you to share or even animate your high-quality graphics in a speech.

Given the challenges with graphics, use them only when they make an important point — or if your content is as complex to explain as Evangelos Simoudis' was. Your designer and publisher are key partners here — follow their advice, and you'll end up with pictures that help tell your story effectively.

Key takeaways

- Hire a professional designer who is expert in printed content to design effective charts and diagrams.
- Make your graphics and charts follow a consistent set of graphical conventions.
- Consider using cartoons to lighten up an otherwise intense and complex topic.
- Deliver graphics in a separate set of files, designed for black-and-white, at the highest resolution possible.

Chapter 14

Coauthors and Ghostwriters

Adopt a disciplined process to collaborate effectively.

Kerry Bodine had always wanted to write a book. So when she re-upped for her second stint as a customer experience (CX) analyst at Forrester, she let her managers know that if they were considering producing a CX book, she'd love to be a part of it.

Harley Manning, the leader of Forrester's CX group, had been at Forrester for 12 years at that point. Forrester's CX research was ramping up and getting more sophisticated, so it was an opportune time to set the organization apart as a CX leader. Shortly after Kerry rejoined the company, Harley and Kerry began brainstorming book concepts. Forrester tapped me to be their editor and sherpa in the book creation process.

Harley and Kerry were well-suited to collaborate. Harley brought decades of corporate experience and work with clients, while Kerry often came at problems from an unexpected and creative angle. Although Harley was a manager and Kerry an individual contributor, they quickly realized that they would have to be on equal footing as coauthors. Working together on the main book idea and table of contents, they began to converge on a set of six customer experience disciplines: strategy, customer understanding, design, measurement, governance, and culture.

These disciplines were the pillars of a "maturity model" that companies could use to benchmark their CX performance. Just as important, Forrester had a slew of potential case studies in each discipline with household-name companies like Boeing, Barclays, the Cleveland Clinic, FedEx, Lego, JetBlue, T-Mobile, and Walgreens. (You can read one of Harley and Kerry's case studies, on Office Depot, in chapter 9).

Harley and Kerry collaborated on a book proposal, which sold to a major publisher. They began to draft chapters. Long familiarity with collaborating on Forrester reports had welded their writing into a single, consistent tone: authoritative and direct, with a bit of an edge. There was a feeling of mutual trust as they built the book together.

Equally important, they fell into a rhythm of weekly planning and review meetings that enabled rapid progress. Their phone meetings typically included Harley and me in Massachusetts and Kerry in California, but with travel schedules, any of us might be connecting from anywhere. We'd critique each other's chapter plans; if one author had drafted a full chapter, the other author and I, as their editor, would review it separately, then we'd all compare notes and ideas at the weekly meeting.

Kerry was surprised at how well the process went as she learned to receive and act on my and Harley's edits — and to offer her own on Harley's chapters. As she told me, "I had always been very self-conscious about my writing; I had had a blog where I would agonize over every eensy paragraph. At Forrester I had flipped like a switch, from hating getting feedback and edits to loving it and seeing how much value it added. Those planning meetings were exhilarating. The most challenging thing for me was editing extra detail out of the case studies, but we looked at the word count, and when it was clear it was too long, we had to make cuts."

As the book came together, we realized it could potentially become an icon in the emerging field of customer experience. Kerry, who was a bit of a perfectionist, put extra effort into refining every last detail of the manuscript and graphics before the deadline to turn it in.

Outside In: The Power of Putting Consumers at the Center of Your Business (New Harvest, 2012) rapidly mapped out a place for Forrester as the leading company analyzing and advising companies on customer experience. Harley and Kerry both scored high-level speaking opportunities, including a European speaking tour for Kerry.

While Harley continued to build CX as a hugely successful revenue center for Forrester, Kerry eventually left Forrester and started her own customer experience advisory and training business. She found that the book opened so many doors that she hardly needed to market herself.

Even now, 10 years after they worked together on the book, *Outside In* continues to make a difference. At a recent event, two young guys asked Kerry if they could take a picture with her. "Your book changed our lives," they said. And that's a pretty good testament to the power of effective collaboration.

Collaboration takes planning

Kerry and Harley make collaboration sound easy. It's not. Unless you and a co-author share a common idea, mutual trust, and an effective system for working together, you're unlikely to reap the kind of gains they did.

The idea of collaboration often begins when you as an author hope to reduce your workload. "I know," you think. "I'll get my colleague or friend to work on the book with me. Then we can finish it quicker, and we'll each have half the work to do." It's not that simple, because coordinating with coauthors generates communications challenges. Both coauthors must be planners, not pantsers, and they have to agree on a plan.

My basic collaboration advice is this: Work on the plan together, define the writing process rigorously, and communicate regularly.

If you hire a ghostwriter to write the book for you, many of these same principles apply; you need a shared vision, a rigorous process, and a system for effective communication. (There's more advice about ghostwriters at the end of this chapter.)

Develop a common understanding

It's hard to share the work if you're headed in different directions. Right at the start, you need a shared vision.

Discuss and agree on your audience. Determine what problem you will solve for them. Talk about your approach: authoritative and detailed or light and witty?

Start with an ideation exercise like the one I describe in chapter 3. This will help you agree, not just on the idea, but also on the title and subtitle. Then write the marketing description together: the flap copy. While I don't normally recommend writing prose by committee, in this case, working together on the marketing text will surface your differences and reinforce your common goals for the project.

Collaborating without a common understanding is foolish. You'll waste a lot of effort, and you'll each start to think the other one is crazy. Settle that in a few collaboration sessions, or you'll waste a lot of effort later.

If you're seeking a traditional publisher, you'll have to create a proposal together, as I describe in chapter 5. That's an excellent exercise to get everybody in sync, because it requires you to agree on ideas and a table of contents and to collaborate on a sample chapter.

Write the table of contents and divide up the tasks

The table of contents is not just a list of chapters, it's a list of tasks to work on. Review my advice from chapter 6 on structure, and then use the reader question method to create a rational list of chapters that you can agree on.

Next divide up the tasks in the project — writing, research, data analysis, whatever. For example: You'll write chapters 1-7 and I'll edit, and I'll write chapters 8-11 and you'll edit. Or, you'll do all the research, and I'll do all the writing.

If everybody does everything in duplicate, you'll drown in a lack of productivity. One person doesn't need to be in charge, but each task needs to have a leader (lead researcher, lead visionary, lead data analyst, person in charge of words, person who negotiates with publishers, and the like).

Agree on a schedule and deadline. Agree on financial sharing terms. Figure out whose name goes first (typically either the more well-known author or the one who originated the idea).

One of you is a better writer. That person should set the tone for the writing and do most of the word crafting. The other author should match their style and tone. (If you both have the same voice, then you must secretly be one person with a schizoid complex.)

Develop an efficient process

As you saw in the case of Harley and Kerry's collaboration, process is crucial. An efficient process gets chapters completed, not just ping-ponged between coauthors endlessly.

Here are some possible processes that work:

- Authors work together on a plan for the chapter and assign it to one author to write. That author drafts the chapter and sends it to the other author for review. First author revises based on comments from second author.
- One author is the primary writer, the other is the visionary. The visionary lays out the plan for the chapter and suggests important points to hit and case studies to write. The writer drafts the chapter and solicits and addresses feedback on the draft from the visionary.
- One author architects the book, but trusts the other author to write it. When the manuscript is complete, the main writer sends it to the first author to review.

These are plans for drafting chapters. You'll also need a process to deal with suggestions from editors or publishers as you get into later stages in the process. And you'll have to decide who's responsible for shepherding the book through the final production process. "We'll all collaborate on everything" is not only wasteful, it's a recipe for conflict.

Design your process so that at any given time, only one author "owns" the text of a chapter that they're working on. If your coauthor is working on a chapter, keep your hands off. If you're editing a chapter, your coauthor must avoid revising it as you edit it. The proliferation of alternate versions is counterproductive and chaotic.

The neat little plans I've laid out obscure a hard truth: Communication between coauthors is crucial. In several projects I helped with, there were weekly video meetings between authors during which they discussed everything — planned content, feedback on chapters, and even ideas for marketing the book. An hour a week sounds like a lot, but it's one way to avoid a lot of wasted work between meetings.

Technology and tools are essential for collaboration. The tools I described in chapter 12 are essential. You must work from a shared planning worksheet and a shared set of folders and be consistent in file naming so it's always possible to see the most recent version of a chapter. (I recommend that coauthors put their initials on the end of each file they write or edit, so it's obvious who's working on what.)

Good communication avoids pitfalls on challenging topics

Ugly jealousy can get in the way of any collaboration. Coauthors need to discuss some contentious subjects. This includes whose name goes first on the cover and how to divide book advances and royalties. Consider what happens if and when you part ways: Who is allowed to do speeches on the book, and who owns the intellectual property? Fail to decide these issues, and you'll find yourself in a custody battle.

And one more thing. Two authors are hard enough to manage. With three authors, you end up with politics, two against one. Anyone who's participated in a three-author project can show you the scars. Properly managed, two authors can create a book more efficiently than one, but three is just asking for trouble.

How to work with a ghostwriter

Ghostwriters are writers you pay to write a book for you. There is nothing shady about this. As long as the book is based on your ideas, it's still your book, you're just outsourcing some parts of the work. The ghostwriter may be the writer, but you are still the author.

The main fallacy that authors seem to have about ghostwriters is that hiring one means they no longer have to work very hard. A ghostwriter rarely goes off and creates a whole book without frequent and intense interactions with the author.

For 14 years, Dan Gerstein has run one of the premier ghostwriting agencies, Gotham Ghostwriters. His primary advice to authors is this: "Make sure this is a priority for you. Both you and the ghostwriter will have to invest a lot of time, emotional energy, and money if you are going to get this collaboration to work."

Where will you find the right ghostwriter? A ghostwriting agency can help with sourcing writers. For example, if you work with Gotham Ghostwriters, they'll send out an anonymized description of the project to their pool of thousands of writers, field proposals from writers who are interested, screen them, and then let you interview the ones who seem promising so you can choose. This is a valuable service, so of course they get compensated. Once there's a solid match between client and writer, Gotham brokers the agreement and receives a placement fee from the client and an agency commission on the payments to the writer.

Of course, you don't need to work through an agency. Many business authors have a sideline as ghostwriters. (Check their professional sites to find out.) If you're reading a book where the cover has a "with" line (for example, "by Sam Parnia, M.D., with Josh Young"), then the "with" name is a ghostwriter. If you want to create a similar book, contact the ghostwriter and see if it's a fit.

Here are some questions to ask to qualify a ghostwriter.

- What sort of writing do you specialize in? (Don't hire a memoir expert to craft a how-to book, or vice versa.)
- Which of your work best represents the ghostwriting that you do? (Read it, and decide if it sounds anything like you.)
- What do you really think of my idea? How would you expand on it? (In a good ghostwriting relationship, the ghostwriter contributes ideas, but they should be subordinate to the author's vision.)
- What process do you use for working with authors? (An experienced ghostwriter will propose several disciplined processes and work with you to choose one.)
- How much do you know about my topic? (Ghostwriters need not be expert in your topic — they generally don't specialize to that extent. But a complete lack of familiarity would suggest a long learning curve.)
- How much will this cost? (Don't waste time attempting to hire ghostwriters outside of your price range.)

How to work with a ghostwriter

Every ghostwriting project should start with an exploration of the book's main idea. Who is the audience? What problem is the book trying to solve? What is the story that the book will tell?

While the author is in charge, this is a collaborative process. The author shares as much as possible about the challenge that the readers are facing, while the ghostwriter contributes ideas about how a well-structured book could help with those challenges. As in the idea development sessions that I described in chapter 3, the output of this work should be a "treatment" that promises what readers will get.

The author and ghostwriter should then collaborate on a table of contents, using the reader question method as described in chapter 6.

Ideally, these efforts will generate a common understanding of what the book must do and how the chapters will accomplish that goal. If the author seeks a traditional publishing deal and has not yet sold a proposal, the author and ghostwriter can then collaborate on a proposal and work on pitching it to agents and publishers.

This collaborative work creates a firm foundation. To turn that foundation into a book, the author and ghostwriter must answer two questions.

- **Where will the source material come from?** How will the author communicate their intentions to the ghostwriter? Some authors prefer to dictate and record content — that's typical for a memoir, for example. Others would prefer to discuss content in a voice or video call. In other cases, authors supply a collection of already-written raw material to work from. Some authors will provide a detailed plan for what's to be included in a chapter; others prefer to deliver disorganized content and let the ghostwriter sort it out. Some authors will supply case study candidates and may even conduct those interviews — others will leave all research, including finding and pursuing case studies, to the ghostwriter. There's no standard way to proceed, which is why it's important to settle the methods for the source material up front.

- **What process will we use to create and review chapters?** As with the coauthor collaboration I described earlier in this chapter, you should create a rigorous process for the development of chapters. I recommend that, after some discussion of the goals of the chapter and some research, the ghostwriter creates a fat outline for the chapter, as described in chapter 11. This fat outline basically roughs out everything that belongs in the chapter, in order. The author should review it, add feedback, and discuss it with the ghostwriter. With that feedback, the ghostwriter is well-positioned to create a chapter. Because that chapter will closely match the fat outline, the author knows what to expect and should be able to provide useful feedback.

How to pay a ghostwriter

When it comes to price, Dan says, you need to understand the relationship between cost and caliber and know what you want to invest. "If you want a Rolls Royce writer and you have a Honda budget, that's not going to work." A mid-tier writer with experience writing the kind of books you want — say strategy, or memoir — will charge $60,000 to $120,000 depending on the amount of work necessary. A higher-end writer who has already written bestsellers is a proven commodity and will charge even more.

Ghostwriters generally bill by the project, not by the hour — this provides some predictability to the expenses and ensures that the author client doesn't have to worry about whether the ghostwriter is wasting time. Authors should expect to pay one-third to one-half of the project price up front to secure the ghostwriter's time. After that, the statement of work in the ghostwriting contract generally describes payments for milestones like the completion of a book treatment, the creation of a book proposal, the completion of a first draft, and the completion of the final draft.

Sometimes ghostwriters get a percentage of authors' book advances or royalties. But unless the author is extremely famous and certain to sell hundreds of thousands of copies, it's rare for a ghostwriter to work purely for a share of the book revenues. A ghostwriting project can take six months or more, and the writer needs to be able to count on payment during that work, not just sit around and hope for a share of some potential book deal.

One last contract term needs to be settled: the ghostwriter's billing. Will the ghostwriter be listed on the cover by name as "with" — indicating that they helped write the book? If the ghostwriter is well known from writing their own books, their name on the cover may help with sales. But such billing also helps the ghostwriter, because it advertises that they're available for high-profile ghost-writing projects. If the author prefers not to list the ghostwriter on the cover, they're usually recognized in the book's acknowledgements.

Key takeaways

- Coauthors must develop a shared vision, including a shared idea of the audience, the main ideas in the book, and the title.
- Develop the table of contents together and divide up the tasks.
- For orderly collaboration, agree on a rigorous review process with shared online planning tools.
- Work out ahead of time who owns the revenue and ideas after the book is published.
- When working with ghostwriters, invest time up front in planning and developing ideas, then settle where the source material will come from and what process you'll use for reviews. Expect to pay a portion up front and more as the ghostwriter hits specific content milestones.

Chapter 15

Editing and Revising

Turn first drafts into a publishable manuscript without endless toil.

In 2009, my coauthor Ted Schadler and I had a problem. We were nearing the manuscript deadline for our book *Empowered: Unleash Your Employees, Energize Your Customers, and Transform Your Business* for Harvard Business Review Press. The front half of the book, about consumers and marketing, was holding together pretty well. But the back half, about workers and corporate technology, wasn't.

We'd done the interviews and written up the case studies. We'd come up with the concepts and frameworks. We had whole chapters written. But structurally, we knew it was problematic. Parts were redundant. In other places, it wasn't clear what order things went in. One chapter was way too heavy in data. So Ted and I reserved a small conference room and resolved to fix it.

Before our meeting, I'd deconstructed the whole second half of the book into sticky notes: blue for full case studies, green for shorter one- or two-paragraph examples, yellow for concepts, and pink for data frameworks. I put them into neat columns on the whiteboard, one for each chapter. The whole second half of the book was lined up in front of our eyes.

Ted and I tossed around ideas for restructuring things. We figured out that three of the chapters were particularly entangled with each other, and we rethought the organization of those chapters. We rethought the order of the chapters, too. Then we started moving stickies around.

In about an hour, we'd come up with a solution we liked. A few examples and concepts ended up on the floor, but that was fine — the book was already too long. I re-collated the sticky notes and stapled them together into little sheafs, one for each of the newly structured chapters. The plan for the rewrite touched 130 pages, seven chapters, and 30,000 words of the book. Implementing it was my job.

The next day, I got to work on the rewrite. I cut and pasted the pieces into the new order. Then I rewrote about 3,000 words of transitions, connections, and backward and forward references throughout the new chapters. In some cases, I changed the emphasis or "moral" of a case study or deleted elements that we no longer needed. I wrote a couple of short sections that our new arrangement demanded. I resisted the urge to tinker with the rest of the text.

Because we had been disciplined in how we structured things, the pieces were as modular as possible. Ted and I had agreed beforehand on what made up a chapter, and we'd both written in a way that preserved those principles. As a result, I was able to finish the entire revision in one day. You'd think that rewriting 130 pages would be a nightmare, but because we had a good plan and solid content to work with, it was remarkably stress-free.

The pieces were in great shape. The book wasn't a mess, only the structure was.

We met our deadline, and we were both happy with the result. And I have no doubt it was easier for readers to understand.

Self-editing and developmental editors

No writers create perfect prose on the first draft. But unlike smaller pieces of writing like blog posts or even white papers, revising a book is more complex. As veteran editor David Moldawer says, "Authors often know how to write a blog post, but they don't understand how a business book actually works and how chapters function."

The relationships among all the parts of a 40,000- or 60,000-word manuscript create challenges, since pulling on text in one spot can distort text in other places.

Self-editing can solve many problems. When you write a chapter, don't obsess over perfection. But once it's written, you may want to come back in a day or two and revise it. Are the pieces in the right order? Is there redundant text? Is a necessary explanation missing or illogical? Revise the chapter with a little perspective, and it will become tighter and more logical.

But there are limits to what you can do on your own. That's when it's useful to bring in an outside editor.

You might think that the publisher's editorial staff will fulfill that function. But these days, they often don't. What you need is a developmental editor who will help improve everything from the ideas in the book to the language.

Hollis Heimbouch, the 25-year publishing veteran editor, SVP, and Publisher at Harper Business that I mentioned in chapter 4, explained it to me this way. "A developmental editor usually is deeply involved in development of the ideas writing, research, and interviews, including really close editing and rewriting and coaching. That is typically not something done in house by commercial publishers. The expectation is that the author will bring that person on board. As part of the contractual agreement, delivering a finished manuscript is the job of the author."

Other publishers are more hands-on. According to Richard Narramore, the executive editor at Wiley, "We do a lot of handholding and development, working on shaping the table of contents to push the reader's buttons, working on key pains and gains. We don't do this on every book, but on the majority of books, we give intensive feedback."

My experience more closely matches what Hollis described. On my first book, the feedback was "Add more international examples." On the second (*Empowered*, the book I described at the start of this chapter), the feedback was "Cut 10,000 words," with no suggestion of where or what to cut. And on *Writing Without Bullshit,* the feedback was, "Add a section on the writing challenges unique to women." None of that is developmental editing, since none of it provides detailed guidance.

It's always useful to get an outside perspective from an expert in business books and how they work. So unless your publisher is as hands-on as Richard Narramore, you'll probably have to hire one. If you want editorial help that makes a significant improvement, your outside editing work is likely to cost at least $5,000 and could easily top $15,000 if your manuscript needs a lot of help.

Work intensively on a sample chapter

The best way to learn to write a great chapter is to work with an editor to review and optimize a single chapter. The objective is twofold. Obviously, you want to end up with a usable chapter, but it's also a chance for you, the author, to learn what it takes to write a chapter. (If you're putting a sample chapter into a book proposal, this is one way to make it the best it can be.)

Here's how to modify the chapter-drafting advice I gave in chapter 11 to include help from a developmental editor.

First, do the research and create a fat outline. Share the fat outline with your developmental editor. Discuss the question that the chapter is answering for the reader and the storyline of the chapter. Because fat outlines are short and easy to create, this gives the editor a chance to quickly review your plan and coach you about the storyline *before* you actually write anything. Revising the fat outline based on your editor's feedback will give you confidence when it's time to write.

After you've written the chapter, you'll get more feedback from the editor. That feedback may include any of the following:

- Is the main idea of the chapter clear?
- Have you structured the chapter in a way that's easy to read and make sense of? Should you have presented things in a different order?
- Have you done a good job telling the story in your case studies? What do you need to do to be a better storyteller?
- Have you tied the story or stories to key points you're trying to make?
- Have you done a skillful job weaving in quotes, statistics, and other research?
- Have you structured your concepts or advice in a way that makes sense?
- Are your arguments convincing? Where are there flaws?
- Do you repeat yourself? How could you restructure the chapter to bring like ideas together and reduce redundancy?
- Do you have any distracting writing tics like words you repeat, passive voice, malformed sentences, breathless prose, exclamation marks, profanity, excessive use of italics, impenetrable jargon, overlong sentences, endless paragraphs, selfish musings, or any other writing sins that detract from getting your meaning across effectively?

- Have you wrapped everything up with recommendations or takeaways for the reader?

To make best use of this feedback, have a discussion with the editor, then revise the chapter based on their advice. Then send the chapter to the editor for another pass to see if your revisions have improved the text and review the challenges that still remain.

Editing the whole manuscript

Authors will often assemble an entire manuscript before passing it off to a developmental editor. This approach reduces the learning you can get by iterating a single chapter, but it has the advantage of enabling the editor to see the whole project at once.

An editor providing feedback on a manuscript like this doesn't just read it one sentence at a time and fix the sentences. (That would be pretty silly if, for example, the sentence is in a portion or chapter that the editor thinks the writer should completely revise or delete.) Instead, the editor provides feedback on the text at all levels, from the conceptual to the detailed. You can expect to get feedback on the quality of your idea, the storyline of the whole book, the chapter order and organization, consistency across chapters, how content is organized within chapters, repetition, and logical errors, along with every possible weakness at the sentence and paragraph level.

A good editor does more than mark up the text; they provide an "edit memo" with feedback on global issues with the manuscript and suggestions on how to fix them. To give you an idea of the type of feedback you can expect, here are some excerpts from edits memos I've created for some of the 20 books I've edited, organized generally from the highest-level feedback to the lowest:

- I've rearranged some of the chapters to make what I feel is a much clearer organization. It now looks like this [followed by a new proposed table of contents].

- There is one overarching weakness that I know you will be eager to fix. That weakness is: *You don't take your own advice about getting to the point.* The opening chapters are long and get in the way of getting to the point of the book. Here's how to fix that . . .
- The biggest challenge is the repetition of the same examples over and over. The reader, encountering the analysis of Netflix for the fourth or fifth time will be sure to react with exasperation. A failure to deal constructively with this problem is a fatal flaw in an otherwise excellent manuscript. The solution is (1) up front in the introduction, list all the companies that form the basis of the narrative, and explain why they are there and that you will refer to them repeatedly, (2) Delete some mentions or cut them back to avoid repeating, not just the same companies, but the same facts and sometimes the same quotes about the same companies, (3) Explicitly refer back, for example, "As we described in chapter 3 regarding Netflix, . . ."
- The text is extremely wordy. Sentences throughout are too long with multiple clauses, making them hard to follow, and this problem is pervasive throughout the manuscript. I have suggested quite a lot of detailed edits to fix these problems. Please review the edits carefully, as you should make sure I have not changed the meaning. Cutting extraneous words, sentences, and paragraphs has reduced the manuscript from 74,000 words to 71,000 words, a reduction of 4%. I believe the manuscript is better off at that length.
- You tend to open chapters with a description that says, "we'll explain this later." That creates a potential in the reader's brain to look out for something coming in the future, which creates uneasiness. It's a lot better to dive right in with an example or give an overview that lays out the organization of what's coming.
- Buried leads. You often have the best summary of the section at the end of the section. Bring it to the top. It will keep people interested.
- Too much passive voice. Passive is a particular problem in a how-to book like this, since a passive sentence doesn't tell who is responsible for doing things (e.g., "Law enforcement must be notified" — who notifies them?). I would estimate that 80% of the line edits here are rewriting

passive sentences in the active voice. While this is a crapload of edits, I feel that, taken together, they help transform the book into an actual advice book, since they tell you what to do.

- Too many exclamation points. You have 59 exclamation points in an 18,000 word document, or about one every 300 words. Each one says "I am not a serious writer, and I need to shout to get you to believe me."

- Antecedents. Where you use words like "this" and "it," if it was unclear what you were referring to, I revised to clarify.

- You repeat some words over and over. They become a litany that annoys the reader. I've deleted a bunch, changed others to be less intrusive, and left a few. The result will be to make the ones that remain more believable and improve the overall text. I did a few searches on the whole text to demonstrate the repetition problem. Here are the numbers: *Very* (270 uses). Obviously, you need this word, but this level of repetition makes it impotent. *Many* (183). Meaningless, but repeated endlessly. *Focus* (93). You can't focus on 93 things. I reduced the number of instances. *Leverage* (74). This is a verb rather than an adjective or adverb, but despite its murky meaning it seems to be your all-purpose verb. Your repetition of this word comes off as a writing tic; every reader will notice it. Because its meaning is indefinite, it makes all your writing seem less specific and effective. I've eliminated as many uses of this as I can. . . .

- Statistics. You quote many. You have no sources. In some cases where I looked them up, the information was neither definitive nor believable. This interferes with your credibility.

As you can see, a good editor explains not just *what* is wrong, but *why* it is a problem. This gives the author the freedom to solve the problem in some way other than what the editor is suggesting.

Don't get too intimidated by red ink. A slew of edits doesn't necessarily mean big problems. In one book I edited, the author tended to go off on long rambling musings about himself and his view of the world — they drove me crazy until I realized he could just delete all that filler, leaving a book that was free of distractions and full of pithy insights. In another book, the authors seemed to write nearly every sentence in passive voice. It was a massive job, but once we revised all the sentences to active voice, the book became a powerful and clear set of recommendations on business strategy.

There is always a final editing pass that takes place when the manuscript is done and ready for the publisher to turn it into a book. This is copy editing, a process I describe in chapter 17. Even though you will have a copy editor, try to find and fix as many grammatical and spelling errors as possible before handing the manuscript in. The closer to final the manuscript is when it goes to the publisher, the less work for you in the production process and the higher quality the final book will be.

Work in passes, rather than gathering continuous feedback

Revisions and editing can get to feel like a treadmill. If you share a manuscript with multiple people and keep making changes, you'll be tweaking it forever. The objective is to get to a version ready to turn over for final copy edits and page layout, not to keep polishing over and over.

To escape from the treadmill of continuous review, I suggest the following:

- If you have a chapter you're worried about, share it with several people and collate their feedback, then rewrite.
- Once you have a nearly complete manuscript, even if it's the first draft, share it with trusted reviewers or an editor and get feedback before revising.
- When you think the manuscript is complete and nearly done, ask someone with an eye for detail to look it over. Resist the urge to show it to a bunch of people more likely to question the whole concept than to provide useful, detailed feedback.
- Fix everything possible before turning the manuscript in to the publisher. Avoid late changes when the text is already in the copy editing and production process.

Working in phases this way will keep you feeling like you're making improvements toward a goal, rather than trudging around in circles.

Key takeaways

- If you write in modular pieces, it's easier to edit your manuscript for structure.
- Revise a single sample chapter several times until it becomes a template for all the other chapters.
- Developmental editors will review your manuscript and find problems both global and specific. You'll usually have to hire your own editor because these days, few publishers provide that service.
- Get reviews and revise in distinct passes to avoid feeling like you're on a continuous editing treadmill.

Chapter 16

Facts, Footnotes, and Back Matter

Keep sources clear and verify quotes.

I once worked with an author who had a personal story in his book. As we neared the point where we would turn the book in to the publisher, he revealed that he'd fudged some facts in his story. "You need to fix it," I told him. "Why?" he asked. "No one will ever know."

A little later on, he solicited a book endorsement quote from a friend. She identified herself in that quote as a CMO — chief marketing officer. I checked her background, and while she'd done some freelance CMO work for companies, she'd never held the title of CMO at any company. "You can't put that endorsement in your book with that attribution," I warned him.

He reluctantly edited the personal story, but the CMO quote remains in the book — he was too timid to change it.

This author charges a lot for his expert advice. I hope it's true. I still trust what he says, 99%. But it would be better if there was no room for doubt.

Don't lie

When people ask me what I do, I say, "I'm an author." Then they'll ask, "Do you write fiction?"

"Not on purpose," I respond.

Of all the principles in this book, the foundational one is "Nonfiction authors don't lie."

Unlike the author in the opening story of this chapter, you would probably never lie on purpose. But an inadvertent lie is just as bad.

I'm talking about facts that are wrong. Quotes that are inaccurate. Or even facts that are obviously taken from other sources, but don't have any citation.

If your book includes inaccurate information, that blows a hole in your reputation. Creating a book that matters means ensuring that it's accurate and that the facts you cite are from reliable sources. If you cut corners on those tasks, you'll get a reputation for shading the truth. And that undermines your goal: to create a book that matters.

In this chapter, I'll talk about three ways to make sure you don't lie, even by accident: organizing citations and footnotes, checking facts, and verifying original content with sources. I'll also describe a few bits of text that first-time authors tend to forget, like the acknowledgments and the author bio.

Citations and footnotes

Most authors hate footnotes. Editors do, too. They're a pain in the ass. Why bother?

Because any quote, fact, or number you cite should have a verifiable source. If I tell you that the famous venture capitalist Ben Horowitz said, "Babies born today will probably never read anything in print," readers who are skeptical deserve to know when he said it (2012) and where the quote came from (an article in the trade journal *Adweek*).[10] And if I tell you that the average reader spends 36 seconds on the average news article, you should be able to check where that came

---

10 "'Is Print Dead?' and Other Tough Topics from the MPA Conference," by Emma Bazilian, *Adweek*, October 16, 2012. See https://wobs.co/BBBBHorowitz.

from — in this case, my previous book, *Writing Without Bullshit* (p. 20), based on data collected by the online news tracking company Chartbeat.[11]

Readers want to be sure you're not making things up, understand your sources, and check them if they want to. As a member of the fellowship of authors, you should give other authors credit for their work — and expect them to give you credit when they quote you. It's how we help each other out.

If you've kept track of the links and sources for all the research you did, then this is an administrative task you can manage. I recently created 134 footnotes for a book I edited (I don't generally do this, but the author was a dear friend). It took nine hours. That may seem like a lot, but for a book that took many hundreds of hours to create, it's a drop in the bucket.

You may have unresolved trauma from trying to match a very specific citation format in papers you did in college. But what readers want isn't perfect footnote formatting. They just want to see the name of the source so they can check it. If you're persnickety, you can use a tool like EasyBib to manage the footnote references, but it may not be necessary. Forget the librarian looking over your shoulder, just think of the reader and what they want to know about the source (who wrote it, what publication, what date, what link).

If you've got more than a few citations, use endnotes rather than footnotes. They're easy to insert with tools like Microsoft Word. As you assemble the manuscript, your footnotes will accumulate in order, neatly numbered, at the end of the text. Using endnotes keeps the sources separate from the rest of the text, so they don't distract readers who would rather just keep reading.

Here's one more trick to make it easy for readers to check sources. To start, always include a link to online sources. While this works well in ebooks, in the print book, you may end up with a long URL like this one, for the *Adweek* article I cited earlier: https://www.adweek.com/performance-marketing/print-dead-and-other-tough-topics-mpa-conference-144509/ .

If a reader is reading that in print, it's hard to type without making a mistake. So you can use a link shortener like Bitly and replace it with a short link like this, which goes to the same place: https://bit.ly/3ghoci6 .

---

11 *Writing Without Bullshit: Boost Your Career by Saying What You Mean* (Harper Business, 2016) by Josh Bernoff, p. 20. Statistic from Joshua Schwartz, Chief Technology Officer, Chartbeat.

But if you want to get a bit more sophisticated, you can create a free Bitly account and link it to a domain you own (in my books, that's wobs.co). You can then customize each link name. Since the book you're currently reading is called *Build a Better Business Book,* I can start all the customized links with "BBBB" (which is useful, since nobody else is using links with four capital B's like that, so they're all available). The link for the same *Adweek* article could be something easy to type and remember, like this: https://wobs.co/BBBBHorowitz .

As an added bonus, your free Bitly account allows you to see how many people clicked on each link. So you can even track how popular your footnotes are.

Check facts

If your book is not supposed to have any lies, then all the facts in it must be true. But what exactly do we mean by "fact?"

Basically, everything in your book is one of three things:

- An assertion of truth. For example, statistics, quotes, or descriptions.
- A statement of opinion. For example, in this book, I have stated that the best business books are made of stories. That is an opinion, not a verifiable fact.
- A prediction. If you say that cryptocurrency is going to be the way most people pay for things by the 2030s, that is a prediction.

You don't need to verify opinions or predictions — while they can be wrong, you don't need sources for them. But you do need sources for facts.

As I described in chapter 10, there are two types of facts:

1. Existing facts you got from elsewhere, such as an online source (secondary research).
2. New facts you created yourself, such as quotes from your interviews and data that you analyzed (primary research).

Once your manuscript is close to final, you should go back and verify whether all the secondary research facts are actually true. Sometimes, this requires deeper research than what you put in quickly when you originally wrote the chapter.

For example, you might include the quote, "The single biggest problem in communication is the illusion that it has taken place," widely attributed to George Bernard Shaw. After all, that's what "BrainyQuote" says.[12] But it turns out, if you do a little digging, that perhaps George Bernard Shaw didn't actually say that. According to Quote Investigator, "There is no substantive evidence that George Bernard Shaw who died in 1950 made this statement. The saying has been linked to Shaw only in very recent decades."[13] Despite the hundreds of articles that quote Shaw saying this, there's no documented evidence that he said it.

Or if we're talking numbers, you might cite the "fact" that there are 100,000 commercial child pornography websites. But if you chase down that number from source to source, it originally comes from Kevin Delli-Colli, a US Customs official, who apparently just made it up and then shared it with a reporter for the *Christian Science Monitor*, after which it began to appear all over the place.[14]

If you have enough facts from enough sources, this verification can become onerous. But it's worth it because you don't want to end up with egg on your face, or even on the wrong end of a libel lawsuit. Jimmy Soni, whose book *The Founders* I talked about in chapter 12, hired a fact-checker to verify all the thousands of facts in his voluminous book about the origins of entrepreneurs, including Elon Musk, Reid Hoffman, and Peter Thiel. Why? Because the people he was writing about are prominent, and he didn't want to risk getting anything wrong.

Check back with your sources

If you've interviewed people to get case studies and then quoted them, are the quotes accurate? And are the facts about those people and events true?

To ensure that they are, you should re-contact every source you quote and

12 From Brainyquote.com, George Bernard Shaw quote. See https://wobs.co/BBBBshaw.
13 From Quote Investigator, "The Biggest Problem in Communication Is the Illusion That It Has Taken Place," August 31, 2014. See https://wobs.co/BBBBquote.
14 "Retirement is Long Overdue for Some Aging Statistics" by Carl Bialik, *The Wall Street Journal*, April 22, 2005. See https://wobs.co/BBBBstats.

get a verification. While journalists will record people and quote them "on the record" without checking, authors of business books typically take a more friendly approach.

You generally want the subjects of your case studies to look good — they're usually representing some sort of best practice. But you also want to maintain accuracy, rather than have them whitewash all the elements of their story until it's no longer interesting.

When you interviewed them, ideally, you mentioned that you were conducting an on-the-record interview and would be quoting them, as I recommended in chapter 9. You should never promise a source that they will get to review and approve quotes, only that they will get to verify facts for accuracy.

So at the fact verification stage, make a spreadsheet of all the people you quoted. Create little files, one for each snippet that talks about an interview subject and their company. And then send an email to each one that looks like this:

> Subject: [Company name] fact verification for [Name of book project] — please respond by [due date]
>
> Hi, [name]
>
> Thanks for agreeing to be interviewed for our book. I've attached a short document that includes the part where we quote you.
>
> Please review this and let me know the following:
>
> Have we used your name and title correctly?
>
> Do the quotes from you accurately reflect what you meant to say?
>
> Are any of the facts in error?
>
> If any of these need correcting, just respond to this email with corrections. If it's fine, let us know that, too.
>
> The deadline for responding is [due date], so we can get any corrections done before the book goes to the publisher.
>
> We'd also like to send you a copy of the book when it is done. If you could let us know your address, that would be helpful.
>
> Thanks again for your help with this book. The book will be published on [publication date].

Note a few things about this carefully worded email. It never promises approval.

And it only pertains to accuracy. If someone wants to change the wording of their quote, you should generally allow it, if it doesn't upend the point you're making. If you got a number wrong, such as the number of stores a retailer has, then this is a chance to fix it. But you are under no obligation to change a reference to "salesforce.com" to read "the market-leading customer relationship management system salesforce.com." And there is no need to include trademark symbols in the text, regardless of what any company's lawyer tells you. In the end, if you are sure of your facts and your sources, you can publish them whether the original person interviewed responds or not.

What matters is that you're telling the truth. And these fact verification steps are the way you make sure that you are.

Front and back matter: the text that first-time authors often forget

When you've completed and fact-checked all the chapters and created all the footnotes, you're done, right?

Almost, but not quite. New authors may not realize they're responsible for the extra bits of text, known as front matter and back matter, that appear before or after the main book content. If you don't want to scramble to assemble those in a hurry — and risk introducing errors in your haste — here are a few pieces you'll need to draft to complete your manuscript. I've also listed the pieces the publisher does for you, so you don't have to worry about those.

- **Copyright page.** The publisher typically takes care of this. But be clear about who owns the copyright — you, a company you've set up for your own business, or your employer.
- **Title page.** The publisher takes care of this. There are typically two title pages: a "half-title" page with just the title alone and a full title page. When you sign a book for a fan, you sign it on the half-title page.
- **Dedication.** You can dedicate the book to someone who inspired you, but it's not required. Authors often dedicate their books to their spouses

and families who had to put up with them being inordinately busy and irritable while they were writing.

- **Table of contents.** The publisher will automatically create this for you. But pay attention to the text in the chapter titles and how they appear together; as I mentioned in chapter 6, parallelism and consistency here can make your table of contents look more enticing.

- **Foreword.** Some authors will tap a famous friend to write a foreword, hoping to get that famous person's name on the cover ("With a foreword by Bill Gates"). If you think a foreword like this will help you out, mention it as soon as you can to your famous friend so they have time to prepare something. Forewords are typically no more than 1,000 words. You may have to share an early copy of the manuscript with the person writing it, or they may even ask you to ghostwrite the foreword for them. Some authors pay people to write their forewords.

- **Introduction.** Authors think they need to write an introduction to ease readers into their content. I'll repeat my advice from my chapter 1: you're better off without it. Because some readers read introductions and some don't, an introduction means you don't know where their head is at when they start chapter 1. Better to just plunge into the scare-the-crap-out-of-them immediacy of chapter 1. Some of the boring stuff that usually goes into introductions (who this book is for, what's coming up in the rest of the book) can just go into the end of chapter 1.

- **Acknowledgments.** This is where you thank everyone who helped with the book: friends, colleagues, editors, publicists, graphic artists, your mentor, your spouse, your children, your mom, your third-grade teacher, and so on. Don't be stingy, and there's no need to attempt to be creative; it's basically a list of names. Some people put acknowledgments at the front of the book, but they're better off at the end where they don't interfere with plunging the reader directly into the story.

- **About the author.** You need a bio. It should be about 500 words long. If you already have a bio, revise it before you publish it here to make it deliver on the two purposes it serves. First, you want to list your most impressive accomplishments, and second, you want to give the reader, who has just finished your book, a chance to connect with you further, for example, to hire you for a speech or retain you as a consultant. To further the latter aim, be sure to include a link to your author website. Be aware, as well, that (the laziest of) people introducing you at events will often read your bio from the book out loud. So make sure the first paragraph hits the highlights. While you're working on this, you may also want to create a super-short version of the bio (30 to 40 words) that will go on the back book flap or the back of the book under your photo.

- **Additional notes.** At the top of the endnotes page, you can optionally include technical information, such as how you gathered data in surveys or how you conducted interviews. If you have other useful information online, such as a list of instructional videos or an instrument readers can use to evaluate themselves, you can provide links to those items here.

- **Appendices.** If there's information that's valuable to include but would detract from the flow of the text, such as a detailed technical explanation, you can optionally include it in an appendix.

- **List of services.** This is optional. But if one purpose of your book is to get business for yourself, you can include a list of paid services you offer. This is the only part of the book where selling is permissible, and it should be brief and written in descriptive, not salesy, language. If the reader loves your ideas, they'll use this to hire you, and there's rarely a need to push them very hard.

- **Index.** Once the pages are laid out and it's settled what information is on each page, an indexer creates an appendix. Most authors don't have the skills or the patience to create their own index, but some do. The publisher may deduct the charge for the indexer's work from your advance, at a cost of $1,000 or more depending on the length of the book. If you're hybrid publishing or self-publishing, you will have to pay for this yourself and may even need to find an indexer. Since indexes must be completed quickly at the end of the book project, some authors and publishers are now omitting them. This is a mistake; if somebody has read your print book and wants to look up something that was useful to them, the index will help them find it.

There's a temptation to spend less effort on the front and back matter, since they're not strictly part of the main book content. But they're part of the book, so they shouldn't be crappy. Try to create these pieces with the same level of detail that went into the rest of the book.

Key takeaways

- Tell the truth.
- Include a footnote for each fact you cite from books or online sources.
- Verify facts for correctness; track down the original source for numbers and quotes.
- Email the people you've quoted in interviews to verify quotes and facts, but don't imply that they have final approval on the text.
- Don't forget the back matter, such as the acknowledgments and "about the author" pages.

PART III

MANUSCRIPT INTO BOOK

Chapter 17

Turning a Manuscript into a Book

Don't lose focus during the book production stage.

I once worked with an author. For reasons that will become clear, I won't share his real name. Let's call him Caleb.

Caleb was writing a highly detailed book of advice on a technical topic. He was a true expert in a hot and hotly debated area at the intersection of technology and business. And he was a perfectionist, often hired at great expense by companies to perfect their technology strategy.

Despite his expertise and perfectionism, his original manuscript was a poorly organized and repetitive 75,000-word behemoth. After several months of editing, though, we trimmed duplicative material and reorganized the rest into a respectable manuscript. It was time to turn it over to the publisher for the first stage in book production: copy editing.

In any normal process, that's basically the end of revising the manuscript. But Caleb had a bad case of "author's remorse."

He began talking to his editor at the publishing company about whether the main idea of the book needed changing. (She sent me a short email about it, the sum total of which was a single word: "Fuck.") He wanted to redefine terms. He requested a bunch of edits and new passages be added after the copy edit was supposedly done. He submitted new, highly detailed graphics that were virtually impossible to render, causing enormous havoc as the pages were laid out. And then he asked for revisions to those graphics in the midst of the production process.

Everyone involved was frustrated, upset, and stressed by the impending pages-to-printer deadline. But we staggered through to the end of the process as best we could. Eventually, the book was published and generated positive reviews and significant publicity for the author, including follow-on articles in impressive business publications.

The book also had embarrassing mistakes on page 227 and 232. We caught them — but only after the book had gone to print.

Author's remorse has consequences. Caleb had put his heart, soul, and intellect into his book. He, his editor, and I had painfully dragged it across the finish line. And now, regardless of what anybody else thinks, Caleb the perfectionist author will always know that his creation has flaws — flaws that could have been caught and fixed if he'd been more disciplined during the last stages of the publishing process.

What authors do — and what they must never do — in the book production process

When a book goes to copy edit, the content should be 99.5% done. This is not a recommendation. It is a principle you must embrace at the risk of enormous stress for you and potential errors in your book, like those that Caleb suffered.

While your creative work on the book is done, the rest of your work is not. Once you hand over the manuscript file, the publisher (or in the case of a self-published book, publishing services company) begins book production: the set of steps necessary to turn a manuscript into a book. To maintain your book's integrity, you must remain engaged throughout the production process.

Kristin Perry, VP of Operations for my publisher Amplify, has supervised dozens of books through the production process. She warns authors about the temptation to turn in the manuscript and say, "I'm done, I'm ready to move on."

Your job is now carefully reviewing the publisher's work and correcting problems, making only small and necessary changes.

There is a temptation to mess with the text once you see it as a set of pages. This temptation feels irresistible. Resist.

Late changes create ripples. You can introduce more errors that the copy editor doesn't get a chance to catch. You can create inconsistencies. You can disrupt the page layout, which is costly and screws up the index. If you have coauthors, you can create anguish for them. Late changes introduce risk that's more likely to undermine the book than to improve it. Focus, people.

When books are published with errors, like Caleb's, chances are pretty good that they got introduced in the final stages. That undermines your reputation. That's a high cost to pay for all that work you did to create the book in the first place.

This chapter will explain your responsibilities during the publisher's rigorous production process. What you are about to read comes from my experience, not just as an author and editor, but also as a former head of production for a publishing company.

If you're working with a publisher, the book production process includes the following steps:

- Author or publisher creates marketing copy for the cover.
- Publisher's designer designs a cover.
- Publisher's copy editor reviews the manuscript to identify the errors in grammar and consistency; author addresses those errors.
- Publisher's designer designs the book's interior (fonts and layout for headings, body text, bullets, and so on).
- Publisher's design staff or author re-renders graphics for publication.
- Publisher's design staff lays out the text in pages.
- Publisher optionally creates advanced reader copies (ARCs).
- Publisher's designer formats the text for distribution as an ebook.
- Publisher's indexer creates an index.
- Publisher gets the book printed and distributed to warehouses and bookstores.

If you're self-publishing, your publishing services company performs the steps listed above as the publisher's responsibility, or you may have to hire freelancers to do these tasks for you.

I'll describe what happens in these steps in the rest of this chapter, with two exceptions. I already covered graphics in chapter 13, and I'll explain what to do about book covers in the next chapter.

Create marketing copy

For simplicity, publishers and authors should create one set of marketing copy and use it everywhere: on your publisher's book page, on retailers' pages for the book (for example, the Amazon page), and on the dust jacket book flaps (for hardbacks) or the back of the book (for paperbacks).

Your publisher often proposes to write this. But authors usually understand their own books better than their publishers do, so you should draft this copy yourself if you can. If you did a book treatment as I described in chapter 3, you have the start of this written already.

Your marketing copy should begin with a startling statement that draws the reader in. It should also entice the reader with samples of the best ideas, stories, and advice in the book. And all of that should happen in a tight 350 or so words of copy.

For example, here's the marketing copy from Jay Baer and Daniel Lemin's *Talk Triggers*, the book I described in chapter 1.

> *Talk Triggers* is the definitive, practical guide on how to use bold operational differentiators to create customer conversations, written by best-selling authors and marketing experts Jay Baer and Daniel Lemin.
>
> Word of mouth is directly responsible for 19% of all purchases, and influences as much as 90%. Every human on earth relies on word of mouth to make buying decisions. Yet even today, fewer than 1% of companies have an actual strategy for generating these crucial customer conversations. *Talk Triggers* provides that strategy in a compelling, relevant, timely book that can be put into practice immediately, by any business.

The key to activating customer chatter is the realization that same is lame. Nobody says "let me tell you about this perfectly adequate experience I had last night." The strategic, operational differentiator is what gives customers something to tell a story about. Companies (including the 30+ profiled in *Talk Triggers*) must dare to be different and exceed expectations in one or more palpable ways. That's when word of mouth becomes involuntary: the customers of these businesses simply must tell someone else.

Talk Triggers contains:

- Proprietary research into why and how customers talk
- More than 30 detailed case studies of extraordinary results from DoubleTree Hotels by Hilton and their warm cookie upon arrival, The Cheesecake Factory and their giant menu, Five Guys Burgers and their extra fries in the bag, Penn & Teller and their nightly meet and greet sessions, and a host of delightful small businesses
- The 4-5-6 learning system (the 4 requirements for a differentiator to be a talk trigger; the 5 types of talk triggers; and the 6-step process for creating talk triggers)
- Surprises in the text that are (of course) word of mouth propellants

Consumers are wired to discuss what is different, and ignore what is average. *Talk Triggers* not only dares the reader to differentiate, it includes the precise formula for doing it.

Combining compelling stories, inspirational examples, and practical how-tos, *Talk Triggers* is the first indispensable book about word of mouth. It's a book that will create conversation about the power of conversation.

Notice how this copy tells the story of the book, including the main idea right at the top along with promises about content (proprietary research, 30 case studies, the 4-5-6 process). And it names names. If you profile prominent companies or individuals in your book, be sure to mention them.

Before you write flap copy, look up your favorite business books on Amazon. com and observe how they've written the marketing descriptions. Take notes on what you like. Then use those techniques to write copy for your own book.

Address copy edits

A copy editor is a specialized editor who finds, flags, and suggests fixes to elements of a finished manuscript that are inaccurate, inconsistent, confusing, or contrary to the rules of usage and grammar.

People use the words copy editor and proofreader pretty much interchangeably. Technically, proofreaders compare rendered copy to the previous version, but colloquially, "proofreading" just means "finding errors the writer missed," which is part of what copy editors do.

As I mentioned in the previous chapter, you should turn a manuscript that is as close to perfect as you can, rather than use the copy editor as a backstop for your own sloppiness. The copy editor will still find problems — there are always errors that you have missed — but the copy editing process goes much more smoothly if you fix most of the problems *before* the copy editor gets to see them. And it wastes everybody's time for copy editors to review text that's not final, because whatever you change after the copy edit will slip in unseen by the copy editor and, as a result, possibly include errors (like the ones in Caleb's book).

Realistically, late interview responses and late-breaking news sometimes mean that you must make changes after copy edits are done. If Elon Musk responds to your request for an interview but the piece is already in copy edit, you're not going to say no. But when you subvert the process, you invite the possibility for errors. As Amplify's Kristin Perry explains, "I'm okay with small edits during book production, but if you are going to rewrite six pages and rearrange paragraphs, you have to have a really good reason. That would have to be something in the marketplace that makes a difference and, if you don't address it, would create a severe gap or have a major impact on how the book is received."

Copy editors are modest by nature. They like writing and want to make it great, but they also recognize that they are the last line of defense against error. As a result, a copy editor will find and flag the following:

- **Grammatical errors.** You used "that" when you should have used "which." You put the period on the wrong side of the quotation mark.
- **Spelling errors.** You wrote "hole" when you meant "whole" or used "colour" on the wrong side of the Atlantic.
- **Rendering of names**. A good copy editor will check and tell you that you wrote Thomson Reuters when you really meant Thomson Consumer Electronics, or that Paul McCartney is Sir Paul, not Sir McCartney.
- **Consistency.** For example, you've been writing "Walmart" in chapters 1 through 4, but called it "Wal-Mart" in chapter 5.
- **Style.** Most organizations base their style on either *The Associated Press Stylebook* or *The Chicago Manual of Style*; adherents of these rival groups have been known to come to blows over the use of commas.[15] Regardless of which your publisher chooses, there are always idiosyncratic tweaks based on its "house style."
- **Accuracy.** In some cases, copy editors will check facts, like dates and numbers. Don't count on them catching every error of this type; check your facts yourself, too.
- **What you ask them to look for.** It's helpful to flag known problems with grammar or consistency if you'd like the copy editor to watch for them. You can ask a copy editor to flag passive voice, clichés, or overuse of the word "cloud" if you're worried about them.
- **Just good sense.** Copy editors flag things that just don't seem right — sentences that don't make sense, definitions that seem odd, inconsistencies in head levels. Many are the times that a copy editor has noticed a problem in my prose that everyone else had missed, but that caused me to smack myself in the head and say "Augh. What a dummy!"

Your job, as the writer, is to review each copy edit and either accept it, address it some other way, or reject it (by writing "stet," which means "let it stand"). Follow your publisher's instructions on how to accept and reject problems using, for example, Microsoft Word's markup features.

---

15 "4 Copy Editors Killed In Ongoing AP Style, Chicago Manual Gang Violence," *The Onion*, January 7, 2013. See https://wobs.co/BBBBonion.

Kristin urges you to respect the expertise of copy editors who have a full-time job working on written content. "If a copy editor says something doesn't work, it's probably worth flagging." But she agrees, "It can be really hard to deal with that criticism."

Don't get into fights with copy editors, just decide how to address the issues they raise. They're simply applying a set of rules, and you're damn lucky they've got the patience to wade through whatever you wrote.

If you like to italicize a few too many words or use colloquial expressions and the copy editor flags them, you can still revert the text to your preferred version with a simple "stet." "Stet" wins every argument. Never ruin your prose just because a copy editor says so. Find a way to keep the beauty and meaning of what you wrote and obey the rules, too.

Copy editing sometimes requires two rounds of review, if there are little problems that still need to be resolved. More than two passes mean something is very wrong between you and your publisher regarding your understanding of the English language.

Review interior designs and page proofs

Concurrently with the copy-editing process, you'll get a look at how the interior of the book will look. The publisher or publishing services company will send you a few pages of sample text that include headings, margins, body text, bullets, graphics, part dividers, and other elements from your book. The interior design is rarely a problem; publishers choose page layout options that match the cover design, fit the page size you've agreed on, and maximize the readability and attractiveness of the text.

Professional publishers rarely create ugly or inappropriate designs. But amateurs do. If you're self-publishing, reject designs that feature margins that seem too wide or too narrow, and make sure that there is a larger margin in the center of two-page spreads (the "gutter") than at the edges. Bad margins are a dead giveaway that a book was (poorly) self-published.[16] Avoid large blocks of sans-serif text as well; professional books use serif fonts for body text to maximize readability.

Once the copy edits are done and the interior design is settled, the publisher will move to lay the book out as pages. The publisher or publishing services company pours the text into design software, typically Adobe InDesign, to paginate it. You'd think publishers could do this flawlessly by now, but in my experience, there are always problems. Here's what to check for at the "page proofs" stage:

- Are there big gaps at the bottoms of pages because of poor placement of graphics or heads?
- Are graphics placed as close as possible to where they're referenced in the text? This is the most likely thing you'll need to catch and fix. Designers normally place graphics after the reference to the graphic ("See Figure 3-1"), on either the same page or the page directly following. Sometimes, if there are multiple graphics in a chapter, you and the publisher will need a few tries to find the least awkward way to position them.
- Do the graphics look okay visually? Be certain that the size and font of text in the graphics is readable and that any shading is appropriate.
- Are there widows (single lines of type separated from the rest of a paragraph by a page break) or orphans (tiny bits of text alone on a line at the end of a paragraph)?
- Are tables rendered properly? Tables are a pain in the butt. They're a great way to communicate information in a small space, but laying them out properly is often a source of errors. Carefully check each table for both layout and content. (One of the errors in Caleb's book, unsurprisingly, was in a table.)
- Are head levels correct? If you have both major and minor section headings in the text, make sure that each heading uses the appropriate style for its head level.
- Are bulleted lists, numbered lists, and block quotes rendered properly?

---

16 "How to spot a crappy self-published book (and make sure yours isn't)," by Josh Bernoff, Withoutbullshit.com, February 15, 2019. See https://wobs.co/BBBBcrappy.

- Have special characters (for example, accented letters in names, emojis, dashes, or mathematical symbols) mysteriously disappeared?
- Are there straight vertical quote marks where there should be curved opening or closing quotes or apostrophes?
- Are any words at the end of lines hyphenated incorrectly? (It looks pretty dumb if you have "Ne-" on one line and "tflix" on the next.)
- Are there lines of type that appear overcrowded, stretched out with extra space between words or letters, or set in the wrong font?
- Did they spell your name or the name of the book wrong on the running heads at the top of the pages? (Yes, it happens, and yes, it is mondo embarrassing.)
- Do the endnotes look right, and are they noted in the right place in the text?

Unless you find major problems, this first pass of the page layout is what publishers use to create advanced reader copies (ARCs). ARCs are paperbound "uncorrected" pre-publication proofs that publishers and publicists send to reviewers to start the process of marketing the book.

It typically takes at least two passes, and often three or four, to get every single page layout issue settled properly. In the last few passes, you'll likely just be dealing with a few annoying leftover issues, such as graphics placement.

Sometimes you need to make small text changes at the page layout stage. You find an error that the copy editor missed, or a news event is just too juicy to leave out of the manuscript, or a final fact check requires a minor change. Any such changes that cause repagination will slow the process down and can introduce a cascade of further pagination issues. So keep such changes to a minimum.

Once the pages are settled, the publisher will use the final text to format an ebook. I've yet to find any publishers who allow authors to review the ebook formatting. Usually, if the printed pages are laid out well, the ebook formatting doesn't introduce any problems.

Making an index

Once the contents of the pages are settled, an indexer can do their work. (For obvious reasons, you can't make an index until you know what page everything is on.) The indexer usually has to work in a hurry, since they're trying to complete the index while you're dealing with the last remaining problems with the page layout.

A few authors are also indexers. (I'm one of the rare ones who do their own indexes.) Given the speed required, authors rarely get to do a detailed review of the indexer's work, but it's worth a few spot checks to make sure all the names that you care about are included, and that they line up properly with the page numbers.

Printing and distribution

If you're doing print-on-demand, make sure to obtain and review a proof copy of the book before it goes on sale online to the public. Print-on-demand sometimes doesn't generate the same perfect-looking book that your publishing services company had you review.

If you're working with a traditional or hybrid publisher, trust the publisher to deal with getting books where they belong. It often takes a month or so for books to go from the printer into warehouses and, if bookstores decide to order it, on bookstore shelves.

Luckily, somewhere in there, you'll probably receive a box of books from the publisher and have a little joyful moment as you open it up.

How to use your extra time during the final production process

The publication, printing, and distribution process is usually far less intense than it was to write the book. You need to pay attention, but it's far from a full-time task. It seems like a good time to relax.

Don't.

This natural lull in the process is when you should be finalizing all the elements of your marketing plan. That's how you make sure you're ready for launch day, as I describe in chapter 21.

Key takeaways

- Make sure you've settled the text completely before submitting your manuscript to the publisher's production process.
- Write marketing copy that draws the reader in and makes promises about the great things in the book.
- A copy editor will find your grammar, spelling, and factual mistakes, but you must decide which of these to fix and which to leave alone ("stet").
- During the page layout stage, be vigilant for formatting errors, especially problems with placement and rendering of graphics and tables.
- Use the relative calm of the production and printing process to plan your book launch.

Chapter 18

Covers

Put your best face forward.

M y first book was almost done. My coauthor Charlene Li and I were excitedly preparing for the launch. And a very important moment had arrived: We were about to see what the book cover would look like.

Our first book was called *Groundswell: Winning in a World Transformed by Social Technologies,* and we had big ambitions for it. Ours was the first book to actually describe and show case studies for how businesses could use social media like Facebook, blogs, and YouTube for everything from marketing to customer service. At the time it was published, in 2008, social media was perceived as a silly distraction, but we had pretty good proof that it would shake up marketing and disrupt many other parts of nearly every business.

When the cover arrived in my email inbox, I eagerly clicked on it . . . and my screen was filled with a bunch of concentric stripes in lime green and lemon yellow. I felt nauseated. A second or two later, I zoomed the display out and got the whole picture — which was curiously askew, with the word "groundswell' in all lowercase, sans-serif, broken in two, across the lower right corner.

Outraged, I forwarded the cover to Charlene. "Can you believe this?" I wrote. "It's awful!"

Charlene responded quickly (it was morning in Boston and very early where she was in California, but she always started work before the rest of the state was awake). "I think it looks okay," she wrote back. We quickly got on the phone. She was pleased with the cover but agreed that if I couldn't stomach it, it had to go.

So I pulled it up on my laptop screen and started showing it to my colleagues.

"That looks awesome," one said. "That's pretty neat," said another. I probably showed it to ten people. They all loved it.

Stephani Finks, the design director at our publisher Harvard Business Review Press and the designer of this cover, sent a color mockup over to our office. I stood a copy of it up next to my desk. People would come by and tilt their heads and smile.

Was I wrong?

I stared at it. It was starting to grow on me.

I went to Stephani's office and asked to see the other designs she'd come up with. None of them were anywhere near as good as the one she'd shared with us.

And I started to realize that I was wrong, and her cover design was shocking, disruptive, attention-getting, intentionally unbalanced, and . . . truly a great illustration of the tremors that social media was about to send through the business world.

We used Stephani's cover. I got business cards printed with it on the back. The design became the backdrop for the book's website. *Groundswell* sold 150,000 copies and led to hundreds of speeches for Charlene and me. Charlene quit her job and started a successful company based in part on the reputation *Groundswell* had created.

Visuals are hard. But I'd learned a lesson. Don't walk away from greatness when it hits you right between the eyes (see Figure 18-1).

Communicating with artists can be challenging

Covers are important. You wouldn't go to a fancy party in jeans and a T-shirt: You'd wear something that shows off what kind of style you have. A book cover is like that. It must work with the title text to communicate the emotions associated with the book. It must promise that you are witty, professional, practical, bold, thrilling, elegant, or whatever other adjectives fit your book and your personality.

Figure 18-1: *Groundswell* cover

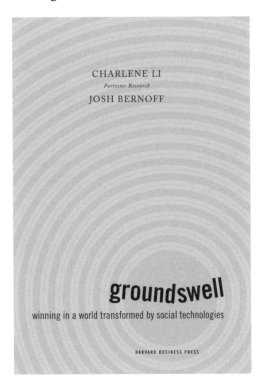

The challenge here is one of communication and translation. The designer uses a visual language of color and type. As a writer, you speak a language of ideas and words. Somehow, you need to bridge the gulf between the conceptual and the visual to create a cover that speaks to the content.

If you have a publisher — traditional or hybrid — they will act as the conduit between you and the designer. (Stephani likes to talk to authors personally, but many publishers insist on representing you to the designer rather than permitting a direct connection.) If the publisher's art director is competent, they're a big help in translating your ideas into a form that the designer can use. If they're not, it will seem like they're putting up barriers that prevent the designer from recognizing what you want.

If you're self-publishing, you'll have to hire a cover designer — and you'll still have to find someone who can translate your vision into reality.

Create a cover brief

The key to communicating with an artist is to *write down what you want* in a way that the artist can understand. That cover brief — with possible additions from the art director — becomes the key communications tool between you the graphic artist. As Torrey Sharp, owner of the Faceout Studio design house, which has produced more than 12,000 covers, told me, "Good design flows from good communication on the front end, with everyone on the same page with the author's strategy."

Here are a few things that belong in the brief that you or the art director share with the designers:

- **What is the format and book size?** For example, is this a hardback book six inches by nine inches with a paper dust jacket? That's typical for a business book. Or is it a paperback book? The publisher and you must finalize a format and size so that the artist knows what size easel they're painting on.
- **What is the exact text on the cover?** The designer can't work until the title, subtitle, author's name, and any other text on the cover are final. (The book you are now reading once had a different, longer title. We got back a nice cover design but had to scrap it because it made no sense once we had changed the title and subtitle.)
- **What emotions do you want the cover/book jacket to evoke?** Stephani, who has designed five covers for me since *Groundswell,* says she wants to hear more about what you want the cover to convey. Is it commanding? Approachable? Subtle? Bold? Precise? A cover design can convey any of those things.
- **What other book covers do you like?** According to Torrey, Faceout's designers want to know what covers have caught the author's eye in the past. That doesn't necessarily mean business books, either — if you liked the cover of a children's book or novel, he'll take a look at those, too.
- **Are there any graphical elements that could inform the cover?** If you have powerful and iconic graphics inside the book — as I described in chapter 13 — they can make their way into the cover design. (That's what happened with the icons in Evangelos Simoudis' *Transportation*

Transformation.) If your book is about ideas in the form of a pyramid, a two-by-two matrix, or a four-step cycle, it may make sense for those elements to appear on the cover.

- **Are there any graphical elements that you hate?** You might say "I hate yellow" or "I hate designs where everything is centered." Tell the designer so they don't create something that you'd never approve.
- **What books will you be competing with?** Your book will appear on the shelf — and in other contexts — along with other books. If it looks similar to the rest, well, that communicates that it belongs, but doesn't stand out. One of the things I like about the *Groundswell* cover is that it *didn't* look like all the other business strategy books — it looked like an earthquake, and we felt like the book was an earthquake. Explain what books and authors you'll be beside, and whether you're trying to look like you fit in or want to be set apart.
- **Don't give specific design instructions.** Telling a designer exactly what to design is like telling Misty Copeland how to point her feet properly in a ballet. Rather than specifying specific elements like background colors, typefaces, and placement, allow the designer to use whatever graphical tools will match the emotions you want to get across. Leave the graphics to the artist.

As an example, here is the brief I wrote for the publisher and graphic artists for my previous book, *Writing Without Bullshit: Boost Your Career by Saying What You Mean:*

> Emotionally, our biggest problem will be people thinking this is a joke. I want to get people to think of this book as bold, useful, and provocative. And a little fun, but not a joke.
>
> Your [meaning the publisher's] "Leadership BS" cover is in the right direction, at least as far as graphical tone goes.
>
> Now I will break my own rule and talk about graphics. I think we can all agree that there will be neither bulls nor shit on the cover. My face will not sell books, either.

Let's not get cute with the Bullshit either, as they did on the cover of "Go the F**k to Sleep." If you're offended by profanity, you won't buy this book, regardless of the cover. So let's own the world "Bullshit" and make it work for us. Here are some examples of people who did that successfully: [Here I linked to Jason Falls and Erik Decker's "No Bullshit Social Media" and Penn & Teller's video series "Bullshit."]

I know [the editor] had suggested putting the word "Bullshit" in script to sort of get you to take notice and play against expectations. I'm not a fan of that approach, I'm afraid. I want people to notice the word.

Also, I have future books planned that will include "Without Bullshit" in the title, so I'd like that pair of words to have some graphical unity that could connect to a word other than "Writing."

Giving feedback

You'll probably get back several possible designs. At Faceout, for example, the objective is to give the author three choices.

Remember, as you evaluate these choices, that the job of the cover is *not* to explain the book. No graphic design could do that. It is to represent the book in the reader's mind — to attract attention and connect that attention with an idea.

As you evaluate the possible designs, ask a few questions:

- Do I like it? If you hate it, you'll never be comfortable with the book. (But you might change your mind, as I did on *Groundswell*.)
- How does this make me feel? Did the cover evoke the emotions you were seeking? Did it evoke some undesirable emotions instead?
- If you like some parts but not others, what is working and what isn't? As Torrey from Faceout says, try to be "diagnostic, not prescriptive." That is, tell the design team that it looks too informal, not that the sans-serif type should be replaced with Garamond Bold.
- How will it look on a screen at three-quarters of an inch tall? Because that's how it will appear in many online applications, like lists of books on Amazon. At that size, the title should be readable and the design

recognizable. But don't expect to be able to read the subtitle or distinguish small and subtle graphical elements.

- How will it look on the shelf next to other books? Here's where you and your competing books need to live together on somebody's bookshelf. Will it be easy to pick out?

Send your feedback to the designer, if necessary, through the publisher's art director. Remember, it is typically within your power as author to reject all of the designs — it's your book, after all — but you'll have more success if you can say *why* the designs aren't working or which elements you still like.

If you can't make up your mind, take a poll. On one book I worked on, we had two possible cover designs: one with a stylized lightning bolt, and the other with a stylized superhero flying through the air. My coauthor and I liked both designs, so I walked them around the office to get opinions. Many people — especially women — found the superhero disturbing; a typical comment was, "Why am I looking at a guy in his underwear?" After hearing that a couple dozen times, we picked the lightning bolt. You can do an online poll of your friends in a similar way on a platform like Facebook or LinkedIn. Don't crowdsource design — that tends to fail, because design is personal — but you can ask the crowd to vote to see what resonates more with your audience.

It's not just a cover

You'll be approving a rectangular graphic. But once you do, the designer's work is not done. They'll have to create a graphical treatment for the spine and the back. If the book is a hardback with a dust jacket, they need to design the book flaps as well. And the same design will likely appear in some variations on the ebook and audiobook. Competent book designers will easily and precisely create those files, provided that they have accurate dimensions for the book (including the page count, which determines the spine width).

There is one piece you'll need to supply: an author photo. So make sure you have a good, high-resolution, professional photo available for placement on the back of the book or the inside book flap, as opposed to whatever random mobile phone photo you're using for social media accounts. A new book is a good excuse to hire a professional photographer and update your photo.

If the cover design elements are strong enough, you can leverage them for business cards and other branding elements. As Torrey Sharp says, when viewing covers, "authors should be thinking in terms of their brand" and whether the design can enhance it.

Somebody — typically the publisher — will be paying at least $2,000 for a cover design. If you're self-publishing, don't skimp here. Cheap designers make cheap-looking covers — and that's not what you need if you're publishing a book that matters.

Key takeaways

- Create a design brief that communicates the emotions you want your cover to evoke.
- Provide feedback that's diagnostic, not prescriptive.
- Apply iconic cover designs as a branding element.
- Your cover is your book in visual form; don't skimp and don't give up, or you'll end up with a cheap and amateurish cover.

Chapter 19

Blurbs and Endorsements

Cultivate and publish prominent endorsements.

The name of the book was *Digital Disruption: Unleashing the Next Wave of Innovation.* In 2013, the idea of disruption had not yet become the overused cliché it is now — it was still new and shiny and trendy. James McQuivey, a leading media analyst at Forrester, had written the definitive treatise on how disruption enabled by digital technologies was different from the classical idea of disruptive innovation, first described by Harvard Business School professor Clayton Christensen in his groundbreaking book *The Innovator's Dilemma: When New Technologies Cause Great Firms to Fail* (Harvard Business Review Press, 1997).

But James knew that standing out from other potential disruption books was crucial, and that meant getting endorsements from top business authors and thinkers. He'd reached out to leaders including *Newsweek* CEO Baba Shetty, Newark mayor (and later, US Senator from New Jersey) Cory Booker, Penguin Random House CEO Markus Dohle, and author Seth Godin. All were lined up to provide quotes. But would Clayton Christensen himself, icon of disruption, endorse the book? How could James even reach him?

He brainstormed with friends and colleagues seeking a connection. James and Clayton were both Mormons, members of the Church of Jesus Christ of

Latter-day Saints, and both lived and worked in the Boston area. But there were thousands of Mormons in Boston. It wasn't much of a connection.

James realized that he went to the same Mormon meetinghouse as Clayton's business partner. So one day after church, he reached out to the business partner and agreed to get him a copy of the manuscript. The business partner promised to ask Clayton to review it.

Clayton and James had a short conversation about disruption. Clayton began to look at the book. The weeks ticked by. The print deadline for the cover was fast approaching, and, with it, the last chance to get any endorsement onto the book jacket. Word trickled back that Clayton was actually reading the whole book — which few potential endorsers do. And then at the absolute last minute, James received an email with a quote from Clayton.

"I have studied disruptive innovation for more than two decades. Here, McQuivey offers insights about disruption — and about the accelerating pace of disruption — that I truly hadn't understood before. This is a very important book about what tomorrow holds in store; it shows us both what will happen and how to address it. I recommend it enthusiastically."

James was floored. The wizard of disruption had not only liked the book, but also felt it had novel insights. It was as if LeBron James had read a book on basketball and said, "Ah, this guy knows stuff about basketball that I'd never really understood."

The quote went onto the back of the book jacket, with a shortened version at the top of the front cover. Clayton, the acknowledged wizard of disruption, continued to have conversations with James on the topic. After a long and productive life as a business thinker, Clayton died in 2020. *Digital Disruption* is the only disruption book he ever endorsed.

Blurbs add credibility

Nearly every author pursues endorsement quotes, colloquially known as blurbs. In my author survey, 72% of authors pursued blurbs. Blurbs won't propel a book to prominence by themselves, but they add credibility and often tip potential buyers toward purchase. They reduce objections by communicating that people who matter think this is a book that matters.

Certainly, to anyone considering a book on disruption, an endorsement by Clayton Christensen makes a big difference.

But how do you get endorsements? And how do you handle the important and often thorny people who provide them?

Get the timing right

Make sure you get the timing right on your blurb pitches. You generally need to give people about five or six weeks before the print deadline. At that point in the book process, you'll have a complete manuscript to share, but it may not be copy edited yet.

Find out from your publisher or publishing services partner what the absolute final deadline is for getting text onto the back cover or back of the book jacket. But never share that deadline with blurb prospects. Tell them the deadline is two weeks earlier to give you some wiggle room in case someone is a few days late.

Make a prospect list

Start a spreadsheet of prospective endorsers weeks before your manuscript is complete. An ideal endorser has a reason to say something nice about your book and credibility with your audience. If you've written a book on marketing, you want senior marketing people, marketing authors, ad agency executives, or executives at big, well-known brands. If your book is about personal productivity, you want recognizable names who write about that.

Everyone on your list should have one of two qualities: They're well-known, or they're familiar with you.

Regrettably, unless you are famous, these two qualities are inversely related. Your sister's dentist treats Malcolm Gladwell, while your best friend is director of marketing at a start-up nobody has heard of.

If you're fortunate enough to have a famous friend, add them to the list. But as you build your list, you should have four or five "sure things" (people with reasonably impressive titles who you know will help), a dozen or so "could reasonably be expected to help" (people with more impressive titles that you don't know as well), and six or eight "reaches" (powerful people who you have some way to reach out to).

Don't be shy about using personal connections. Look at how James McQuivey got to Clayton Christensen. On one book I worked on, we got *Forbes* publisher Steve Forbes to endorse because he was friendly with the author's sister-in-law.

If you have a publicist or corporate PR department to help you, take advantage of it. PR professionals often have relationships with prominent people and other authors.

You'll end up with a list of 25 or so targets. But your yield will not be 100%. This many targets may reasonably yield the four or five great cover quotes you need.

How to ask for endorsements

Write a personal email to each individual on the list. In the email, use language that refers to your connection to the potential reviewer, their qualifications, why the book is relevant, and how grateful you would be. Include a deadline (two weeks before the actual publisher's deadline).

Don't promise to put an endorsement on the back cover. Promise to use it. If you get too many, there may not be room for them all. Extra ones can go on the Amazon page and on an interior page in the book.

Do not send a mass email to everyone on the list. You'll just offend people. If you received a "Dear generic friend" request to endorse, wouldn't you be offended?

Be prepared to send the book in the form of a PDF file, a Microsoft Word file, or a link to a Google Doc. Some people send the book in the first email, but it's more respectful to ask first before sending a huge file to someone. And make sure it's all together. One author that hoped for my endorsement sent me a link to a folder full of files — essentially an "assemble it yourself" version of the book. I don't have time to do that, and neither do your potential endorsers.

Some people insist on printed copies. Be prepared with a bound version of the manuscript text from your local copy shop or a paperbound proof ("advanced reader copy") if your publisher has made a bunch of those.

In the case of famous and powerful people, you may end up dealing with their admins or PR staff. These folks are far more responsive. Treat them well and connect with them frequently.

Send the first email yourself (unless you're tapping a friend's connection — if so, have that friend send it). You can have your own publicist or admin send follow-ups.

Send a reminder after a week or two, especially if you got a "sure I'm interested" response but haven't heard anything since.

Be alert for corporate permissions roadblocks. Some of your professional friends may provide a quote along with, "Oh, yeah, I need to run it by legal or PR." That tends to slow things way down. (If the person "forgets" to contact legal or PR, it's very rare that there's a problem, but your contact will likely be aware of how sensitive these groups are at their company.)

Curate your cover quotes

Ideally, your back cover includes a mix of quotes: some where the quote is great, and some where the endorser is well-known. (Regrettably, the most impressive endorsers rarely deliver the juiciest quotes.) Include some fellow authors and some business practitioners in your field. An ideal mix includes both men and women. Endorsements from start-ups and big companies, or from US and foreign companies, add to the variety.

How to edit quotes — and how not to

Most endorsers provide quotes that are too long. Unless they have explicitly told you that you must use the entire quote, you can trim the quote down. It's far better to have two great sentences than four sentences of which two are great and two are confusing and extraneous.

Do not change quotes without checking. People are sensitive. Twice, I've had people make what seemed like minor changes in quotes from me that I felt changed the meaning. That left me mightily annoyed.

Amazingly, some endorsers are happy to help but have no idea what to say. If so, offer to ghostwrite a quote for them. Try to match what you think they'd say. Some authors actually send sample quotes along with their pitch; I think that approach risks insulting the prospects.

Sometimes you can negotiate. This is especially important with powerful endorsers who may not have provided the best quote. This is a delicate negotiation.

For example, in two books I worked on, we had similar situations: The CEO of a huge technology company had agreed to write the quote, then supplied a quote that wasn't quite usable as is. In both cases, I ended up negotiating with the PR contact at the company.

In one case, the PR guy and I went back and forth. He clearly knew why I needed to make the changes, and he also knew what his CEO would agree to. I didn't ask for changes to make the quote more effusive, just to make it accurate. We negotiated the details and the endorsement appeared — and it was impressive.

In the second case, the quote supplied was unusable since it didn't mention the authors or the book or apply to the book in any way. I tried to get the PR guy to add "As [book title] describes" to one sentence, but he said the CEO would not change a word. We didn't use the quote at all, because it said nothing about the book.

I don't recommend trying to beef up quotes to make them over-the-top. If they're good, keep them. If they're potentially good but too long or confusing or otherwise unusable, negotiate. People understand the need to make the quote fit, but they won't be very happy if you're attempting to make them sound like gushing sycophants.

Verify names and titles

In many cases (especially authors), the endorser requests a specific identification. For example, if you use a quote from me, I'd like it to read "Josh Bernoff, best-selling author of *Writing Without Bullshit*." If the endorser hasn't supplied the language for their endorsement, you need to check the name and title for accuracy before submitting it to go on the cover. How do they spell Kristin? Do they use a middle initial? Do they go by "Charles" or "Chuck" professionally? How do they describe their title? LinkedIn can help guide you, but it's best to send a note back saying "Is it okay if we list you this way?"

Don't let blurbers lie about their qualifications. A bestselling author is an author whose book has appeared on a national bestseller list, not one who got an orange ribbon in a subcategory for an hour on Amazon. You don't want lies about qualifications published on the back of your book.

End your negotiation by getting their address. Then, when the book is published, send them a copy as a thank you.

Key takeaways

- About six weeks before the print deadline, reach out to a target list of about 25 people.
- Include people you know well and very famous people.
- Curate quotes to reflect a diverse set of endorsers.
- Don't make changes to contributed quotes without checking.
- Verify endorsers' names, titles, and addresses.

Chapter 20

Audiobooks

Read to your readers.

When my first book *Groundswell* was nearing publication, the publisher put me in touch with an audiobook publisher to whom they'd sold the audio rights. I didn't know much about audiobooks, but I was aware that lots of people preferred to consume books in that format.

And I knew how to read aloud. After all, I'd read countless stories to my kids over their childhoods.

So I reached out to the audiobook publisher and suggested that I could narrate the book. Their response was quick: Send us a sample, and we'll see if you're good enough.

I needed to audition to narrate my own book.

I recorded myself reading a few pages. Response: good enough, but just barely. Work on it. So I did. I practiced and learned what it takes, not just to read your book out loud, but to read it in a way that connects with the people listening.

A little later I spent parts of four days in a little recording studio with an expert audio producer, Kenny Pappaconstantinou, listening. He'd stop me from time to time and point out where I'd flubbed, bumped the microphone, backed away from the microphone and gotten too faint, varied my tone, misread words, skipped words, rustled pages, or squeaked my chair. And that didn't even count the times I stopped myself.

Reading aloud, I found six typos in the text that both I and the copy editors had missed. For the most part, I felt pride in what I'd written, but I found a few places where I'd created difficult-to-read sentences that really should have been rewritten.

Reading my own prose felt natural. I'd drafted most of the chapters in that book, but my coauthor Charlene Li had drafted some parts. Even though Charlene wrote in a style virtually identical to mine, it was far harder to read her parts aloud. The text just didn't sit quite as naturally in the reading-aloud part of my brain.

It took 14 hours to record eight hours of audio.

I read the whole text aloud and almost completely verbatim, but with one change. The original text included two F-bombs, both where I was quoting other people. My print publisher had insisted on deleting one of those (the other, in a quote from Samuel L. Jackson, was apparently too essential to the meaning to delete). This had bugged me. So as I read the audiobook, I restored the missing F-word.

As it turned out, lots of people apparently acquired the audiobook and listened to it while exercising, driving, cooking, or doing other things. I know because they sometimes live-tweeted their experience, including the guy who was listening with his toddler in the car and was startled by the F-bombs. Sorry, dude, I wasn't writing with your toddler in mind.

Narrating my first book was work. But it was worth it. Because no actor could understand what I wanted to say the way I could.

Do you need an audiobook?

Should your book be available in audio format?

Absolutely.

Audiobooks are growing. In the decade from 2012 to 2021, there was a double-digit increase in audiobook sales every year, including a 25% increase in 2021.[17]

---

17 "Audiobook Growth Continues," by Shannon Maughan, *Publishers Weekly,* June 8, 2022. See https://wobs.co/BBBBaudio.

Audiobooks represented 8.1% of US book trade revenues in 2021.[18] And I hear from authors all the time who tell me that their revenues from audiobooks rival or even exceed what they get from book advances or royalties.

More importantly, recognize that there are a class of business book readers who consume books only by audio. Some of those are travelers who would rather not take bulky books on flights and prefer to listen on their mobile phones. Others listen on their commute or while exercising. Whoever they are, it's a mistake to leave them behind. Your audiobook will reach them even if they'd never pick up your print book or ebook.

There is a small class of business books that won't translate well into audio: books that are heavy with diagrams, for example, or reference books. But for the rest, failing to create an audiobook would represent a major waste.

If you have a traditional publisher, they've likely secured the audio rights along with the print rights. Check your contract. And as soon as you can, find out how the audiobook will be produced and distributed. Often publishers have their own audiobook division; in other cases, as with my first book, they will contract with an independent audio publisher. Reach out to that audio publisher and find out the plans and schedule for the audiobook.

If you have a hybrid publisher, they may be able to recommend audio publishers they've worked with before. And if you're self-publishing, you can work with a service like ACX or Findaway to get your audiobook produced and distributed through services including Amazon's Audible. Your objective is to have the audiobook ready and available at the same time as your print book launches so that readers who hear about it can immediately put it into their audio queues.

Should you narrate your own book?

If you get the chance to narrate your book, take it. It's a rewarding experience and a more direct way to connect with readers. While a print book allows you

---

18 "Audiobooks: Every Minute Counts," by Karl Berglund, *Public Books,* October 5, 2022. See https://wobs.co/BBBBaudio2.

to get into the mind's ear of the reader, an audiobook gets you into their *actual* ear. Your voice has the potential to be even more persuasive than the text alone.

There are plenty of reasons you might not want to narrate your audiobook. You may not be willing to spend ten or 20 hours recording, you may hate your voice, you may be shy, or you may have a strong accent, a stutter, or some other speech impairment that makes it difficult for you to read aloud or hard for listeners to understand you.

Effective business book narration is about communicating meaning. It's not about having the voice quality and discipline of an opera singer. If your voice is scratchy, nasal, or lightly accented, that just makes it more interesting. Think of Bob Dylan. He's no opera singer, but when he sings, his scratchy voice puts emotion into his words in a way that's superior to what a "classically beautiful" voice could do. It's the same for a book author.

If you can spend the time and are willing to put in the work, you should narrate your audiobook. Because no voice actor can possibly understand what you're trying to say as well as you can.

How to do audio narration

While you should narrate your own book if you can, that doesn't mean you should do the audio recording. Experienced audio producers and recordists have the specialized skills to produce your audio session, coach you, identify problems, and edit and assemble the finished audio into the formats that audiobook services require.

In past years, recording the narration typically meant conducting sessions over several days at a recording studio. Now, the producer may be listening in a control room nearby or may be remote at another location. Either way, they'll likely be communicating with you over headphones and may play back pieces of your audio for you to evaluate. If you have a high-quality microphone and home recording studio, as many podcasters do, you can still benefit from the supervision and work of an audio producer. If you're producing the audio yourself, you'll pay the producer for their work; if your publisher is releasing the audio, they'll line up the producer and pay them.

My most important tip for audio is this: Don't read, *perform*. My audio producer, Kenny Pappaconstantinou, whose company Elephant Audiobooks has produced more than 500 audiobooks, talks about finding your narrative voice — the tone and cadence you want to use to connect with reader-listeners.

Your narrative voice must communicate emotion. When you're reading something funny, smile. When you're saying something important, slow down and be dramatic. Use pauses and vary the volume a little to play up important phrases. Develop a storytelling tone for case studies and a more even, informational tone for factual material and information. Paradoxically, if you're reading something shocking, it's often more effective to just say it than to shout it.

If you've done acting, this will make sense to you. But even if you haven't, don't think of yourself as reading. Think of yourself as *telling the reader what you know*. If you can visualize that audience member, you can communicate to them. You may even want to put a photo of a reader next to where you're reading to remind you who you're trying to connect with.

You may have heard highly produced audiobooks like Malcolm Gladwell's that include music and actual recordings of people from interviews. And there are narrators who do voices, like Jim Dale, the amazing narrator of the Harry Potter audiobooks. You don't need anywhere near that much drama. You shouldn't do voices. You just need to be you, performing your own story. One of the most effective audiobooks I ever heard was Mel Brooks' autobiography, because his authentic and scratchy voice, Brooklyn accent, sense of humor, and *joie de vivre* came through in every story he told. If he can do that in his nineties, you can do a little of it, too.

Audio narration tips

Here are a few ideas that will help you prepare for and perform your book.

- **Practice reading aloud.** Reading aloud is not something we do every day. You should get used to it. Sit down in a room, start reading, and record yourself to see how you sound. Kenny from Elephant Audiobooks says he sometimes has author-narrators who haven't practiced come in, start recording, and then once they've figured out how they want to sound, ask to rerecord the first few hours. You can avoid that by practicing ahead of time.

- **Consider coaching.** If you want to sound like a pro, learn from a pro. Audiobook coaches like Sean Pratt, narrator of more than 1,000 audiobooks, will coach you through narration techniques to develop the narrative voice that's right for you.

- **Dedicate the time.** You can't rush a narration. You can probably read about 8,000 words per hour, or 100 to 150 words per minute. But it will take up to twice that long in the studio to lay down the recording. You need to allow time for mistakes and for breaks — nobody can read for two hours at a stretch. And you need to concentrate. If your mind is elsewhere because of all those hours, your recording will reflect it. Good author-narrators sound authoritative, not anxious.

- **Keep a glass of liquid lubrication nearby.** Some readers prefer room-temperature water. Others add a few drops of lemon. Just don't drink anything that will make you burp.

- **Use audible punctuation.** Readers have punctuation to guide them. Audiobook listeners don't. That means you need to use your voice to communicate how to parse the words and sentences. You'll develop a standard-length pause at the end of a sentence, maybe half a second. Pause a little longer at the end of a paragraph. Pause longer at the end of a section or chapter. Pause for every comma, but a little less. Make your questions sound like questions. When narrating a series, use the tone of your voice to help the listener recognize that they're hearing a list: up, up, up, and down. And you need a way to indicate a chapter title or section heading — likely an even intonation, going down a bit, and a longer pause after that. The reader hears that sentence fragment and says, ah, that's a heading.

- **Create workarounds for visual elements.** If your text has graphics or tables, you won't read them. That creates gaps. You'll have to leave out portions of the text that say things like "See Figure 2." And nobody wants to hear you read a table. You could put those graphics online on your book site and read a note that refers audiobook listeners to them.

- **Prepare for words and names that are difficult to pronounce.** Track down the pronunciation of names or places you may not be familiar with.

In one book I narrated, there was a case study about an Italian executive named Guido Jouret. I contacted him and confirmed that his name was pronounced Ghee-dough, not Gwee-dough. And before I read a section that referred to Zappos founder Tony Hsieh, I asked my social media friends how to pronounce his last name (it's "Shay"). These are problems you can ignore when writing, but not when reading aloud. If your text includes a word that's long or unfamiliar, say it a bunch of times until you're comfortable with it. If you stumble on omnichannel or transubstantiation each time you mention them, it's going to be a long day at the studio. (Everyone has these problems; for example, actor Benedict Cumberbatch, when narrating a nature documentary, discovered that he was virtually unable to correctly pronounce the word "penguin.")

- **Prepare for emotional parts, too.** It's not just words that will trip you up. There are parts of your text that are funny or sad or shocking. That's great in writing. But you can't be laughing or crying as you narrate. Read them aloud. Read them again. Read them again, until you can get through them without cracking. Emotion in your narration is fine, so long as it doesn't interfere with recording your words.

- **Take breaks when you are tired.** When you are tired, you will make mistakes. You'll skip words or mispronounce them. Your producer will likely catch these errors, but it will take you longer to lay down the audio. You're better off taking 15 minutes off, or breaking for lunch, and coming back to it with a fresh head. And don't schedule an 8-hour reading session. You're not impressing anyone; nobody cares that you did the reading in one sitting. Break it up across several days, and the quality of the result will be better.

- **Take note of errors.** The best time to do the audiobook is when the copy edits are done and the text is rock solid, but the page layout is not quite complete. Reading aloud is a good way to catch little mistakes. Take note when you do. And fix the errors before you finalize the pages.

You may not be an actor, but you can act out your book and connect with readers. It's a chance you shouldn't pass up.

Key takeaways

- Your book needs an audiobook, and you should narrate it if possible.
- Don't just read your book, *tell* it to the reader; use emotion to connect and communicate.
- Prepare for your performance by practicing reading aloud, reviewing difficult portions of the text, and developing ways to communicate visual elements like lists and headings.

PART IV

SUCCESS

Chapter 21

Launch and Promotion

Generate visibility with diverse marketing tactics.

Rohit Bhargava identifies trends — he calls himself a "non-obvious trend curator." By 2020, he had published ten annual books in a series called *Non Obvious*, each cataloguing the past year's counterintuitive trends for strategists and marketers. In January of 2020, he was planning to publish the capstone of the series, a book called *Non Obvious Megatrends: How to See What Others Miss and Predict the Future.* He hoped to use it to launch a platform featuring blog posts and podcasts. For Rohit, the success of *Non Obvious Megatrends* was crucial.

As I described in chapter 4, Rohit is also the proprietor of his own hybrid publisher, Ideapress Publishing, which opened the door to all sorts of imaginative promotions. It was time to unleash what he called his "crazy ideas." And while you can't do everything Rohit did, nothing is stopping you from using promotion strategies as creative and diverse as his.

Rohit's promotional strategy around the end of 2019 and the start of 2020 began with his mailing list of 15,000 interested potential readers from previous book launches. But just poking this list would be insufficient. He used the list to recruit 800 true fans who would be willing to participate in a launch, gathering

350 of those into a private Facebook group where he could energize them further. To pique the group's enthusiasm, he shared all sorts of intriguing insider content, like a speeded-up video of his "haystack method" of organizing interesting bits of news to identify the trends they portend.[19]

He engaged the group by asking their opinion on which of two types of promotional socks would be better. He shared a bizarre behind-the-scenes outtake from the photo shoot for an interview he did with Microsoft, featuring him covered head to toe in thousands of colored sticky notes.[20]

Most importantly, he shared an early copy of the book with the fan group. He got them cued up to post Amazon reviews as soon as the book went live, with a goal of 100 reviews posted on the week of the launch. While he didn't tell reviewers what to write, the reviews were overwhelmingly positive. Throughout the program, he sent them surprising and whimsical gifts, such as branded mugs, socks, a full set of the previous books in the series, and a banana slicer (which he frequently mentions in his speeches).

Some of the fan reviewers also posted on their own platforms, such as blogs and podcasts. Rohit agreed to appear as a guest on some of these. He reached out to a few Instagram book influencers with big followings. Others among his fan base secured bulk book sales at their companies. Rohit arranged to send signed books to some of those or to participate in an hour-long call to answer their strategy questions.

Because of the way bestseller lists work, bulk sales are more likely to contribute if they're spread across multiple retailers. As the publisher as well as the author, Rohit was able to route bulk sales through independent bookstores across the country, Barnes & Noble, bulk book sellers like Porchlight, and even Books-A-Million. Total bulk orders passed 8,000 in the first week after publication, which Rohit and his team directed through more than 100 different retailers.

Many people do book tours. Rohit turned his into a set of local promotional mini-events. He'd start with an intimate appearance for his friends in a city. He'd arrange for digital ads in elevators and taxicabs and radio ads to play in conjunction

---

19 You can see one of Rohit's haystack videos on YouTube. See https://wobs.co/BBBBrohit.
20 There are some absurd visuals in the Microsoft article. See "Rohit Bhargava: A 'near-futurist' scours data for hidden clues about how the world works," by Mark Mobley, Microsoft Story Labs, August 14, 2018. See https://wobs.co/BBBBmicrosoft.

with his appearance. The local ads mentioned not only the book, but also a local bookstore where you could buy it. Bookstores were happy to carry the book in exchange for the promotion, which drove foot traffic to their locations.

Rohit also conceived and executed two of the most unusual promotions I'd ever heard of.

The first was a bookstore scavenger hunt. His team identified 143 local bookstores that would take phone orders. They then contacted each one and ordered the book in the name of an imaginary customer: Al Bunbury (a name drawn from an Oscar Wilde play). Then his team held a scavenger hunt. Local people who signed up could get a golden ticket in Bunbury's name, show the ticket to the store manager, and pick up the book. Store owners would post photos on social media, highlighting how Rohit had brought people into the store (and incidentally, deepening the relationship between Ideapress Publishing and the bookstore for future books).

The second unusual promotion occurred in hotels. Jane Ubell-Meyer, a book marketing wizard, had started a program called "Bedside Reading," working with hotels to place books on guests' bedside tables. When Rohit became a client, she placed copies of his book in rooms in 12 hotels around the country in January and February of 2020, timed to coincide with the book launch date. The hotels loved the program and some even gave Rohit a break on food and space rental in his local book promotion events at their hotels.

In an insane example of publicity begetting its own publicity, an article about Bedside Reading appeared in the travel section of *The Wall Street Journal*, including details about the book and a photo of the *Non Obvious Megatrends* book glowing on a bedside table in a Boston hotel room.

This wasn't cheap. Rohit invested tens of thousands of dollars in all of this promotion. But it was worth it. He got buzz for his capstone book, feeding future speaking opportunities. He got royalties on all those bulk book buys. His book won the Eric Hoffer Book Award. And with all those purchases spread across all those retailers, his book debuted at the top of the bestseller list for business books in *The Wall Street Journal*. Rohit's Non Obvious business plan was off and running.

You put all that effort into your story. Now tell it!

What Rohit did may seem like an awful lot of work. It's intimidating to realize that after everything you did to research, write, and publish your book, your work is not done. Is there no rest for the weary author?

Regrettably, I've watched many authors invest all their efforts in creating a book and none in promoting it. "If it's good, my target readers will seek it out," they think. Not likely.

Promoting your book is every bit as essential as creating it. You must be just as systematic in planning and executing that promotion as you were in creating the book in the first place. More than half of the authors in my survey cited book promotion as one of their biggest challenges after publication.

My survey revealed that authors used a wide variety of marketing tactics, taking advantage of traditional tools like publicity campaigns as well as social media promotion. As you can see from Table 21-1 and Table 21-2, their levels of success with these tactics varied.

Table 21-1: Promotional tactics used by nonfiction authors
Source: Bernoff.com author survey 2019-2022 (N=172 published authors)

Promotional tactic	% who used	% of those who said it worked
Back cover blurbs	72%	59%
Encouraged reviews on Amazon, similar sites	70%	55%
Public speaking	70%	67%
Contributed articles to media sites	57%	47%
Outreach to press	56%	44%
ARC distribution	51%	52%
Publisher's publicity team	50%	22%
Outreach to podcasters	40%	63%
Soliciting book reviews from media	37%	33%
Outreach to bloggers	34%	49%
Hire book publicist	30%	46%

Most authors pay to tap outside resources and expertise for promotion. The average author in my survey with a publisher — either traditional or hybrid — spent $10,000, while the average self-published author spent $1,500 (see Table 21-3).

Table 21-2: Social media tactics used by nonfiction authors

Source: Bernoff.com author survey 2019-2022 (N=172 published authors)

Social media tactic	% who used	% of those who said it worked
Promote on Facebook profile/page	64%	45%
Promote on own/corporate Twitter	62%	36%
Promote on own/corporate blog	60%	55%
Post articles on LinkedIn	59%	50%
Produce and share video content	44%	57%
Promote on own/company Instagram	31%	31%
Post on Forbes, similar sites	23%	57%
Produce and share infographics	19%	33%
Promote on own/corporate podcast	16%	57%
Amazon ads	12%	45%

Table 21-3: Money spent by authors or their companies to promote books

Source: Bernoff.com nonfiction author survey of published authors, 2019-2022

Promotional spending	Traditional publisher (N=79)	Hybrid publisher (N=37)	Self-published (N=48)
Median spend	$10,000	$10,000	$1,500
Percentage who spent $0	15%	8%	27%
Percentage who spent at least $10,000	52%	54%	27%
Percentage who spent at least $50,000	18%	13%	10%

After hearing about Rohit's extensive promotion plan and reviewing the variety of tactics in these tables, you may feel a bit overwhelmed. You need a system to identify what promotion will work best for you, your book, your skills, and the resources you have. That starts with a systematic approach to building a successful promotion plan.

The five key elements of book promotion

The objective of book promotion is not to get everyone in the world to hear about your book. It is to get as many people as possible *in your target market* to know the book exists and to understand what problem it solves. Since the people in your target market have a lot in common (for example, they're all building contractors or they're all tech executives), they tend to gather and talk to each other. This is central to your book promotion strategy.

Despite the variety of possible promotion tactics, all successful book promotion plans are based on five elements, which you can remember by the initialism PQRST:

1. **Positioning.** Who is the target market, and what kind of book is it (for example, strategy, leadership, marketing, personal productivity, or memoir)?
2. **Question.** What big question are you answering for the people in the target market?
3. **Reach.** What resources will you use to create awareness in as many individuals in the target market as possible?
4. **Spread.** How will you make it easy for people who like the book to share their positive impressions with others in the target market?
5. **Timing.** How will you ensure that the bulk of your promotion hits around the publication date, so that individuals in the target market hear about the book multiple times?

Let's see how this applies to Rohit's book promotion plan for *Non Obvious Megatrends*:

- Positioning: A trends book for corporate marketers and strategists.
- Question: How can strategists identify major trends emerging now?
- Reach: Tactics included contacting Rohit's existing mailing list, seeding books in hotels, giving speeches in local markets, appearing on podcasts, and giving interviews.
- Spread: Rohit catalyzed the spread of information by assembling his fan group and feeding it sharable assets like the haystack video and the picture of him covered with sticky notes.
- Timing: He made sure the bulk of his promotional activities happened in January and February of 2020, around the launch of the book, including getting lots of Amazon reviews so potential buyers could feel comfortable that the book was a purchase worth making.

You can't execute Rohit's plan, because you don't have the same book or the same resources he does. But like Rohit, your plan should include the positioning, question, reach, spread, and timing that are unique to you and your skills and assets.

I'll get to all five elements in detail in a moment. But first, let me answer the question that's probably in the back of your mind: Isn't the publisher supposed to be marketing the book?

What will your publisher do?

Not much.

Your publisher's marketing group focuses on its paying customers: bookstores. Publisher reps will contact buyers at both bricks-and-mortar and online bookstores and talk about what sets your book apart. In the same conversation, they'll also be talking about all the other new books they represent. As a result of their marketing work, some bookstores might order a copy or two of your book.

Your publisher also has a publicity group, with publicists that will try to get you reviews and media coverage. They'll work on your book for a few weeks on either side of the publication date, after which they'll be off to promote somebody else's book.

The publisher's marketers and publicists are not lazy. But their staff probably consists of three to five people who are working on 20 or 50 books a year. This limits the amount of their marketing resources that are available to you.

A traditional publisher will often send an advanced reader copy of your book to all the usual book reviewers (who get hundreds of such books each year). They might contact some news media that they think would be interested. They might place an excerpt. This activity can work: In my own most recent book launch, the publicity staff for the publisher Harper Business generated book reviews in *Harper's Magazine* and the largest newspaper in Toronto, placed an excerpt in *The New York Observer,* and arranged for *The Daily Beast* to publish an article I wrote about the topic of the book. That was it. I had to do all the rest of the marketing myself.

Nearly every author I've ever worked with has been disappointed in the publisher's marketing and publicity work. If you look back at Table 21-1, you'll notice that only 22% of those who worked with the publisher's publicity staff said the tactic worked, the lowest effectiveness of all the tactics authors tried.

Some authors become resentful about this. Don't waste your dudgeon. Just reset your expectations. Accept that publishers can't and won't do much. You need to step up and do it yourself.

Mind your P's and Q's: your positioning and the question you answer

The point of book promotion is to spread a message about your book. If the message is "This author has a book," you have failed, because that alone won't interest people. All of your efforts should focus on the positioning, including the target market and the question you are answering for that group. That's the P and Q of PQRST.

Jane Wesman, president of Jane Wesman Public Relations, is an expert on book publicity and marketing. She helps authors step outside themselves and figure out who their audience is and how the book will benefit that audience. "What are your audience's problems?" she asks authors. "What are their pain points, and what are they concerned about? And how does your book solve those problems?"

Answering that may sound easy and obvious, but for inward-focused authors who are writing mostly from their own expertise, it can be hard to get outside their own heads and consider a reader's point of view.

Sandra Poirier Smith, CEO of the renowned book publicity firm Smith Publicity, suggests a focus on what makes your book unique. "Writing about a topic that is old or saturated is not going to fly," she says. "Focus on what is new, against conventional wisdom, or hitting a stress point in someone's life. That's when the media reacts, 'This is new, this is exciting.'"

If you started your book with the idea development techniques in chapter 3, you have what you need for this. If not, you can do it now. Describe your target market. Tell what question you answer for them, and what is unique about your answer. If you need help, look at the questions your chapters answer, as I described in chapter 6, and what they add up to.

Let's look at some P's and Q's from the authors I've profiled so far.

Jay Baer's *Talk Triggers* is a business strategy book aimed at marketers and strategists that answers the question, "How can you get people talking about your business?"

Laura Gassner Otting's *Limitless* is a personal growth book aimed at people rethinking their careers; it answers the question, "How can you make sure what you do for work actually makes you happy?"

Evangelos Simoudis' *Transportation Transformation* is a trends book aimed at executives in the auto industry that answers the question, "What is the future of transportation, and how can you position yourself to benefit from it?"

Take this opportunity to look back at your book and figure out why it exists. Write down your positioning (target market and type of book) and the question you answer for readers.

Now you're ready to plan how to spread the word about your book through reach.

Build reach through your platform: the channels you own

Three types of channels generate reach for your book: owned, earned, and paid. Owned channels are channels you control and can put anything you want into. Earned channels refer to mentions you get in other people's media, such as news sites. Paid media is advertising.

Let's start with owned media that you control. Taken together, the assets you control are your *platform*.

At the center of this platform is a website for the book and the author. You must make sure that anyone who hears about your book and searches for it finds something enticing. And as Carolyn Monaco, a publishing consultant for business experts who has helped launch more than 200 books says, your site should serve not just your book, but also your goals for your business for the next several years.

Your book site (or the section of your personal or corporate site that describes the book) should feature a big and prominent graphic of the book cover, which is necessary to remind people that yes, you wrote a book about this stuff. Describe the book in enticing terms; reuse or modify the marketing copy I described in chapter 17. Write down what big question you answer for readers, and what subsidiary or follow-on problems you solve as well.

Obviously, include links on your site for where people can buy the book, such as Amazon, Bookshop.org, and Audible.com for the audiobook. (Yes, I've seen people forget this.) Include a link for people who want to hire you to give a speech as well.

"The site should reflect who you are to your audience, the preeminent expert on your topic," says Carolyn Monaco. And, she says, it should also explain "how the author can help them accomplish their goals."

Your platform extends well beyond your site to include any place where you regularly communicate with followers. It might include a blog, a podcast, a video series on YouTube, a Twitter account, a Facebook Page, an Instagram account, a LinkedIn profile, an email list, a regular newsletter, a Substack, a stream of content on Medium, a column in a trade media site or on *Forbes* or elsewhere, or anywhere else where you regularly post content for potential readers. (Table 21-2 at the start of this chapter includes some of the channels in authors' platforms.)

Smart authors cultivate channels in their platform well in advance of their book launches. Identify where you have the biggest following or where you feel you can build a following. Then start communicating on a regular basis, at least every couple of weeks. Cultivating these channels has multiple benefits. It puts you in touch with potential readers, so you can learn their needs. It enables you to create trial balloons for content, so you can see what resonates and include it in your book. And finally, it enables you to build up an audience that you can tap into at the time of your book launch.

Your platform is most effective when you use it not just to blast out content, but also as a two-way communications conduit. Listen and engage. If you post, be prepared to respond to those who find your posts interesting. The more you engage, the more likely they are to be helpful when it's time to spread the word about your book.

Build reach through earned media coverage, with the help of a publicist

Channels you own typically have a smaller reach than existing media channels. If you can get featured in newspapers, magazines, radio, television, blogs, and podcasts, your reach will expand. The best way to do that is with an expert on publicity: a paid book publicist. Book publicists are public relations professionals who are expert in book promotion, including Cave Henricks Communications, Mark Fortier's Fortier Public Relations, or the two firms I've mentioned already, Smith Publicity and Jane Wesman Public Relations. If your company has a solid PR department, you can often tap into book promotion resources there.

Fees for a good independent publicity firm typically start at $4,000 a month; they'll usually work on publicizing the book for two to four months, and sometimes more, around the publication date. But it's not even worth hiring them unless you can make available to them your main promotional resource: yourself. Especially in the days around the book's release, you need to be ready at a moment's notice to go on radio or television or participate in an interview. If the "Today" show wants you on camera on the day after your book launch, you'd better not be galivanting around New Zealand.

As veteran book publicist Barbara Henricks, president of Cave Henricks Communications, points out, many media outlets will consider articles that run under your byline, allowing you to spread awareness about your book and share your ideas. You can contribute to newspaper opinion pages with an op-ed (or as *The New York Times* calls it, a "guest essay"). You can also create content that may run in sites like *Fast Company, Inc., Forbes*, or the *Harvard Business Review*. For example, the excellent publicity staff at my former employer Forrester sourced a dozen different opportunities for bylined articles about my book with Ted Schadler, *Empowered.* I rapidly wrote articles based on book content, and, as a result, publicity about the ideas in *Empowered* seemed to be everywhere you looked.

Writing content adapted from your book is work, but it's a lot easier than creating the content in the first place. Your publicist is the best up-to-date guide on which sites are appropriate for your type of content and their rules around contributed content. You generally can't do a hard sell in such a column — "buy my book" is right out — but sites may permit more subtle mentions or allow you to name yourself as the author of your book in the byline at the end of the article.

Before I leave the topic of earned media for reach, I need to hit on one more key tactic: speeches. Among authors I surveyed, this was the most effective promotional tactic: 67% who did speeches thought that they worked well. There's no more powerful way to make an impression than to deliver a speech about the book. Identify the main conferences that those in your target market attend, and apply to speak there, typically on track sessions or panels. Since such events line up speakers eight months to a year ahead of time, you'll need to plan your speeches well in advance of your book launch. Even if you are a paid speaker, the time around your book launch may be the right time to do a few extra speeches for free or at a reduced rate to generate exposure and awareness. And events often have bookstores that will carry your book, giving those who hear you speak an immediate opportunity to buy a copy. If you don't already have a speaking career, this is a good way to start, as I describe in the next chapter.

Create content that spreads

After positioning, question, and reach comes spread. As you near the launch date for your book, concentrate on sharing content that will spread. Ideally, every person who reads what you share is a potential vector to get that content out to their own aggregated set of contacts.

You already have a deep well of content to draw on, having spent six months or more researching and assembling fascinating content for your book. Write, post, or share audio or video about your case studies, statistics, major conclusions, how-to steps, or graphics. Any of those tactics can work, but don't forget to reference your book and link to it in each piece of content that you post.

A great tool here is Melanie Deziel's book *The Content Fuel Framework: How to Generate Unlimited Story Ideas* (StoryFuel Press, 2020). She recommends considering ten possible content "focuses" including people, history, and process, as well as ten formats: writing, infographic, audio, video, live video, image gallery, timeline, quiz, tool, and map. The tools in her book will stimulate your thinking on what you can create that will attract an audience.

Naturally, Melanie used her book's recommended tactics to launch the book. She turned ideas in the book into attractive and sharable graphics. She recruited 35 people (including me) into a Facebook group, promising them early access to the book and encouraging them to post about it around the time of the launch. She sent her recruited fans a couple postcards with graphics illustrating her ideas along with the book.

She posted the blurbs she'd collected from popular content marketers like Ann Handley and Jay Baer as attractive graphics on Twitter, which of course generated retweets from those blurbers to their many thousands of followers. And she encouraged everyone she'd formed relationships with to write Amazon reviews. Her personal outreach also generated interviews on 21 podcasts.

As a result, on launch day, the book reached number one in big categories on Amazon, including creativity and communications skills, and was in the top ten in web marketing and e-commerce. It accumulated 56 Amazon reviews, all five stars, which is a great haul for a self-published book.

Melanie and Rohit's promotions were effective, but relatively staid compared with one author I interviewed: James Fell. If you're interested in more provocative tactics, you could learn from his experience.

James started with a platform as a fitness and self-help author, which included a Facebook following of 80,000 people. He wanted to break out of his self-help niche and write about things he found more interesting, based on his background as a history major. In 2020, he wrote his first "sweary history" post, a tirade about Martin Luther and the Holy Roman Emperor laced liberally with F-bombs. He followed it up with a hugely popular post on Mae West, who had been sentenced to ten days in jail for "corrupting the morals of youth" in a Broadway play about sex. James was off and running, and his audience was growing.

After creating a year's worth of daily posts, he compiled them into a book, *On This Day in History, Sh!t Went Down* (BFW Publishing, 2021), filled with absolutely outrageous, totally opinionated, not-remotely-safe-for-work daily history lessons. No publisher would touch it, so he published it himself and promoted it to his Facebook following, which had since grown to 287,000 fans of profane history tirades. He made money from proprietary content on Patreon and then took a huge bonus to move his audience to Substack. His first history book has sold 48,000 copies so far and led to a successful sequel. James is far from shy — consonant with the outrageous language in his posts — and in his current Facebook posts he repeatedly exhorts people to *buy the book*. The result of his new popularity has been adoring coverage in his local paper, the *Calgary Herald*, and a steady stream of revenue from book sales and Substack subscribers.

Whether you're creating intriguing videos like Rohit, clever graphics like Melanie, or outrageous text posts like James, the key is to create content that your target audience will find useful, interesting, or entertaining, then figure out how to get that content to spread effectively. All three of these authors collected their fans into a group and tapped that group to launch their content, which is a terrific way to start.

The key to starting and energizing a fan base is to be personal, rather than efficient. Reach out, individually, to fans to create a fan group. Recruit people with a personalized message. Give them an inside picture of what's going on. Give them tools and tasks for promotion that are closely tied to the ideas that energized you and them in the first place.

Go for sales, reviews, posts, and social sharing, and you'll create the impression that the book is everywhere and everyone is talking about it.

Timing knits all the promotion together

Of the five elements of PQRST, I've now covered positioning, question, reach, and spread. What's left? Timing.

Timing matters because it maximizes the efficiency of your other efforts. Here's a thought experiment. Imagine that efforts like the ones I describe in this chapter create 50 opportunities for visibility: sharable videos, blog posts, bylined articles in media sites, interviews on podcasts, and so on.

If those 50 hits are spread across six months, each one creates a little ripple, but in total, those ripples may just attenuate without effect.

But if you orchestrate your timing so that they all hit in the same three-week period, they are additive. A potential reader sees how a fan of yours shared an infographic on Instagram. Then they read a review on a blog they follow. They see that you're speaking at a conference; maybe they attend your talk. Then they hear you interviewed on NPR. All those impressions create the idea that the book is everywhere — it's the hot new thing. Each is another opportunity to get a buyer thinking, "This is the next new thing, I should get this." And that's what creates book sales — hitting that reader with impressions from all sides in a short period of time.

Many promotion efforts continue well after the book launch. Once you've got the publicity rolling, you can extend it over months and years. But a big bang around the publication date is the ideal way to maximize the effectiveness of all the work you've put in.

A clever timing tactic: newsjacking

If it's happening now, you should be posting about it now. That, in brief, is the philosophy of newsjacking, a term invented by David Meerman Scott and described in detail in his book *Newsjacking: How to Inject your Ideas into a Breaking News Story and Generate Tons of Media Coverage* (Wiley, 2011).

Barbara Henricks at Cave Henricks Communications emphasizes the importance of remaining agile in a campaign, including watching for opportunities to weigh in on current news stories. "When you're able to contribute to the dialogue in a meaningful way *and* get your book front-and-center," she says, "that's rocket fuel." Authors should be watching the news with an eye to relevant things to comment on, because latching onto news stories is a great way to create content that spreads.

Here's the newsjacking formula:

- **As you read the news, notice topics on which you have a perspective worth sharing.** For example, if you write about reputation, a famous person's reaction to accusations of sexual harassment is fair game. If you're an expert on corporate culture, every large business merger is an opportunity to opine on how corporate cultures may or may not combine effectively.
- **Describe briefly what happened, then segue quickly into your unique perspective on it.** Write about what the news item means for creativity, or start-up funding, or accounting fraud, or whatever is likely to interest your segment of readers.
- **Tell what the lesson is.** Stuff happened. Fine. You have an opinion on it. Interesting, perhaps. Here's what it means for your readers. Ah, now we've created useful content.
- **Create a great title that's not clickbait.** Use the names of companies and individuals to signal that it's about the news people are reading, but make your own take clear in the title.
- **Post and promote *quickly*.** As David Meerman Scott's diagram shows, the value of newsjacking is perishable; if you wait more than a day, it becomes far less effective (see Figure 21-1). Share your newsjacking posts on social media as quickly as possible.

Avoid "bestseller programs"

While we're on the topic of timing, there's one tactic you'll hear about that just might get you onto a bestseller list. It's called a distributed buying program, or a bestseller program. Unfortunately, I don't recommend it.

Figure 21-1: Newsjacking interest peaks and then dies off rapidly
Adapted with permission of David Meerman Scott.[21]

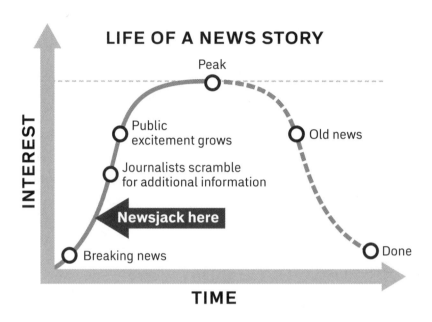

Basically, you can hire a specialized company to place bulk buys of your book through a variety of retailers in a way that increases your chances of hitting the bestseller lists. Those buys might come from your clients, places where you are giving speeches, or directly from you or your company. For a fee that's typically $30,000 or more, the company distributes those buys among many different bookstores and creates the impression that they come from lots of individual buyers. If you're successful, all those book buys get tallied by whatever method *The New York Times* or another bestseller list uses, and you've fooled them into thinking your book is a bestseller.[22]

There are three small problems with this, and one big one.

First off, it's expensive. If your book costs $25 at retail, and the buying program

---

21 For more detail and the original version of this diagram, visit newsjacking.com.

22 An article in *Esquire* sheds some light on the arcane methods that *The New York Times* uses to make its bestseller list and companies like Book Highlight that authors use to game the list. "The Murky Path To Becoming a *New York Times* Best Seller," by Sophie Vershbow, *Esquire,* December 9, 2022. See https://wobs.co/BBBBbestseller.

buys 5,000 copies — which is a minimum to get you a chance at a spot on the bestseller lists — then the cost of the books alone is $125,000. Someone is going to have to pay that, whether it's places that hire you to speak, bulk buyers at your clients, or you. Add to that the fee for the bestseller program company itself, and you're well into six figures.

Second, it doesn't always work. The bestseller lists are on the lookout for these types of purchases. If they feel they've spotted such tactics, they'll keep you off the list, even if you qualify on a numerical basis.

And third, being on a bestseller list for one week isn't sustainable. It simply doesn't have an outsized impact on your book sales in the long term.

The biggest problem, of course, is that this is a dishonest tactic. People who find out you did it will question your integrity. Most book promotion tactics look smart in the light of day — this one just looks sneaky and manipulative. You can distribute all those books to places where you're speaking, but in the end, you're just trying to fool people.

If you have bulk sales happening anyway and can direct them to different retailers — as Rohit did — I have no problem with that. But don't twist yourself out of shape or spend tens of thousands of dollars to buy your way onto a bestseller list.

Spend your time on more honest efforts. Promotion is hard work, and there are no shortcuts.

Promotion is a big topic, but you can master it

There's a reason this chapter is the longest one in the book. There are so many dimensions to book promotion that it can seem overwhelming. And with fees for helpers doing book publicity and marketing, the costs can easily exceed $10,000.

The key is to pick the tactics that match what you're good at, leverage the resources you have, and tap into what is most promotable about your book. That's PQRST: identify your positioning, clarify what question you answer, exploit reach tactics, find ways to spread the word, and focus on timing everything to crescendo just before and after the book's publication date. You'll create the impression that your book's success is inevitable. And that's a self-fulfilling prophecy.

Key takeaways

- Build your own marketing and publicity program to augment your publisher's limited efforts.

- Develop your book promotion based on PQRST: positioning, question, reach, spread, and timing.

- Start with your target market positioning and the question you will answer.

- Build reach around your author platform: assets you control such as your website, social media accounts, and regular places you can post attractive content.

- Expand your reach with earned media publicity, including contributed bylined articles and speeches; a publicist can help with these.

- Create assets that spread easily like video and infographics; organize a group of your fans or friends that can help share your content.

- Time all of your efforts to come to fruition right around the time of your book launch.

- Use newsjacking — tying your shared content to current news — to insert your book's ideas into the current zeitgeist.

- Avoid distributed buying programs; they're expensive, risky, and appear dishonest.

Chapter 22

Public Speaking

Book yourself for visibility and profit.

What stands out about Jay Acunzo is the way he sees the world. If ten people look at a situation and see one thing, Jay looks at the same situation and sees something completely different — and revealing. He's pretty awesome at telling stories based on what's unique about people and relating those stories back to people who are listening.

That's great for a book, because books are made of stories. And it's great on stage, because speeches are made of stories, too. But, at least to start, Jay wasn't a public speaker. He was just a guy who liked to spot unique things and tell stories about them.

Jay started a little group called "Boston Content" full of people who liked to create things — blogs, video, podcasts — especially things related to marketing and stories. Fellow group members invited him to present at "lunch and learn" sessions at their companies. He didn't have one set speech, and he rarely got paid. And it didn't add up to much. "There wasn't much traction," as he puts it.

But then Jay started to assemble his stories with an eye to a pattern they had in common.

There was the Death Wish Coffee guy who figured out that instead of making coffee out of arabica beans, which make coffee that tastes good, he could make coffee from robusta beans: coffee that's crammed full of caffeine. It turned out to be the kind of coffee that was perfect for truck drivers, construction workers, and other types who were ready to work themselves to death — hence Death Wish Coffee.

There were the people at the Merriam-Webster dictionary, who would tweet about words that were happening in the news — words like "sedition" and "impeachment." These communications from the dictionary staff stood out because they were timely and had an attitude, rarely qualities you associate with dictionaries.

And there was the animal shelter that got gobs of publicity by advertising really bad, nasty dogs that would be a nightmare to adopt. Those posts spread like mad, because they were so radically different from the typical warm, fuzzy, and forgettable marketing that most shelters use.

Jay collected a whole bunch of stories like that. They all had a similar moral. Best practices are average. Do the unthinkable. Trust your intuition.

These kind of stories aren't easy to find. But with Jay's unique perspective on the world, he could spot them. He was relentlessly curious. He had a different mindset from what you'd expect in an author — or a speaker. Not "I am the expert." But "I will find these things out and learn how they work and figure it out and bring it back to you — and tell you the story in the most engaging way possible."

He started giving (free) talks in track sessions at conferences. He still didn't get much traction. That is, until he got another insight, with help from the speech coach Andrew Davis. The idea wasn't to give good speeches. It was to give the *same* speech so many times that you could polish it and make it sparkle. Eventually, he gave the top-rated track session speech at the huge Content Marketing World conference in Cleveland. That top rating comes with an invitation to speak on the main stage in front of many hundreds of people the following year, which is what he did.

He also realized that it wasn't sufficient to be giving speeches. He collected the stories and profiled the people in them in a highly polished and popular podcast called Unthinkable. And he assembled them into a self-published book called

Break the Wheel: Question Best Practices, Hone Your Intuition, and Do Your Best Work (Unthinkable Media, 2018).

While that first main stage speech at Content Marketing World didn't pay, it generated interest: leads. People who heard Jay — or heard about him — hired him to give speeches at conferences on heating and ventilation systems or kitchen and bath design. They didn't want a highly customized speech. They wanted a version of the speech he gave at Content Marketing World. And since top-rated speakers don't speak at heating system conferences for free, they paid.

Eventually, he was giving 20 to 25 paid speeches a year. His speeches weren't just inspiration — because we're all sick of the "Rah, rah, you can do it" type of speaker. They weren't just entertaining, because he's more than a performer. And they weren't just educational, because people don't enjoy lectures very much. They used stories to combine inspiration, entertainment, and education to drive home a useful point. That's what caught on. As Jay told me, "Very few things are more practical than perspective-changing ideas."

Why do authors speak?

Authors give speeches. Everybody knows that. But as I looked into that, I began to ponder an uncomfortable question: Why are authors so frequently also public speakers? After all, authors sit in their writing rooms and type — they're often introverts and thinkers, not performers. If authors aren't entertainers, why do so many of them end up on stages?

Once you analyze it a little more deeply, you begin to understand why it makes sense.

Starting in chapter 1, I've made the point that business books are full of stories. And stories are a big part of what it takes to be a successful public speaker, too. So long as you're collecting and organizing stories, why not use them in print and on stage, too?

Authors crave audiences. If you're going to work on a book for a year, you must really want to share something with the world. And what better way to do that then on stage in front of hundreds of people at a time? In my survey, authors' two top goals were "Share the knowledge I had" (75% wanted to do that) and "Boost my reputation" (65%). Giving speeches enhances both goals.

The through line of a book also sets you up to build a speech, because both are really just a big story about how to solve a problem. That big story — the big idea, the "aha" insight, the justification for that idea, and the advice — is perfect for a 30- or 40-minute speech.

That said, there are crucial differences between speakers and authors.

Speakers must hone their crafts with lots of practice and repetition, as Jay did. If they've collected the ideas in a book, they need to choose the most dramatic and interesting elements of their books and leave the rest out. The difference between a book and a speech comes down to what you leave in and what you leave out. Luckily, a book has so much in it that there's usually a rich collection of content to pick from.

And the same challenge goes the other way. If you've got a great speech, you may have the *structure* of a book. But you're going to need a lot more proof that what you're saying is true; people who read books aren't going to get caught up in your performance and suspend disbelief the way that audiences at speeches sometimes do. You'll also need a lot more detailed advice. Advice far too detailed and pedantic for a speech turns out to be essential for a book that's attempting to be not just entertaining, but also useful.

If you do both books and speaking, though, they tend to reinforce one another. As Jay says, "It is such a natural way to monetize your ideas; speaking and writing books goes hand in hand."

Speaking and being an author are mutually supportive activities

Speakers with books know the books will help market them by spreading the word about their ideas. In my survey, 40% of authors said they had a goal of getting more paid speaking gigs. And three out of four of those felt the book had helped them to accomplish the goal.

Conversely, 79% of the authors in my survey used public speaking to promote their books; it was the third-most-popular promotional tactic, after back cover blurbs and encouraging reviews on sites like Amazon. And it tends to work. Two-thirds of those who used speaking to promote books said that it worked, making it the most successful promotional tactic that authors attempted.

There's no rule that says that authors belong on stage. If you're happy in your writing room and scared to death of speaking in front of an audience, feel free to stay that way.

But if you collect content and stories with both modes of delivery in mind, you'll find what so many other authors have: Speaking and writing support each other.

Tips for authors who want to be public speakers

While this isn't a book on public speaking, I can point you to one, cowritten by Jay Acunzo's speech coach: *The Referable Speaker: Your Guide to Building a Sustainable Speaking Career — No Fame Required* (Page Two, 2021) by Michael Port and Andrew Davis.

The book's other coauthor, Michael Port, runs a company called Heroic Public Speaking, which has coached hundreds of successful speakers. His advice is to think hard about what kind of speech you want to give. How-to-do-it speeches are great for breakout rooms. Authors who write how-to-do-it type advice books can succeed with speeches like that, since they attract an audience that's likely to follow up, not just by buying the book, but also by hiring the author. (The book you're reading right now is a book like that, and it's not likely to win me many paid speaking gigs.)

But the other kind of speeches are "change how you see the world," speeches. They're appropriate for big idea books, and they're what you need to become a successful, paid keynote speaker, like Jay Acunzo.

For a speaker like that, the key is to do what Jay did: Practice and polish and hone one "change how you see the world" speech until everyone who hears it is blown away. As Michael says, "The only way you get better at it is by working at it." That's what generates stage-side leads — the people who come up to you after the speech and ask if you can do it for their organization or conference and change how *they* see the world.

According to Michael, a successful speech like that has five foundational elements:

1. Make a clear promise to the audience.
2. Demonstrate that you understand how the world looks to that audience.
3. Describe a big idea that promises a new way of looking at the world.
4. Describe the consequences of not pursuing that promise.
5. Describe the rewards — financial, emotional, physical, or spiritual — of going after the promise.

After hearing that, I realized that Michael and I are in sync — because his steps 4 and 5 are the same fear and greed I've told you to put into chapter 1 of your book.

You might or might not want to do the work it will take to be a successful public speaker. But if you do, it's sure to reinforce your book, and your book will reinforce your speaking career. Both will spread your influence further. That's why so many authors are public speakers, too.

Key takeaways

- Books and speeches are both made of stories.
- Speaking and being an author are mutually reinforcing goals.
- Get help from a coach to polish your speaking ability, and get so good at giving variants on one speech that you get referrals to paid gigs.

Chapter 23

Making Money

Make your books pay your bills.

In 2007, Joe Pulizzi had just left his job at Penton Media. He was jazzed about an idea called "content marketing." The central premise of content marketing is that creating useful content generates interest, which generates traffic, which generates business. That powerful idea has since achieved massive resonance in the marketing world, but in 2007, content marketing was brand new, and Joe was little known. As he explains it, "I had no credibility."

So he put what he knew into a book, written with coauthor Newt Barrett, called *Get Content, Get Customers: Turn Prospects into Buyers with Content Marketing*, and self-published it in 2008. Word began to spread, offers to speak began to appear, and McGraw Hill, which was looking for a book on the new topic, made a deal with Joe to republish the book under a new cover.

The book was part of a broader strategy for Joe. It helped promote his blog, subsequently generating 15,000 subscribers. The challenge, of course, was how to turn all that popular content into actual cash. By 2010, he recognized that if he was ever going to succeed, his work needed to be more visible in more places — including places people would pay for. A careful review of the responses to his blog and the emails he was getting told him where that revenue might come from: events and training.

He and his team renamed the platform they were working from, creating an organization called the Content Marketing Institute (CMI). He created training courses. CMI started an event called Content Marketing World and sold sponsorships to fund it. The event grew and became highly profitable. To support the event, the blog, and the training, Joe created more content marketing books, three traditionally published with McGraw Hill and one self-published. He also branched out into a regular content marketing podcast. Joe and his coauthors cranked out a new book every couple of years to keep the content and the ideas fresh and up to date.

Where did the vision for this self-reinforcing set of content come from? Joe admits it was "stolen" from a 1957 diagram that Walt Disney created detailing his plans for the Disney company.[23]

In Walt Disney's 1957 diagram, the films feed the TV shows, which feed the music. Everything drives people to Disneyland, where they can buy plenty of licensed merchandise. The same content feeds the comic books and magazines. Every piece of content feeds every channel, which strengthens every other piece of content. In the 2020s, the age of the Marvel Cinematic Universe, this might seem obvious, but in 1957, it was visionary. You can see Joe's version of the same picture in Figure 23-1.

Like Disney in 1957, Joe's Content Marketing Institute generated content in books, podcasts, blog posts, and newsletters, which fed demand for Content Marketing World and training courses, which generated further interest in more content, and on and on around the diagram. By building his business that way, Joe turned a little-known idea into a solid marketing concept, with himself and his organization at the center of it.

Joe has a few pieces of advice for authors dreaming of building an empire around their ideas.

The first is this: "If you're going to publish, it has to be differentiated in some way — a small audience where you are the leading expert in the world."

---

23 I was unable to obtain permission to reprint Disney's diagram, but you can see a copy in this article: "This 1957 drawing reveals the brilliant strategy behind Disney's lasting success," by Steven Benna, *Insider*, July 17, 2015. See https://wobs.co/BBBBdisney.

Figure 23-1: Content Marketing Institute strategy

Reprinted with permission of Content Marketing Institute.

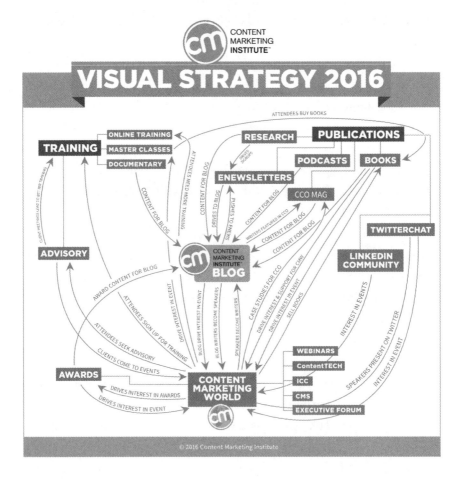

Unless you have a unique perspective on the world and can articulate that perspective in a unique way, nobody is likely to pay attention to you — or remember you. A book is, fundamentally, the expression of that perspective.

Joe's second insight is equally powerful. *Give everything away.* In a world awash in content, it makes sense to publish a free blog, a free podcast, or a free set of YouTube videos. It makes sense to offer sections of your book for free. Joe and his partners didn't worry that they might be giving away bits and pieces of proprietary content. Instead, what they argued most about was, "Are we giving enough away?"

This is counterintuitive. But if you have training courses and events and paid webinars and consulting, the objective of your content is to get people to say, "Wow, I gotta hire the people who created this." The events cost money, and they make money. So do the sponsorships and the training. And the demand for all of those comes because the free (or cheap) ideas in the books and the rest of the content convinces people with money that they want to immerse themselves in the world those authors have created. They want to learn from the experts.

Do authors make money from books?

Joe Pulizzi made plenty of money from books. But he'd be the first to tell you that it was the other elements of his content diagram that brought in most of the revenue.

To understand why that is, let's get a little deeper into the economics of books. Because until you understand those economics, you might think that publishing a book, by itself, is going to make you rich — and it almost certainly won't.

Imagine for a moment that you write your first book. You get a publishing contract with a traditional publisher. We'll assume the publisher gives you a $100,000 advance, which is pretty generous for a first book. (Of the traditionally published authors in my survey, only 23% received an advance that large.)

Now let's further assume that due to your excellent promotional efforts and the sparkling quality of your book, it sells well. Let's assume it sells 30,000 copies over the first two years at a list price of $30. (There are various other considerations here such as sales of ebooks, audiobooks, and foreign rights, but for the purposes of this exercise, the sales of print copies are a fair approximation.)

A typical publishing contract will offer you royalties of up to 15% of the list price. That means you're getting $4.50 per book. Multiply that by the 30,000 copies and you've made $135,000. But what about that $100,000 advance? Well, that's an *advance against royalties*. That means you don't get paid royalties until the total accounting for the royalties passes the amount of the advance. So you'll bank the $100,000 advance and the $35,000 in additional royalties.

244 I BUILD A BETTER BUSINESS BOOK

This moderately successful book has now generated $135,000 over the year it took you to write it and the two years it was on sale. A take of $135,000 over three years is nice, but if that's all the money you make, you probably can't quit your day job — especially if you've spent tens of thousands of dollars on book promotion to make the book successful.

But wait, you might say. What if I self-publish? A self-published $30 book might make you $18 a copy (remember, the bookstore or online bookseller still takes its cut of the retail price). But unless you're very unusual, your "successful" self-published book is likely selling about 10,000 copies. Now you've made $180,000, but you've also had to pay for your own editor and publishing services along with your promotional expenses. You're not way ahead relative to the traditionally published author, and your risk is much higher.

The bottom line is that authors make money, but not from book sales alone. Moderately successful authors like the examples I just described make money from other sources. And truly successful authors that are selling hundreds of thousands of copies? The elite authors — the Malcolm Gladwells and Daniel Pinks and Tony Robbinses — may make millions of dollars from book sales, but they're also making $50,000 a speech and making lots of other cash from sponsorships or other sources. So even the elite nonfiction authors are not living solely off of book sales.

Ways to monetize your book

Even if you don't make a living selling books, your books may help you make a living in other ways. In Chapter 2, I listed the goals authors had for their books. Now take a look at Table 23-1, which shows the same goals with data on whether they paid off. Note that only 20% accomplished a goal of making money from book sales, but many more accomplished a variety of other goals.

Two-thirds of authors hoped to boost their reputations, and 60% actually did. And many of the other goals come down to that: a greater reach among the target audience and a bigger reputation for those folks. Getting speaking gigs, generating leads, changing opinions, and boosting a corporate reputation all come down to the goal of boosting your reputation.

Table 23-1: Goals of published authors
Source: Bernoff.com author survey 2019-2022 (N=172 published authors)

Goal	% with goal	% who accomplished goal
Share the knowledge I had	75%	70%
Boost my reputation	65%	60%
Get more paid speaking gigs	40%	30%
Prove I could write a book	38%	36%
Generate leads	30%	20%
Change opinions in my field	28%	21%
Money from book sales	27%	20%
Boost my company's reputation	19%	14%
Credit for academic publication	5%	4%

I'd like to give you a perfect formula to make money from your book. But I can't, because I don't know what you're good at and what your situation is. That's also why you should be skeptical of any one-size-fits-all formula for making money from being an author. Every author is different.

What I can offer you is a list to stimulate your imagination. Which of these ideas? Which sound the most enjoyable and best suited to what you're good at and what you can realistically build on the reputation your book creates?

- Start a paid speaking career (as I described in the previous chapter). Most authors augment their income that way.
- Generate leads for a consulting business. Use the book to demonstrate your expertise.
- Run workshops or training sessions.
- Use the visibility from the book to raise your own reputation and get a promotion.
- Use the visibility from the book to get hired as a college professor or to flesh out your list of publications if you're already in an academic position.

- Raise the visibility of your company's business and use that to create more leads.
- Start a paid content channel using a platform like Patreon or Substack.
- Give online talks for sponsoring companies that they use to generate leads for their own business.
- Write a paid series of posts or pieces for a company, associating your name and content with their business.

I'll share what happened with my book *Groundswell,* just because it fulfilled many of these goals. *Groundswell* received a six-figure advance and sold more than 150,000 copies, which contributed to nearly $500,000 in royalties. At the time we published it, my coauthor Charlene Li and I were both analysts at Forrester, and Forrester owned the copyright, so the company received the royalties. But the company's sales team sent hundreds of copies of the book to prospects and clients, contributing to our reputation and to what likely ended up as many millions of dollars of sales.

I stayed at Forrester and gave almost 200 speeches about the book content, typically at $10,000 to $15,000 per speech. That money went to Forrester, but it made me sufficiently successful at the company to merit a lot of prestige and a promotion to senior vice president. I stayed with the company for seven more years, and then, after I left, I used my reputation as a bestselling author to sell my next book and build a business on consulting with authors and companies.

Charlene left Forrester within a year after the book was published and started her own research and consulting business. She had a lucrative speaking career that the bestselling book helped to launch, and her business was also quite successful — and after a few years, she sold her business to a larger consulting organization.

Charlene's and my paths were different, but both took off in large part because of the success of the book. And this is how you should think, too, regardless of the specific ways you choose to monetize your book's success.

All of this is work. But if you weave the book content throughout all the other pieces you're interested in building, as Joe Pulizzi did, you can generate success. The audience you reach becomes the customers for your business. The story in your book becomes the services you deliver. And that's how most authors make money.

Key takeaways

- Books make money, but often not enough to support authors on their own.
- Authors make money from speeches, consulting, training, generating leads, and a variety of other means.
- Weaving the content through these various offerings — some free, some paid — allows you to build on the ideas in the book to create a successful career.

Chapter 24

Writer to Author

Don't stop at one book.

I started this book with the story of Jay Baer's *Talk Triggers.* He's the author of six books, and by the time you read this, maybe one or two more.

Laura Gassner Otting, whose book *Limitless* was so good that her friend Tara Diab got the cover graphic tattooed on her arm, has a second book coming out right around the time this book will be published.

Denise Lee Yohn has written two books. Phil M. Jones has ten. Shel Israel has five. Scott Stratten has six. Joe Pulizzi has seven business books and a novel.

Counting the book you're reading right now, I have five.

What's gotten into us?

Authors write

Authors will often tell you that writing a book was one of the most difficult things they have ever undertaken. They'll also tell you that they want to do it again.

Among the authors I surveyed, 87% agreed that writing a book was a good decision. And 76% plan to write another nonfiction book within ten years.

There are a lot of reasons for this.

It's not just vanity. Vanity might be sufficient to drive you to write the first book, but it's not what gets you to want to write another.

It's because writing a book is an intellectual activity unlike any other.

It's an act of sheer creation that requires little more than a keyboard, a brain, and a willingness to do research and conduct interviews. No other singular, simple, human creative activity has the same chance to reach and change the lives of so many in a potential audience.

It's a concentrated effort on a single idea that you own and you can direct. That in itself is rewarding and exhilarating.

It focuses your ideas into a platform you can use to speak, to gain clients, and above all, to gain influence.

And once you have done it, you realize that you have learned much of what you need to do it all again.

About that next book

When Kerry Bodine and Harley Manning completed the manuscript for *Outside In,* as I described in chapter 14, Kerry immediately wanted to start writing another book. Her first book wasn't even published, let alone effectively promoted, so I had to talk her down. I've since learned that Kerry's impulse to write more is quite common — nearly every author seems to feel that way. So I have this advice for you.

Finish the first book at a high level of quality before you go to write another. Make that first book matter.

Promote that first book so that it takes flight. Writers don't just write — they promote. And work on ways to monetize that first book. Your options for the next book are a lot wider if you've launched the first book successfully and built a business on it.

Your audience has the clues for what you should write next. Listen to your readers' feedback. What questions are still unanswered? What ideas go beyond what you already wrote? What business stories have you learned that have yet to be told?

Don't just ring the changes on your first idea. Use it as a platform to go higher, farther, and deeper.

And above all, don't lose track of what you need to create a successful new book.

Define or refine your audience.

Create an even more powerful idea.

Collect and share more compelling stories.

Weave them together into a book-length narrative that takes readers to an even greater height of understanding.

And use the platform you've built to promote the new book.

Do all that, and you'll be more than a writer. You'll be an author. It's the best creative life I can imagine, and once you've written a book, no one can ever take that away from you.

Good luck.

Acknowledgments

I had to write this book. After watching so many authors struggle with the same challenges, I was moved to share what I know. So I set out eagerly in 2019 with a solid plan, organized a successful author survey, and began interviewing experts and fellow authors. And I started writing.

Then something happened. I stalled. Some combination of overwhelming client demands, family challenges, several moves, and the pandemic sapped my energy.

So as I write the thank-yous for this book, I'm drawn most powerfully to the people who helped me restart the project and take it successfully to a conclusion.

This starts with my wife, Kimberley. Unlike other authors, I don't expect my wife to read what I write — she's an artist, not a businessperson. But she knows me. And when she heard me, in 2022, tell someone that I was mostly retired, she told me I wasn't. "Don't be silly," she said. "You're not retired. You are happier when you are working." She was right, of course. So I got off my ass and got back to work. And it did make me happy.

The second person I'd like to thank is Tamsen Webster. I knew part of the problem was that my book needed a strong point of differentiation; that lack was part of why I had run out of steam. I took Tamsen's Red Thread workshop in the summer of 2022 and identified that point of differentiation: my belief that business books are stories. Chapter 1 exists because of Tamsen, who gave me the push I needed to relaunch myself. Tamsen for me is sort of like the therapist's therapist. Because I help authors, I know what creative people with ideas need, and I knew she had what I needed but couldn't do on my own.

I am surrounded by a community of fellow authors who have supported me throughout this process. They likely don't realize that one great way they have helped me is by asking questions and, in the process, revealing what the content for this book needs to be. Many of those authors are profiled in this book. If you read a name in this book, know that I am grateful to them for writing about fascinating topics, asking excellent questions, and being willing to share their experiences honestly. Mitch Joel and Scott Stratten are tied for first among equals in this group, and my gratitude extends especially to them.

Thanks to my author clients for being willing to pay me for work that was so interesting I could turn it into a book. I love you all.

As should become clear from what I said in the last 24 chapters, writing a book is a team effort. I'm grateful to the publishing staff at Amplify, led by the ever-resourceful Naren Aryal and the diligent and nearly perfect Kristin Perry, Nina Spahn, and Myles Schrag, for turning my manuscript into an actual book. And profound thanks to my preferred copy editor, Merlina McGovern, who cleverly got laid off just in time to copy edit this book.

Thanks to Bobbie Carlton and her crew at Carlton PR & Marketing (including a clever young guy named Ray Bernoff) for their promotional plan and execution. And to my posse of fellow authors who were willing to promote the book on social media and write reviews, any success I have would have been impossible without you.

Publishing is a cruel world. But there are two groups of people that make it a wonderful place to be: writers and readers. If you are either (or both), thank you for my livelihood and for making the world endlessly fascinating. Keep reading, and keep writing.

Index

About Josh Bernoff

J osh Bernoff is an expert on how business books can propel thinkers to prominence. Book projects on which he collaborated have generated more than $20 million for their authors.

Josh's most recent book is *Writing Without Bullshit: Boost Your Career by Saying What You Mean* (Harper Business, 2016). Toronto's *Globe and Mail* called it "a Strunk and White for the modern knowledge worker." He is the coauthor of *Groundswell: Winning in a World Transformed by Social Technologies* (Harvard Business Review Press, 2008), which was a *Businessweek* bestseller. He has authored, coauthored, or ghostwritten eight business books.

He works closely with nonfiction authors as an advisor, coach, editor, or ghostwriter. His author clients include Mitch Lowe, former Netflix cofounder and Redbox president; Kevin Tracey, CEO of the Feinstein Institutes for Medical Research; and Stefan Falk, former lead trainer at McKinsey & Company. He has collaborated on more than 45 nonfiction books.

Josh writes a blog post on topics of interest to authors every weekday at Bernoff.com. His blog has generated 4 million views.

He was formerly Senior Vice President, Idea Development at Forrester, where he spent 20 years analyzing technology and business. He appeared on "60 Minutes" and got quoted everywhere from *The Wall Street Journal* to *TV Guide*. The Society for New Communications Research recognized him as "Visionary of the Year." Prior to Forrester, Josh spent 14 years in start-up companies in the Boston area.

Josh has a mathematics degree from The Pennsylvania State University and studied mathematics in the Ph.D. program at MIT.

He lives with his wife, an artist, in Portland, Maine.

Contact Josh on his blog or at josh@bernoff.com.

How I Help Authors

If you're working on a book, I may be able to help you.

Learn more about me and my services at my website Bernoff.com. The Author Services tab lists my services.

I work with authors on ideas and titles, book proposals, and editing manuscripts. I ghostwrite one business book per year. I coach authors. These are paid services; I don't work for free or "for exposure."

My site includes a sample book proposal. Go to wobs.co/BBBBproposal to download my proposal for *Writing Without Bullshit*, which generated multiple offers from publishers and a six-figure advance. The content is proprietary, but feel free to copy the framework.

I blog every weekday on topics of interest to authors at Bernoff.com.

I work exclusively with nonfiction authors. If you write fiction, I can't help you.

I will not be a coauthor on your book. Write your own book or hire a ghostwriter.

Fair warning: I do not accept advertising or guest posts of any kind. If you pitch me for that, I will taunt you publicly and mercilessly on my blog.

You can contact me at josh@bernoff.com; I respond to serious questions and serious authors. Let's succeed together.

Advance Praise, Continued, for

BUILD A BETTER BUSINESS BOOK

Endorsed by more than 50 successful business authors

"Josh Bernoff has put everything he knows about preparing, writing, and launching a successful business book into a masterclass that will improve every part of your book and your career as an author. *Build a Better Business Book* will help you define the success you want and achieve it more efficiently than you thought possible. It's a guaranteed return on your investment." —**William Kilmer, author of *Transformative***

"Got a book in your belly that's itching to get out? You must read Josh Bernoff's *Build a Better Business Book* for a step-by-step guide on how to make it a reality—and not lose your mind or waste your time and money. I'm recommending it to every future author I know!" —**Charlene Li, *New York Times* bestselling author of *The Disruption Mindset***

"Twelve years ago, I was already a professional writer but I had no clue how to create a business book and get it published. Josh guided me and my coauthor through the process to a successful result—now he's captured that guidance in print. It's never boring and always incredibly useful." —**Harley Manning, coauthor of *Outside In: The Power of Putting Customers at the Center of Your Business***

"Business book success does indeed have a secret formula. Josh Bernoff's book reveals it with the turn of every page. From the concrete steps and vast number of examples he offers you know he's the real deal, because he has successfully applied the formula for himself and others dozens of times over." —**James McQuivey, PhD, author of *Digital Disruption***

"Based on two decades of experience editing and writing business books, I can't imagine a more useful starting point for authors than this clear and comprehensive guide." —**David Moldawer, editor of more than 70 books**

"Josh Bernoff's book is the ultimate guide for writing a successful business book. It offers practical advice, eliminates guesswork, and saves authors from costly mistakes. It's an indispensable resource for any aspiring writer." —**Dr. Vince Molinaro, author of** *Accountable Leaders* **and** *The Leadership Contract,* **a** *New York Times* **bestseller**

"For anyone who's ever considered writing a business book but doesn't know where to start, this is the only guide you'll ever need." —**Scott Monty, leadership and communications strategist**

"Writing a business book is easy. Writing a great business book is hard, or at least, it used to be. Josh put together a wonderful resource that will guide you in writing a business book that transcends mediocrity and delivers greatness." —**Jacob Morgan, author of** *Leading with Vulnerability: Unlock Your Greatest Superpower to Transform Yourself, Your Team, and Your Organization*

"Bernoff's book is destined to quickly become the classic guide every first-time and seasoned business book author reads, references, and recommends time and time again." —**Melanie Notkin, bestselling author of** *Savvy Auntie* **and** *Otherhood*

"Josh's subject matter expertise is matched only by his simpatico for fellow authors. If you're a business writer, this is the how-to book you've been waiting for." —**Anita Nowak, PhD, author of** *Purposeful Empathy*

"Writing books is hard. Writing good books is nearly impossible. Josh Bernoff's *Build a Better Business Book* makes it a whole lot easier. It's packed with instructional stories, a clearly defined road map, and actionable advice at each step of the way." —**Laura Gassner Otting, national bestselling author of** *Limitless* **and** *Wonderhell*

"I wish I had read this book five books ago. Josh Bernoff delivers an absolute masterclass guide that will indisputably help business authors build a better business book." —**Dan Pontefract, author of five business books**

"I only wish I had Josh's book before I started out on my business book journey. Whether you are a book newbie or an experienced author, *Build a Better Business Book* will save you from countless mistakes and missed opportunities on your book publishing journey." —**Joe Pulizzi, author *Content Inc.* and *Epic Content Marketing***

"This book is a must-read for any would-be business author. It is to business books what Strunk and White's *The Elements of Style* is to writing and grammar. It's just filled with insight after insight." —**Robert Rose, author of *Killing Marketing* and *Content Marketing Strategy***

"A business book can be magical! It can generate passionate fans of your work, put you on the fast track for promotion, or launch a public speaking career. However, as Josh reveals in this excellent book, there are many elements you need to get right for the magic to happen for you. I wish I had this next to my desk as I was writing my first business book." —**David Meerman Scott, author of twelve books, including *Fanocracy*, a *Wall Street Journal* bestseller**

"Publishing your book is going to change your career. Trust Josh to show you the way." —**Andy Sernovitz, author of the *New York Times* bestseller *Word of Mouth Marketing: How Smart Companies Get People Talking***

"If only I had this book twenty years ago! It's an indispensable resource that would have saved me a ton of time and energy." —**Stephen Shapiro, author of *Invisible Solutions***

"Bernoff has created a veritable treasure chest of invaluable advice that will benefit both first-time authors and experienced scribes." —**Phil Simon, author of *The Nine: The Tectonic Forces Reshaping the Workplace***

"*Build a Better Business Book* by Josh Bernoff is a comprehensive road map every aspiring business author needs to read." —**Sandra Poirier Smith, CEO, Smith Communications**

"There are way too many business books out there, but no guides to business books quite like this. Josh is the architect behind the blueprint for success in this industry." —**Scott Stratten, coauthor of *UnMarketing* and five other bestselling business books**

"Writing a business book will be the best decision of your career, if you know how to execute. But if you are even slightly unsure, then you must read Josh Bernoff's book." —**Robert Tercek, author of *Vaporized: Solid Strategies for Success in a Dematerialized World***

"Your ideas matter. Shouldn't your book? Josh's great guide will help you capture your brilliance and grow your influence." —**Ron Tite, author of *Think. Do. Say.***

"If writing a business book appears as daunting as climbing Mount Everest, this book is like a Sherpa that helps take prospective authors to the summit. I wish it had appeared before I wrote my first book, since it is so full of amazing advice I had to learn the hard way." —**Rishad Tobaccowala, author of *Restoring the Soul of Business: Staying Human in the Age of Data***

"A must-read guide to creating the book that matters. Josh Bernoff is not just an accomplished author; he is a business book whisperer who helped over 40 authors publish books that profoundly affected others." —**Ekaterina Walter, *Wall Street Journal* bestselling author of three business books, including *The Laws of Brand Storytelling***

"No matter what question you have about writing a business book, Josh Bernoff has your answer. And not just any answers: the clear-sighted, no-punches-pulled answers that work based on his and his clients' experience." —**Tamsen Webster, author of *Find Your Red Thread: Make Your Big Ideas Irresistible***

"An indispensable book with rich insight for both would-be and established authors. Delivers straight talk on everything from memorable writing, making money from your work, and coauthors, to bestseller lists and promotion." —**Trena White, co-founder and publisher, Page Two**

"In clear language, Josh Bernoff demystifies the many puzzles of publishing. *Build a Better Business Book* is an invaluable guide that I'll happily recommend to everyone who wants to write a nonfiction title." —**Karen Wickre, author of *Taking the Work Out of Networking: Your Guide to Making and Keeping Great Connections***

"Josh is creative and pragmatic—the ideal combination to help me generate a breakthrough business book title." —**Denise Lee Yohn, author of *What Great Brands Do* and *Fusion***